A Driving Guide

Routes to Roots

Discover the cultural and industrial heritage of southwestern Pennsylvania

Rivers of Steel National Heritage Area

Acknowledgements

Appreciation

Routes to Roots combined the time, talents, and energy of many individuals and organizations. Doris J. Dyen directed the project; other core members of the team included Janis Dofner, Libby Boyarski of Boyarski Design, Joan Guerin of Guerin Design, Barbara E. Klein, and Julie Throckmorton-Meunier. From initial site visits to final field tests, the driving guide has truly been a team effort, constantly enriched with ideas from all members as we grappled with the challenge of how best to present an industrial region and its heritage to visitors.

We thank the many people throughout the Rivers of Steel National Heritage Area who welcomed us to their special places and shared their living traditions with us — and with you!

Funding

Routes to Roots was made possible with support from:

National Park Service,
U. S. Department of the Interior

Pennsylvania Department of Conservation and Natural Resources, Bureau of Recreation and Conservation, Pennsylvania Heritage Parks Program

The Pennsylvania Tourism Office

ISBN 0–9754462–0–7
Copyright © 2004 by Steel Industry Heritage Corporation
All rights reserved. This book or portions thereof may not be reproduced in any form without consent of Steel Industry Heritage Corporation.
Printed and bound in the United States of America
10 9 8 7 6 5 4 3 2 1

Contents

Introduction   4

Nuts & Bolts   5

Three Rivers Route: **Big Steel**   **6**

Ohio-Beaver Route: **Thunder of Protest**   **80**

Alle-Kiski Route: **Mosaic of Industries**   **116**

Youghiogheny Route: **Mountains of Fire**   **146**

Monongahela Route: **Fueling a Revolution**   **182**

Index   218

Introduction

Southwestern Pennsylvania

During the century-long Big Steel Era (1890s–1980s), the entire seven-county Pittsburgh Industrial District resembled a huge creature born and bred for one purpose: steel-related production. The District's rivers and streams were the creature's lifeblood — arteries and veins carrying raw materials, fuel, and finished products. The intricate web of long-distance, short-haul and interurban rail lines and roadways were the nerve and lymph system, connecting the mine patches, mills and markets into a smoothly functioning network. These hard-working communities in turn were the muscles, bones and vital organs, pulling and pushing, sweating and pumping day and night. The creature's head was the City of Pittsburgh, center of corporate board rooms, cultural facilities and institutions of higher learning. And its heart was the chain of huge, densely clustered plants that stretched from the confluence of the Pittsburgh Point several miles along each of the District's three main rivers — the legendary milltowns that gave the whole region its century-long identity as the "Steel Capital of the World."

The scale was immense: Titans of industry such as Andrew Carnegie, Henry Clay Frick, J. P. Morgan, the Mellon Family, B. F. Jones and his partner Laughlin were household names and giant figures on the local scene. Towering furnaces cast their fiery glow across the sky and the rumble of the steel mills rolled unceasingly over the landscape. Thousands of workers recruited from the four corners of the Earth labored day and night to produce the millions of tons of steel that built the Empire State Building, the Golden Gate Bridge, the battleships and tanks that won two World Wars and propelled America to world preeminence.

In the mid-1980s, the Big Steel Era came to an abrupt end. One by one, most of the huge mills and subsidiary plants closed forever. Within about five years, a hundred thousand people were out of work. The unthinkable became the commonplace, as multi-story sheds were torn down, machinery dismantled, and the towering stoves disappeared in clouds of wreckers' dust and smoke. For over a decade former mill sites in and near Pittsburgh lay as desolate brownfields.

Then, in the late 1990s, like a phoenix rising from the ashes of the fiery furnaces, the area began to revive, with new residential/commercial developments such as the Waterfront in Homestead and the South Side Works in Pittsburgh. Riverfront hiking/biking trails were started. U. S. Steel's remaining mills — Edgar Thomson, Irwin and Clairton — were upgraded to become once again world-class steel operations, albeit with far fewer workers. At the same time, the mill towns and mine patches also began efforts to conserve their heritage, both for their own people and for visitors eager to learn about the region. The Rivers of Steel National Heritage Area, headquartered in Homestead, has played a leading role in preserving historic structures and documenting the customs and arts of these communities. Throughout southwestern Pennsylvania, although the steel industry no longer powers the region, the working communities honor the physical reminders of their industrial might and the treasures of cultural tradition that are the living legacy of steel.

BY THE WAY

Route 28 was named in honor of the World War I veterans who served in the 28th Division of the U. S. Army. The insignia on their uniforms was a red keystone.

above: Each "By the Way" relates an interesting fact that we uncovered along the way.

below: Each industry icon identifies an industry you will see as you drive the routes.

If you're heading north from Kittanning through Brady's Bend look for Brady's Bend Corp.'s limestone works.

Nuts & Bolts

While southwestern Pennsylvania's history is long and varied, the places and events in this guide reflect the cultural and industrial heritage of the period from 1875 to the 1980s when this region was the steel-making capital of the world. Every community, every neighborhood, every site has a story to tell within the Rivers of Steel National Heritage Area. We've crisscrossed the National Heritage Area's seven counties: Allegheny, Armstrong, Beaver, Fayette, Greene, Washington and Westmoreland, to bring them to you.

How to Use This Guide

Routes to Roots divides southwestern Pennsylvania into five driving routes named for the region's famous rivers — the Ohio, Beaver, Monongahela, Youghiogheny, Allegheny, and the Kiskiminetas.

Each of the driving routes begins with an introduction about that area's history and folk culture. Each route includes an orientation map with numbered locations showing featured sites and points of interest within that route. In the text, useful information such as addresses, hours, admission, and telephone numbers appear in the site headings. Pay particular attention to the phone symbol ☎. This symbol denotes destinations that may have limited hours of operation or that require you to call ahead for a visit. At the end of each driving route you will find a month-by-month listing of festivals and other events that highlight the region's living traditions.

To help our readers plan their *Routes to Roots* experience, we have grouped the sites into whole-day and half-day itineraries. Driving directions for these itineraries are printed in italics. Even though the driving directions have been carefully tested, southwestern Pennsylvania's terrain can challenge any visitor. We suggest taking along a good road map for your visit. Lastly, we encourage you to engage the folks you'll be meeting along the way. People love to share their stories of life in the region.

An Invitation

In researching this book, we discovered many wonderful places and events. We're sure that you will find others. Please tell us about them so we can share the information with your fellow travelers in upcoming editions. If you are disappointed with a site, we want to hear that too. Please write to:

Rivers of Steel
National Heritage Area
Routes to Roots Driving Guide
623 E. 8th Avenue
Homestead, PA 15120

Note to our Readers

The opinions expressed in this guide are based on the driving guide team's experience at the time of our visit. Those traveling at other times may have different experiences since prices, dates, hours and conditions are always subject to change. Though we made every effort to ensure that this book was as up-to-date as possible before going to press, we urge you to check with sites beforehand to avoid inconvenience or surprises.

Travel is always an adventure. For your safety the author, editors, and publishers encourage you to stay alert and aware of your surroundings to make your visit an enjoyable one.

Now that you have the guidebook to a great experience, visit our website at: www.riversofsteel.com for a look at our online version of the *Routes to Roots* driving guide. The online driving guide offers additional features on southwestern Pennsylvania's traditions and regular updates on new travel adventures within the Rivers of Steel National Heritage Area.

above: The five routes in a seven-county area are named for southwestern Pennsylvania's rivers: the Ohio, Beaver, Monongahela, Youghiogheny, Allegheny and the Kiskiminetas.

below: Symbols designate sites as well as site features.

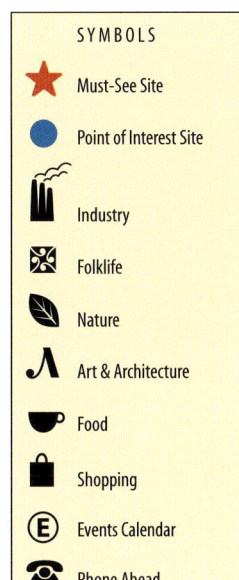

Three Rivers Route

Pittsburgh Area

Big Steel

From Pittsburgh outward, steel and related industries governed the life of riverfront towns. On the Allegheny and Ohio, steel-related companies flourished in towns like Sharpsburg, Etna, Millvale, and Blawnox, McKees Rocks and Neville Island. Within Pittsburgh, Jones & Laughlin's South Side Works, Eliza Furnaces, and Hazelwood Coke Works operated from the 1880s through the 1980s. At the height of the "Big Steel" era, the skies were notoriously dark with soot and smoke at noon, and writers aptly described the whole Pittsburgh region as "hell with the lid off."

The industrial core was the Monongahela River's Steel Valley, stronghold of U. S. Steel. Founded in 1901 as a merger of Andrew Carnegie's holdings with those of financier J. P. Morgan, U. S. Steel's massive mills and furnaces dominated both sides of the river for more than 10 miles. They included the Homestead Works and Carrie Furnaces, where plate steel was made; the Edgar Thomson Works in Braddock, producer of rails and structural steel; the Duquesne Works, famous for its innovations in steel technology; the National Tube Works, maker of steel pipe; the Irvin Works, producer of sheet steel; and the Clairton Works, where bituminous coal from all over the region became coke to fuel the mills. Supporting these huge mills was a host of smaller independent firms: foundries, tool-and-die makers, trucking companies, barge and rail freight carriers, and specialized manufacturers.

U. S. Steel's mills on the lower Monongahela alone spanned 18 contiguous communities from West Homestead to Clairton, and from Swissvale to McKeesport and Glassport. The communities' fortunes rose and fell in rhythm with the industry's worldwide market cycles.

Politically and financially tied to the mills, these towns were home to a mosaic of workers from every European country and beyond. The hulking mill buildings dominated the riverfronts, and the workers lived in their shadow. At first, mill-working families found homes in the so-called "immigrant wards," then later in row houses up the hills behind the mills, but never out of their sight, sound, and smell.

Mingling daily on the job — and often suffering discrimination based on nationality, race, and creed — workers created ethnic oases during their few leisure hours. They built churches, Saturday schools, and clubs where they could maintain the languages, customs, arts, and beliefs of their homelands — their connection to their cultural heritage. Often the company managers not only aided these efforts, but also built community centers and sponsored sports teams, all from a pragmatic goal: to prevent workers from uniting to strike or disrupt production.

opposite page: **Charging Open Hearth 5 at the Homestead Works**
top: **Pinching pierogi**
bottom: **Teeming ingots**

Rivers of Steel Archives

The "hell with the lid off" quote has been attributed to Charles Dickens and Mark Twain among others.

Three Rivers Route

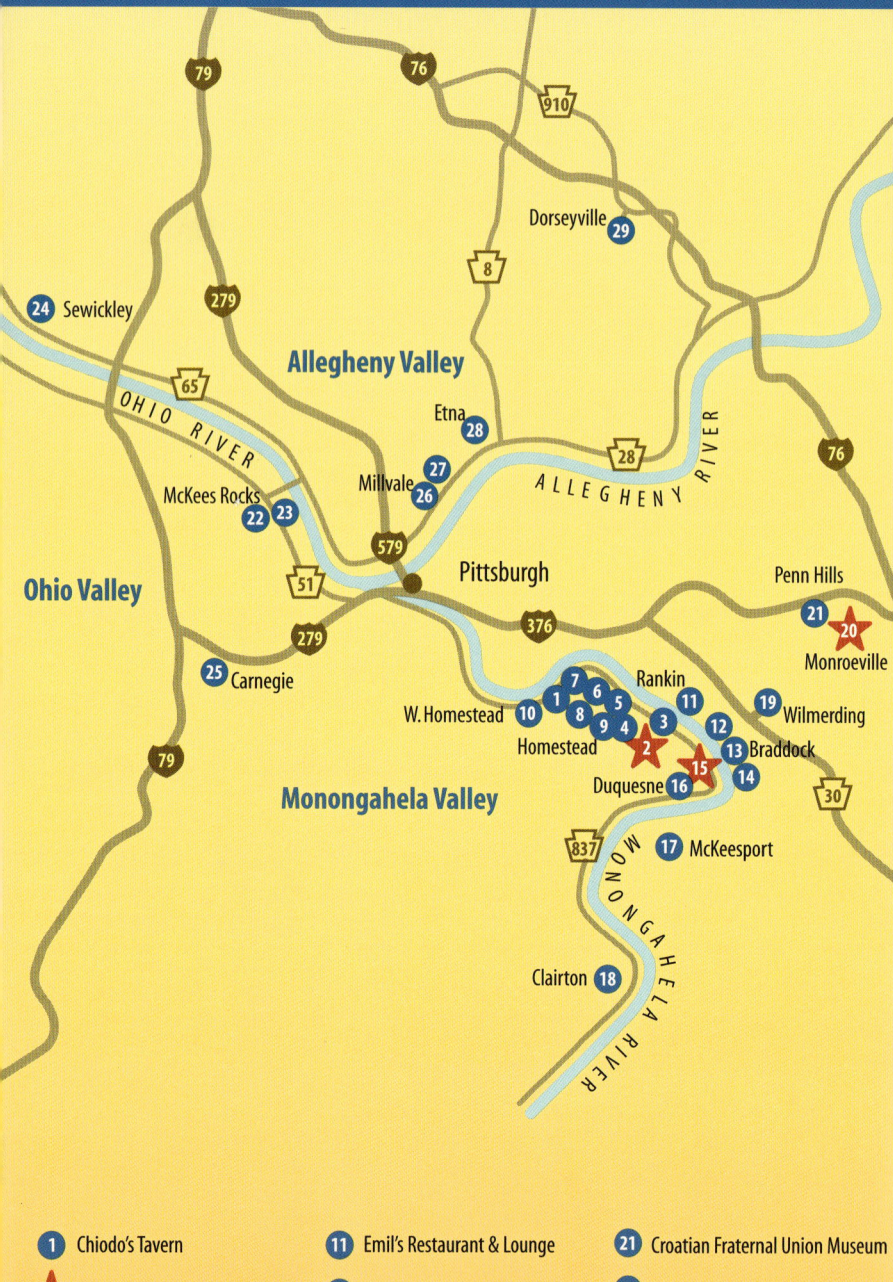

1. Chiodo's Tavern
2. The Bost Building
3. Pump House and Water Tower
4. A & B Bakery
5. Conrad's Catering
6. Art Space 303
7. Blemahdoo's African Market
8. Little Frick Park
9. Carnegie Library of Homestead
10. Bulgarian-Macedonian Center
11. Emil's Restaurant & Lounge
12. Braddock Carnegie Library
13. St. Michael Church
14. U. S. Steel Edgar Thomson Works
15. Kennywood Park
16. Metamorphosis Sculpture Park
17. McKeesport Heritage Center
18. U. S. Steel Clairton Coke Works
19. George Westinghouse Museum
20. Sri Venkateswara Temple
21. Croatian Fraternal Union Museum
22. Mancini's Bakery
23. Pierogies Plus
24. Little Athens of Sewickley
25. SS. Peter & Paul Ukrainian Church
26. St. Nicholas Croatian Church
27. Chatellier's Bakery
28. Blarney Stone Restaurant
29. Council of Three Rivers American Indian Center

Pittsburgh Area

MONONGAHELA VALLEY

From Pittsburgh: *Take I-376 E to Homestead exit 5. Take Beechwood Blvd. to Browns Hill Rd. Cross Homestead High-Level Bridge (Homestead Grays Bridge) into Homestead.*

One-Day Tour: Sites 1–10
Chiodo's Tavern: *Right just after bridge. Chiodo's is on corner. (Parking lot next to building.)* **The Bost Building:** *From Chiodo's parking lot, left on 8th Ave. (PA 837) to Heisel St. The Bost Building is on left.* **Pump House and Water Tower:** *Continue on 8th Ave. Left on Waterfront entrance ramp .25 miles to the Pump House and Water Tower on right.* **A & B Bakery:** *A & B Bakery is across 8th Ave. from Bost Building.* **Conrad's Catering:** *Continue 1 block west on 8th Ave. to Conrad's on left.* ☎ **Art Space 303:** *Continue 1 block west on 8th to Art Space 303 on right.* ☎ **Blemahdoo's:** *Continue 1 block west on 8th Ave. to Blemahdoo's on right.* **Little Frick Park:** *Continue west on 8th Ave. Left on Amity St. up hill. Left on 10th Ave. Little Frick Park is on right.* **Carnegie Library of Homestead:** *Continue on 10th Ave. Right on McClure St. Left on 11th Ave. Go 2 blocks to Library on left.* **Bulgarian-Macedonian Center:** *Continue on 11th Ave. Left on Louise St. Left on 10th Ave. past front of library. Right on McClure St. Left on 8th Ave. Go 1 mile to "Y" in road. Bear left on West 8th Ave. Bulgarian-Macedonian Center is on right.* **Return to Pittsburgh:** *8th Ave. to Homestead High-Level Bridge to Beechwood Blvd. to I-376 W.*

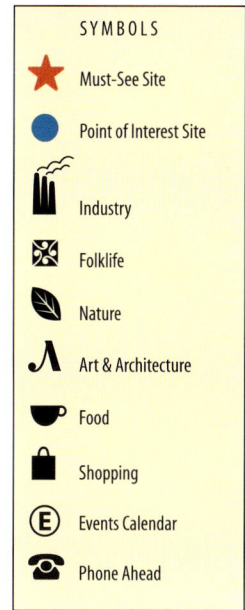

SYMBOLS
- ★ Must-See Site
- ● Point of Interest Site
- Industry
- Folklife
- Nature
- Art & Architecture
- Food
- Shopping
- E Events Calendar
- Phone Ahead

HOMESTEAD

Chiodo's Tavern
412–461–3113
107 West 8th Avenue, Homestead
Weekdays, 10AM–2AM; Sat, 11AM–2AM

When Joe Chiodo opened the watering hole that bears his name in 1947, the mill was just two blocks away and Homestead was a thriving community. Although much has changed since then, Chiodo's Tavern remains. The drinks are still reasonably priced, the food, including the famous Mystery Sandwich, still won't help your cholesterol, and the odd items still hanging from the ceiling are older than some of the patrons.

BY THE WAY

In 2002, the Homestead High-Level Bridge was renamed the Homestead Grays Bridge in honor of the Negro League baseball team. The team began as a group of steelworkers in 1912. The Negro Leagues were formed in the 1920s and continued into the 1950s.

A motorcade carrying Nikita Krushchev, premier of the U.S.S.R., past Chiodo's in 1959.

Three Rivers Route

Steel & Iron Industries

Steel is born of the ancient Greeks' four elements: earth, air, fire, and water. Yet steel does not occur in nature. It is a man-made alloy that combines iron with other materials under intense heat. With coke as the fuel and limestone as a cleanser, iron ore is smelted in a 2,500°F blast furnace to produce pure iron. Melted with zinc, magnesium, or other ingredients, the iron becomes molten steel ready to be cast, forged, or rolled.

Steel and iron dominated southwestern Pennsylvania from the early 19th-century iron furnaces in Fayette County to the 21st-century basic oxygen furnace in Braddock. At the height of the steel era, mills stretched for miles along the region's three major riverfronts, while iron foundries, pattern makers, and other steel-related industries lined their branches. Steel employed more than 100,000 people in the Pittsburgh region. No wonder that iron and steel gave their names to local sports teams, beer, and the region itself.

U. S. Steel was the world's first billion-dollar corporation. But there were many other steel makers vying for position in the region: Jones & Laughlin, Republic, National, Wheeling-Pittsburgh, and, in more recent times, Allegheny Ludlum.

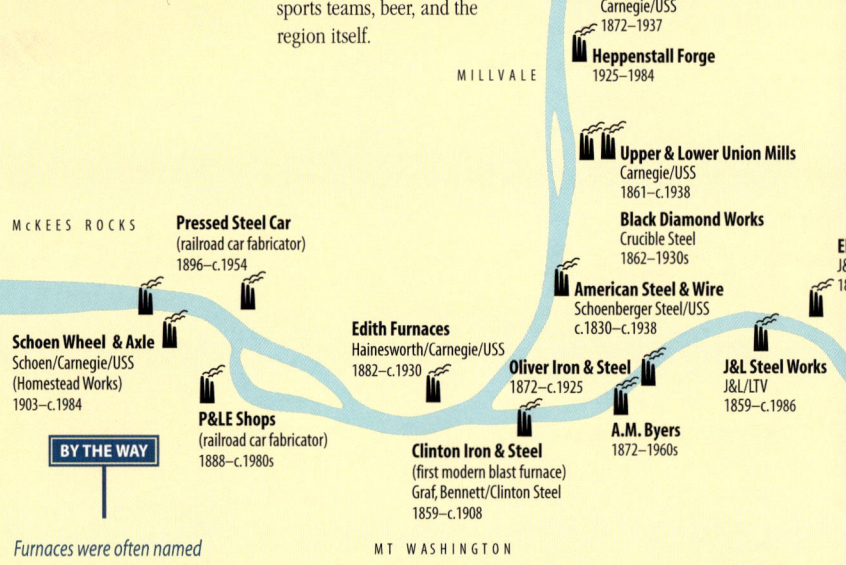

ETNA

Spang-Chalfant
Spang-Chalfant/National Supply
c.1840–1960

Isabella Furnaces
Carnegie/USS
1872–c.1953

Lucy Furnaces
Carnegie/USS
1872–1937

Heppenstall Forge
1925–1984

MILLVALE

Upper & Lower Union Mills
Carnegie/USS
1861–c.1938

Black Diamond Works
Crucible Steel
1862–1930s

American Steel & Wire
Schoenberger Steel/USS
c.1830–c.1938

Oliver Iron & Steel
1872–c.1925

J&L Steel Works
J&L/LTV
1859–c.1986

A.M. Byers
1872–1960s

McKEES ROCKS

Pressed Steel Car
(railroad car fabricator)
1896–c.1954

Schoen Wheel & Axle
Schoen/Carnegie/USS
(Homestead Works)
1903–c.1984

P&LE Shops
(railroad car fabricator)
1888–c.1980s

Edith Furnaces
Hainesworth/Carnegie/USS
1882–c.1930

Clinton Iron & Steel
(first modern blast furnace)
Graf, Bennett/Clinton Steel
1859–c.1908

MT WASHINGTON

BY THE WAY

Furnaces were often named after their owners' wives. Back then, furnaces were thought to be "fiery and unpredictable, like women."

Steel-Making Process

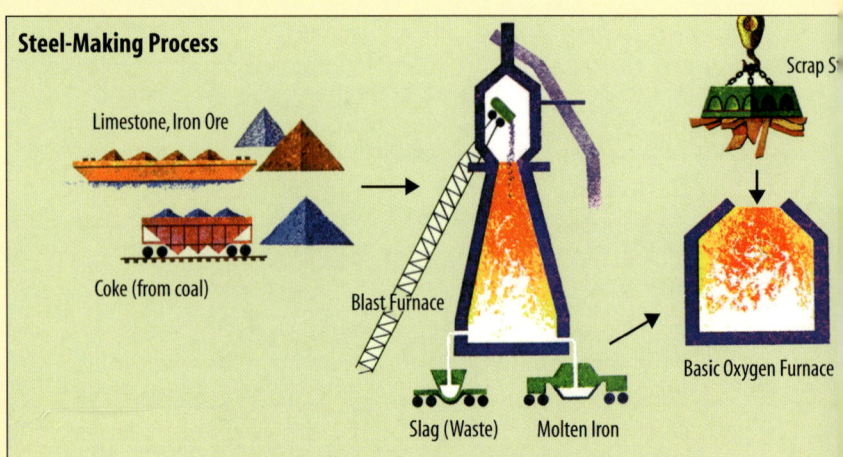

Pittsburgh Area

Steel is more versatile than iron. Iron is brittle and cracks in extreme heat or cold, while steel remains strong and supple. Steel can form straight pins and skyscrapers. Steel rails linked America's east and west coasts, and steel plate armored the ships that fought two world wars. Steel built America.

The 12 stacks at the Waterfront development were vents for the Homestead Steel Works "soaking pits" where ingots were heated evenly before rolling.

BY THE WAY

Steel became America's symbol of strength. Think of "steely-eyed looks," "steel yourself for the blow," and "steel magnolias."

TURTLE CREEK

Westinghouse Air Brake
Westinghouse/WABTEC
c.1870–present

Westinghouse Electric
Westinghouse
c.1880–1980s

SWISSVALE   BRADDOCK

Carrie Furnaces
Fownes/Carnegie/USS
1883–1984

Edgar Thomson Works
Carnegie/USS
1875–present

HOMESTEAD   DUQUESNE

Homestead Works
Pittsburgh Bessemer/Carnegie/USS
c.1880–1986

Duquesne Steel Works
Allegh. Bessemer/Carnegie/USS
1886–1984

HAZELWOOD

...elwood ... Works
...LTV
...80s–1984

Mesta Machine
Mesta/Whemco
(mill equipment supplier)
1899–present

National Tube Works
Boston/National/USS
1898–1987

Harbison-Walker
(refractory brick for furnaces)
1900–1950s

DRAVOSBURG   McKEESPORT

Irvin Works
Carnegie/USS
1930–present

Clairton Works
St. Clair/Carnegie/USS
1901–present

CLAIRTON

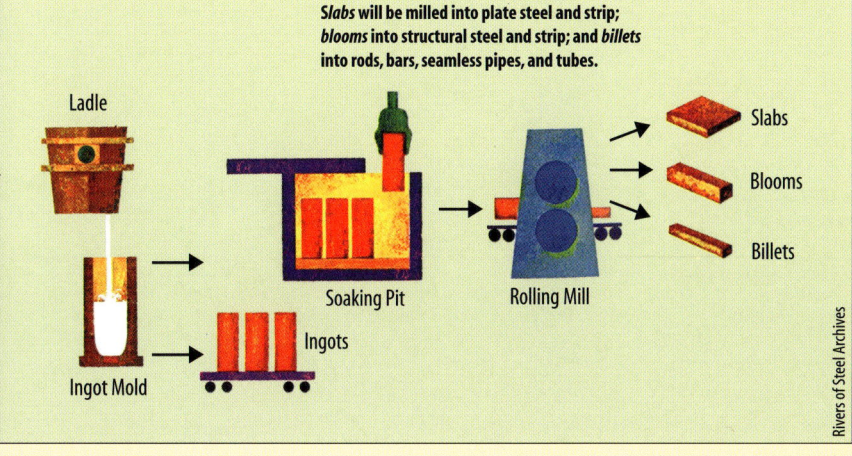

Slabs will be milled into plate steel and strip; *blooms* into structural steel and strip; and *billets* into rods, bars, seamless pipes, and tubes.

Ladle — Soaking Pit — Rolling Mill — Slabs / Blooms / Billets

Ingot Mold — Ingots

Rivers of Steel Archives

Three Rivers Route

Homestead Steel Works

More than any other entity, the Homestead Steel Works marked western Pennsylvania as the Steelmaking Capital of the World. For more than a century, the Homestead Works dominated an industry and defined a community.

Built in 1881 by a handful of businessmen eager to cash in on the industrial boom, the Homestead Works began flourishing after Andrew Carnegie purchased it in 1883.

Its history is both infamous and celebrated. It was the site of one of the nation's most dramatic and deadly labor conflicts, and until it shut down in 1986, it was also one of the world's largest steel mills and the flagship plant for U. S. Steel. With facilities on both sides of the Monongahela River, the Homestead Works encompassed 430 acres and employed more than 200,000 workers through the years.

Carrie Furnaces 6 and 7 were once part of a bank of blast furnaces used to smelt iron for rolling mills across the river. Today they loom above the Monongahela like iron dinosaurs. These fossil furnaces are rare artifacts of America's industrial history. No complete furnace plants from this period still exist in the United States, and all other nonoperative blast furnaces in the Pittsburgh area have been long since torn down.

Measuring 92 feet tall, the Carrie Furnaces' shells were constructed of 2.5-inch-thick steel plate, and lined with refractory brick to withstand more than 3,500° F.

When a furnace was fired up, it began a "campaign" that continued 24 hours a day, seven days a week, for an average of six to seven years. When the Carrie Furnaces were taken off line in 1978, they were producing approximately 2,500 tons of iron a day.

top: **Shift change at the Homestead Works, circa 1955**

bottom: **U. S. Steel Homestead Works, circa 1951**

Pittsburgh Area

Steel Speak

basic oxygen furnace a furnace that refines molten iron and scrap into steel.

Bessemer process a method of making steel by forcing a blast of air through molten iron to remove carbon and impurities.

billet semi-finished steel, 2″ to 7″ square, used for bars, channels, or other structural shapes.

blast furnace a towering cylinder lined with heat-resistant bricks, used by steel mills to smelt iron from ore.

bloom semi-finished steel with a rectangular cross section more than 8″, milled to make I-beams, H-beams, and sheet piling.

carbon steel steel with high carbon content. Most steel is carbon steel.

coil steel strip (less than 1/8″ thick) rolled from slabs and coiled for easy transportation and storage.

coke a processed form of coal that is the basic fuel consumed in blast furnaces.

continuous casting pouring molten steel directly from the furnace to form billets, blooms, or slabs.

flat-rolled steel steel processed on rolls with flat (rather than grooved or cut) faces. Products include sheet, strip, and tin plate.

flux a cleaning agent such as limestone that reacts with impurities in a furnace to form slag.

heat a batch of refined steel.

hot metal the molten iron produced in a blast furnace.

ingot steel cast in a metal mold, ready for rolling or forging.

pickling a process that cleans a steel coil of its rust, dirt, and oil.

plate sheet steel more than 8″ wide and from 1/4″ to more than 12″ thick.

slab most common semi-finished steel. Slabs are 10″ thick and 30″–85″ wide.

stainless steel steel that contains more than 10 percent chromium, resists corrosion and maintains its strength at high temperatures.

teeming pouring hot metal into ingot molds.

above: The Homestead Works 48-inch Mill was the last steam-driven rolling mill in America. (photo circa 1904)

below: This WWII-era promotional page in *U. S. Steel News* stated: "This 12,000-ton hydraulic press can squeeze — as though it were a piece of putty — a hot mass of steel weighing 525,000 pounds. …The forging in the photo, once an ingot, is being shaped to be a propulsion shaft for driving a great ocean liner."

Three Rivers Route

The Bost Building
412–464–4020
623 E. 8th Avenue, Homestead
www.riversofsteel.com
Exhibit hours: Mon–Sat, 11AM–4PM

Built in 1892 as a hotel for the rapidly growing workers' ward of Homestead, the Bost Building served as headquarters for the Amalgamated Association of Iron and Steel Workers. Using the third floor as a watchtower, union officials monitored activities in the mill and along the Monongahela River.

From the building American and British newspaper correspondents filed stories for a world hungrily following the strike that pitted the Carnegie Steel Company against the strongest labor union of the time.

Now a Registered National Historic Landmark, the Bost Building serves as the visitor center for the Rivers of Steel National Heritage Area. Its third floor features restored rooms and changing exhibits.

above: **The Bost Building today**

right: **George Czakoczi and Julie Throckmorton-Meunier view a painting of Joe Magarac, folk hero of eastern European steel workers, at an exhibit on steel heritage in the Bost Building's third-floor gallery.**

Pump House and Water Tower
East Waterfront Drive, Munhall

Part of the former U. S. Steel Homestead Works and scene of the infamous Battle of Homestead in 1892, the Pump House and Water Tower are being redeveloped by the Rivers of Steel National Heritage Area as an interpretive site for the history of the mill and a trailhead for the Steel Valley Heritage Trail.

left: **River view of Carrie Furnaces**
right: **Pump House and Water Tower**

Pittsburgh Area

The Homestead Steel Strike of 1892

Fair wages and safe working conditions were explosive issues in 1892. The Homestead Steel Strike struck a violent spark, but failed to ignite the U.S. labor movement.

A contract dispute between the Amalgamated Association of Iron and Steel Workers and Carnegie Steel turned into one of the bloodiest labor battles ever. On July 6, some 10,000 workers and supporters gathered at the Homestead Works Pump House. Armed with sticks, rocks, and guns, they rushed to meet the barges coming up the Monongahela River. The barges carried 300 Pinkerton guards hired to break the strike and lockout.

After a day of conflict in which strikers as well as Pinkertons died, the guards surrendered. The strike and lockout continued until November, when laborers asked to be released from their strike pledge. Two days later, the strike ended. The union had been broken, and the course of American labor was set for the next 50 years.

The Homestead Strike

We are asking one another as we pass the time of day,
  Why working men resort to arms to get their proper pay.
And why our labor unions they must not be recognized,
  Whilst the actions of a syndicate must not be criticized.
Now the troubles down at Homestead were brought about this way,
  When a grasping corporation had the audacity to say:
"You must all renounce your union and forswear your liberty
  And we will give you a chance to live and die in slavery."

Song collected by folklorist George Korson in New Kensington, Pennsylvania, 1940

above: **Pennsylvania National Guardsmen patrolled Eighth Avenue after the Battle of Homestead.**

center: **During the battle, workers fired on the Pinkertons' barges in the Monongahela River.**

right: **News of the Battle of Homestead riveted the nation.**

Strikers from the 1892 Battle of Homestead are buried in the cemetery that sits atop the hill overlooking Homestead.

15

Three Rivers Route

A & B Bakery
412–462–2322
514 E. 8th Avenue, Munhall
Tues–Sat, 6AM–5PM; Sun, 6AM–1PM

Since 1962, A & B Bakery has served the community with Slovak "cold-dough" filled cookies and holiday *pita* (apricot nut pastry), this bakery's local specialties, as well as doughnuts and other American favorites.

Bakery clerk Pat Trent

> **BY THE WAY**
>
> *There were 26 dialects spoken in Homestead's immigrant wards in 1910.*

Conrad's Catering
412–462–3534
504 E. 8th Avenue, Munhall
www.conradcatering.com
Mon–Th, 10AM–5PM; Fri, 10AM–6PM; Sat, 10AM–5PM

Need a stuffed cabbage fix? Whether you call them *holupki* (Slovak) or *sarma* (Serbo-Croatian), Conrad's is the place to get them any time of year.

Deli owner Becky Savolskis updates the day's menu.

> **BY THE WAY**
>
> *In 1907, Slovaks made up 53% of the workforce in Homestead.*

Pittsburgh Area

❻ Art Space 303
412–326–0100
303 E. 8th Avenue, Homestead
www.steelvalleyarts.org/space303.htm
☎ Phone ahead

Housed in a restored building that dates from the early 1900s, and showing the latest works by contemporary artists of the historic Steel Valley, Art Space 303 skillfully integrates the old with the new.

Courtesy Brian K. Britza

❼ Blemahdoo's African Market Place
412–461–3551
221 E. 8th Avenue, Homestead
☎ Phone ahead

Blemahdoo's African Market Place is crowded with possibilities. There are fabrics yet to be transformed into fashion statements and dresses yet to be discovered by shoppers looking to dazzle. At this store, no two outfits are alike. That's because owner Dee Blemahdoo designs them in her head and then makes them by hand.

Originally from Guinea, West Africa, Dee (with her husband and their three children) now lives on Pittsburgh's North Side. After working hard to develop a loyal following of clients, she decided to open her own boutique on Homestead's main thoroughfare. That was about 10 years ago.

These days, Dee's customers come from near and far for her hand-crafted jewelry, imported African artifacts, and, of course, those intricately embroidered, folded, and flounced dresses. In fact, one of her creations was recently sighted in the *Pittsburgh Post-Gazette*'s Seen column.

But if there's one specialty that distinguishes Dee's handiwork, it's her custom-made wedding gowns. Their vibrant designs summon the rich heritage of Africa, not to mention each bride's personal style. Matching ties and cummerbunds for grooms complete the wedding portrait.

One of Dee Blemahdoo's African-inspired creations

Three Rivers Route

Homestead — A Church on Every Corner

High atop St. Michael Slovak Catholic Church in Homestead, a statue of St. Joseph the Worker keeps silent watch over the Steel Valley. It is a fitting tribute to a community built on a foundation of steel.

But St. Joseph and his church do not stand alone. From the corner of Tenth Avenue and Ann Street in Homestead's "Little" Frick Park, nine houses of worship are in view, and just a few blocks away visitors will find another five.

The relationship between steel and spirituality dates back to the 1870s, when the rise of iron- and steel-making in the Monongahela Valley attracted English, Scots-Irish, Irish, German, and African-American workers. The oldest churches in the area reflected these ethnic groups. At one end of the park is the Irish Catholic St. Mary Magdalene, and midway along Tenth Avenue is the African-American Park Place AME. Nearby are St. John-Mark (a merger of two German Lutheran churches), a Scots-Irish Presbyterian church, an English Episcopal church, and a former Methodist Church (now the Lamb of God Christian Ministries).

above: **St. Joseph the Worker stands atop St. Michael Church.**
center: **St. Michael Church is now one of six churches in St. Maximilian Kolbe Parish.**
below: **Slovak motifs grace St. Michael's sanctuary.**

Look for the Slovak inscriptions over the doorway at St. Michael's Church, then up at the statue of St. Joseph to see a ladle pouring steel over the world.

Pittsburgh Area

Wanting to increase production and solidify the new nonunion operation of the Homestead Works after the Strike of 1892, Andrew Carnegie and Henry Clay Frick recruited more workers from Poland, Slovakia, Lithuania, and Hungary. Homestead boomed as Roman Catholic, Eastern Orthodox, and Jewish laborers poured into the immigrant ward below Eighth Avenue nearest the mill. Most of these immigrants knew little English and faced harsh working conditions and daily discrimination from the English-speaking "Johnny Bull" mill bosses. With the men's first pay, these groups began building their own houses of worship: safe havens in which to gather, speak their own languages, and raise their children.

All this changed as World War II loomed and the government ordered the Homestead Works to expand. Within a year, the immigrant ward was razed and much of its population moved to new homes uphill from the mill. Many of the eastern European congregations based in the ward chose to relocate near Frick Park, where long-established groups already worshipped. Today, across from St. John-Mark is St. Anthony, the Polish Catholic church; halfway down Ann Street is St. Nicholas Greek Orthodox church, and, a block beyond on Tenth Avenue, across from the Episcopal church is the former Rodef Shalom Temple (now the home of the interdenominational Community of the Crucified One). Within easy walking distance are the Hungarian Reformed Church and the former Carpatho-Rusyn St. John the Baptist Byzantine Catholic Cathedral.

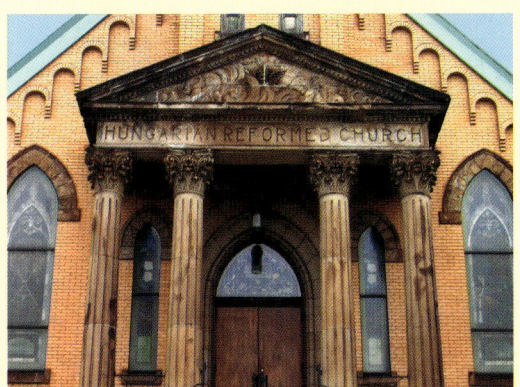

above left: **St. Gregory Russian Orthodox Church**

above right: **St. Nicholas Greek Orthodox Church's steel domes were made at the Homestead Works.**

center: Labor, **a stained-glass window at St. Mary Magdalene. The parish served as the temporary morgue for workers who died in the Battle of Homestead.**

below: **Hungarian Reformed Church**

Three Rivers Route

8
Little Frick Park
10th Avenue between Amity and Ann Streets, Homestead

Called "Little" Frick Park to distinguish it from Pittsburgh's Frick Park, this quiet oasis becomes a hub of activity on Sundays when worshippers flock to the churches surrounding it.

Homestead's Frick Park, circa 1920

BY THE WAY

It's hard to believe that this graceful park was once a trash dump owned by Henry Clay Frick, who later donated the land to the Homestead community.

9
Carnegie Library of Homestead
412–462–3444
510 10th Avenue, Munhall
www.einetwork.net/ein/homested
Mon–Fri, 10AM–7PM; Sat, 9AM–5PM

Guilt can be a powerful force. As history tells the story, it was guilt that prompted Andrew Carnegie, one of the wealthiest, most influential industrialists of the 20th century, to perform philanthropic good deeds. Carnegie's sense of guilt can be traced back to the Homestead Strike of 1892. In the name of the Carnegie Steel Company, Henry Clay Frick hired Pinkerton guards to secure the mill against the locked-out workers. That fateful decision resulted in the death of seven workers.

Perhaps it was guilt, a public relations move, or just an act of good will, but three years after the Homestead Strike, Carnegie decided to donate a library to the Homestead community. (A library bearing his name was already a part of Braddock, home to his Edgar Thomson plant.) Ironically, Carnegie chose to build the library where the state militia had camped during the strike.

Carnegie Library of Homestead, circa 1910

Dedicated on November 5, 1898, the Carnegie Library of Homestead was constructed in the French Renaissance style. Reflecting Carnegie's wish to uplift body, mind, and spirit, the facility boasts a heated swimming pool, an indoor track, a gym, meeting rooms, and an acoustically perfect music hall. U. S. Steel maintained an office there and provided heat and water to the building directly from the Homestead Works plant until well after World War II. Listed on the National Register of Historic Places, the building was restored in 1998 to commemorate its centennial.

WEST HOMESTEAD

The Bulgarian-Macedonian National Educational and Cultural Center
412–461–6188
449 W. 8th Avenue, West Homestead
www.bmnecc.org
Sat, 9AM–5PM; Sun, NOON–5PM

When Patricia Penka Jordanoff French was a child, her mother would make her go to Bulgarian classes every week. "Of course, I fought against it," she recalls. "I wanted to be outside playing with my American friends. But now, as an adult, I thank my mother every day of my life. Because of her, I can speak Bulgarian fluently. She made sure that her children kept their identity."

French has continued to follow her mother's example. Recently, she transformed the Bulgaro-Macedonian Beneficial Association, founded in the mid-1930s to help first-generation immigrants adjust to their new country while giving them a place to enjoy their ethnic traditions, into a new organization. Now, French and her fellow members are looking beyond their own backyards, having set their sights on keeping Bulgarian-Macedonian traditions alive throughout the United States.

Renamed the Bulgarian-Macedonian National Educational and Cultural Center (BMNECC), the organization hosts monthly public *vecherinka* (evening) events, featuring authentic Bulgarian food, music, and dance. From September to May, Saturday mornings are devoted to Soup Sega (Soup Now), a sale of homemade soups using family recipes from different regions of Bulgaria.

With its membership growing once again, the BMNECC has started an archive and museum. As part of its mission, the Center maintains ties with educational and cultural institutions in the homeland and hosts frequent visits by the Bulgarian Ambassador to the United States, as well as other dignitaries.

Pat French's mother would be proud.

above: **Bulgarian crafts on display at the Center**

below: **Soup's on! Center members cook 14 different kinds for the weekly Soup Sega sale.**

The West Homestead Electrical Machine Company (WHEMCO) still manufactures heavy industrial machinery as did its predecessor, Mesta Machine Company.

Three Rivers Route

RANKIN TO CLAIRTON

From Pittsburgh: *Take PA 837 S (Carson Street) to Rankin Bridge.*

One-Day Tour: Sites 11–18

Emil's Lounge: Left across Rankin Bridge. Right exit off bridge. Right at light on Kenmawr Ave., under bridge into Rankin (stay in center lane). Left on 2nd Street/Rankin Blvd. Right on Hawkins Ave. Go 2 blocks to Emil's on right. **Braddock Carnegie Library:** From Emil's, take Hawkins Ave. Go 2 blocks. Left on Rankin Blvd. Bear right on Kenmawr Ave. under bridge (stay in center lane). At light, continue straight 10 blocks on Braddock Ave. Left on Library St. Go 1 block to Library on corner. ☎ **St. Michael/Good Shepherd Church:** From Library, continue 3 blocks on Braddock Ave. to Church on left. **U. S. Steel Edgar Thomson Works:** From Church, continue 2 blocks on Braddock Ave. to mill overlook on right (off-street parking). **Kennywood Park:** From mill, take Braddock Ave. back under Rankin Bridge to first right up ramp. Cross bridge, then left on PA 837 S. Go 2.5 mi. to Kennywood Park on left (parking lot on right). **Metamorphosis Sculpture Park:** From Kennywood parking lot, continue 2 mi. on PA 837 S. Left on Grant Ave. into RIDC Riverplace City Center. Go 1 block to Sculpture Park at corner. **McKeesport Heritage Center:** Continue on PA 837 S. Cross McKeesport Bridge. Follow left ramp on PA 148 N, then right (SE) on Hartman St. Go 1.2 mi. Left into Renziehausen Park (road changes to Eden Park Blvd.). Left on Tulip Dr. Left on Arboretum Dr. Right into Heritage Center parking lot. **U. S. Steel Clairton Works:** From Heritage Center take Tulip Rd., then right on Eden Park Blvd. (becomes Hartman). Left on PA 148 S. Cross McKeesport Bridge. Take PA 837 S to Clairton. Left across Clairton Bridge. Right on Glassport Rd./Lincoln Blvd. for panoramic view of Clairton Works. **Return to Pittsburgh:** Clairton Bridge and PA 837 N.

As you cross the Rankin Bridge, you'll see Carrie Furnaces 6 & 7 on the left, and on the right, Epic Metals Corp., manufacturers of steel deck.

RANKIN

11 ✺ ☕

Emil's Restaurant and Lounge
412–271–9911
414 Hawkins Street, Rankin
Tue–Th, 11am–7pm; Fri, 11am–8pm; Sat, 11am–4pm

Tucked away on a side street is Emil's, a typical Steel Valley tavern where everyone is family. You can munch on a mile-high Reuben or burger while listening to your favorite Croatian tamburitza tunes on an old-fashioned jukebox (four tunes for a dollar). Ask Emil to point out the songs by his son-in-law, Croatian crooner Miroslav Skoro.

Tamburitza music heads the hit parade at Emil's.

Pittsburgh Area

BRADDOCK

Braddock Carnegie Library
412–351–5356 or 412–351–5357
419 Library Street, Braddock
www.einetwork.net/ein/braddock/
Mon & Tues, 10:30AM–6PM; Wed, 10:30AM–7PM; Th, 10:30AM–7:30PM;
Fri, 10:30AM–4PM; Sat, 9AM–4PM

In 1889, Braddock opened the nation's first Carnegie library. The building has changed through the years, but the library now offers books, DVDs and videos, bingo, sports, tutoring programs, and summer camps.

left: **Ornate stonework on the Braddock Carnegie Library's façade**

right: **The library's wrought-iron railings were made at Braddock's mill.**

St. Michael/Good Shepherd Parish
412–271–1515
1101 Braddock Avenue, Braddock
☎ Phone ahead or attend Mass: Sun, 8AM, 10AM;
Mon–Fri, 7AM, 9:30AM; Sat, 9:30AM

Founded in 1891, St. Michael the Archangel of Braddock was the first Slovak Catholic parish in the Pittsburgh Diocese. The parish claimed its place in labor history during the Great Steel Strike of 1919, when the church became local immigrant workers' only safe meeting place. In the 1990s, St. Michael's merged with other Braddock congregations to form Good Shepherd parish.

The Great Steel Strike of 1919

Nicknamed the "Hunky Strike," this struggle was one of the first to involve Slavic workers. After the union's defeat in 1892, steel workers' conditions had worsened. Thinking them docile, companies recruited thousands of Slavic immigrants. But the end of World War I saw a drive to reorganize the mills, fueled by the worker-centered communist ideology arising in eastern Europe. Braddock became a flash-point in this struggle, which culminated in the 1919 Steel Strike. The immigrant workers faced constant harassment from U. S. Steel's Coal and Iron Police. Refusing to be intimidated by company threats of reprisal, Father Adalbert Kazincy, the priest at St. Michael's, opened his church to the activists as a place to meet and organize. The Strike, though unsuccessful, showed that immigrant laborers were just as willing to fight for their rights as those born in the United States.

Three Rivers Route

U. S. Steel Edgar Thomson Works
Braddock Avenue, Braddock
Outdoor observation area

Out of this Furnace

The voice of the mill... came over the wall like the breathing of a giant at work, like the throb of an engine buried deep in the earth. In it were the piping of whistles and the clash of metal on metal; the chuffing of yard locomotives, the rattle of electric cranes and skip hoists, the bump-bump-bump of a train of cars getting into motion; the wide-mouthed blow of the Bessemers, the thud of five-ton ingots dropping six inches as they were stripped of their moulds, the clean, tenpin crack of billets dropping from a magnet, the solid, unhurried grind of the ore dumper, lifting a whole railroad gondola of iron ore and emptying it, delicately; the high whine of the powerhouse dynamos, the brute growl of the limestone and dolomite crushers, the jolting blows of the steam hammers in the blacksmith shop, the distant, earth-shaking thunder of the blooming mill's giant rolls. A hundred discords merged into harmony, the harsh, triumphant song of iron and flame.

—Thomas Bell. *Out of This Furnace*, 1941.

It was in Europe during 1872 that Andrew Carnegie saw for himself how easily and cheaply the new Bessemer steel-making process could produce rails. Upon his return to Pittsburgh, he secured an option on 107 acres of farmland along the Monongahela River in Braddock.

Named for the president of the Pennsylvania Railroad and Carnegie's inaugural customer for steel rail, the Edgar Thomson Works was completed in 1875. ET, as folks in the region call it, was the first large Bessemer plant in the area. (The Bessemer process, which produced steel by forcing a blast of air through molten iron to remove impurities, was introduced in the 1870s in the United States.) Edgar Thomson Works was also Carnegie's first steel mill and the first of his "integrated" or "basic" steelmaking plants in which the full steelmaking process was completed on site and under one management.

Today, ET, no longer a Bessemer plant, is the lone basic steelmaking mill left in Pennsylvania. While its roots go back to the beginnings of the American steel industry, the plant is among the most modern and productive in the world. As other mills were closing in the 1980s, the Edgar Thomson Works was given a new lease on life with the installation of a $250 million continuous caster. Designed to convert liquid steel directly into slabs, the continuous caster eliminated several costly and time-consuming intermediate steps in the process.

During the 1950s, its peak years of production, Edgar Thomson employed 5,000. Today, ET employs approximately 900 and produces a 500,000-pound heat of high-quality steel every 40 minutes — that's enough to make nearly 3,000 refrigerators or 5,000 washing machines. Each year, the plant's 2.8 million tons of raw steel account for 23 percent of the nation's steel production.

Pittsburgh Area

Labor Unions

Southwestern Pennsylvania was not only a cradle of America's second Industrial Revolution, but also the nation's crucible for organized industrial labor. As early as 1845, women textile mill workers in the town of Allegheny (now Pittsburgh's North Side) struck to achieve a 10-hour workday. After the Civil War, the expansion of railroads and the steel-led industrial boom brought heightened visibility to such labor issues as workplace safety, production quotas, hiring practices, and mechanization, as immigrant workers poured into the region from around the globe.

For more than 100 years, industrial workers endured harsh conditions that shortened life spans, and mill and mine disasters that maimed and killed. The region's history was punctuated by labor struggles such as the Great Rail Strike of 1877, battles including the Morewood Mine Massacre of 1891 and the Homestead Steel Strike of 1892, the 1919 "Hunky" Steel Strike, and the 1937 Aliquippa showdown that resulted in the U.S. Supreme Court's validation of the Wagner Act, guaranteeing workers' rights to collective bargaining.

Cleaning the Basic Oxygen Furnace before its next heat. Workplace safety and workers' health are primary concerns of labor unions.

Both the American Federation of Labor and the Congress of Industrial Organizations held their founding conventions in Pittsburgh (the AFL in 1881, the CIO in 1937). Several international unions started in Pittsburgh, including the Ironworkers and the Bakery, Confectionary and Tobacco Workers in the 1890s and the United Steel Workers of America in 1942, as well as a host of local craft unions: Carpenters, Boilermakers, Sheet Metal Workers, Electrical Workers, Bricklayers, and others.

A pantheon of labor's national heroes played significant roles here: William Z. Foster, Fannie Sellins, Mary Harris "Mother" Jones, John L. Lewis, and Philip Murray. Throughout the Rivers of Steel National Heritage Area are historic markers and memorials celebrating events, organizations, and individuals, testaments to the workers' solidarity and resolute strength.

A view of the Edgar Thomson Works from across the Monongahela River

Three Rivers Route

DUQUESNE

Kennywood Park
412–461–0500
4800 Kennywood Boulevard, West Mifflin
www.kennywood.com
Mid-May–Labor Day: Gates open daily, 10:30AM–late evening

BY THE WAY

Look for a panoramic view of U. S. Steel Edgar Thomson Plant from the Carrousel Restaurant on Kennywood Boulevard (PA 837 S).

The year was 1898, and the Monongahela Street Railway Company decided to lease a popular picnic site — Kenny's Grove — and the land surrounding it. Since 1818, the Kenny family had made its living, and fortune, mining coal from this tract of earth, about 12 miles from Pittsburgh proper.

Andrew Mellon held controlling-interest in the Railway Company, and he coined the name Kennywood Park. At the time, Kennywood was one of a number of trolley parks — gathering spots located along the tracks — that were cropping up throughout the country.

In the early days, Kennywood not only boasted beautiful picnic grounds, but also a man-made lake, a dance pavilion, a cafeteria, and a merry-go-round. During the next several years, patrons were treated to new and exciting attractions. 1900 saw the grand opening of the bandstand; 1901, the Old Mill ride; and 1902, a state-of-the-art figure-eight roller coaster.

However, as the challenges of running an amusement park grew more demanding, the Railway Company sought to sever its ties. By 1902, it had subleased Kennywood to a Boston-based firm and later to a group of Aspinwall businessmen. By 1906, the lease, as well as the day-to-day responsibilities, went to A. S. McSwigan and F. W. Henninger.

These two gentlemen and their descendants managed to guide the park through changing lifestyles, economic conditions, and fashions, and a few cataclysmic events. Kennywood has survived several fires and severe storms.

Throughout the decades, visitors have enjoyed now-classic attractions, like the merry-go-round (featuring 50 moving

Nationality Days, Kennywood Park, painting by Kathleen Ferri, mid-1990s

Pittsburgh Area

horses) and Noah's Ark; a variety of old-fashioned but still-thrilling wooden coasters like the Jack Rabbit (built in 1921), the Thunderbolt (built in 1924), and the Racer (rebuilt in 1927); more modern, high-tech rides like Phantom's Revenge and Aero 360; and, of course, food from the Potato Patch.

Encompassing 140-plus acres, Kennywood was named a National Historic Landmark in 1987 and remains a Pittsburgh institution. It is a place for first kisses and first roller coaster rides, a place to be taken to as a child and then to bring your own children. It is also a place to celebrate ethnic heritage and pride.

Kennywood has always welcomed the region's diverse populations. In the beginning, explains Andy Quinn, the park's director of community relations, nationality days simply added ticket sales. Now, they are "ingrained in the fabric of western Pennsylvania."

That tapestry includes Carpatho-Russian, Italian, Slovak, Serbian, Greek, Byzantine, Hungarian, Slovene, Polish, and Croatian Days. But these gatherings are about more than bumper cars and arcade games. "Often," Quinn says, "nationality days feature religious services, programs, and speakers."

Joe Magarac, legendary hero of steel, is one of the attractions at Kennywood.

16 Metamorphosis Sculpture Park

RIDC Riverplace City Center, Duquesne
Outdoors

There are still steelworkers at the Duquesne mill — or more exactly, workers in steel. On a prominent corner at the old U. S. Steel Duquesne Works site stand three figures built from steel plate and hardhats salvaged from the mill, alongside a huge butterfly made of steelworkers' hand tools. In recognition of Duquesne's transformation, the Metamorphosis sculptures were created in the early 1990s by metal artist Tim Kaulen and a crew of former Mon Valley mill workers as part of the site's redevelopment after the plant was demolished.

Duquesne Steel Company introduced the "direct rolling" process in 1886 to compete with Andrew Carnegie in the rail market. Carnegie started a bogus rumor that his rival's new process produced defective rails, putting Duquesne Steel out of business. Carnegie acquired their works in 1889, then refitted his Braddock and Homestead mills to use the same "direct rolling" technology, and earned a profit six times the $1 million purchase price he paid!

Workers of steel and a tool-winged butterfly symbolize pride in a mill town's past and hope for its future.

Three Rivers Route

McKEESPORT

McKeesport Heritage Center
412–678–1832
1832 Arboretum Drive, McKeesport
Tues–Th, 9am–5pm; Sat, 9am–3pm
Admission is free. Ring the doorbell to enter.

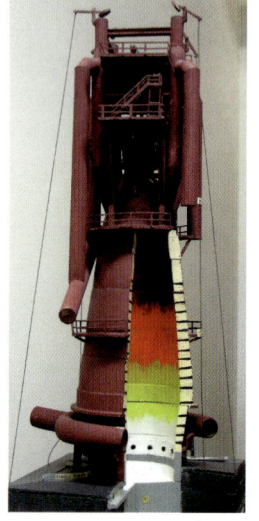

A model blast furnace

They didn't call McKeesport "Tube City" for nothing. From 1871 to 1987, McKeesport was home to National Tube Works, one of the world's largest producers of iron and steel pipe. It became a division of U. S. Steel in 1901. Weekdays, McKeesport's modest population of 55,000 would swell as workers from surrounding communities arrived to punch the clock at National Tube, at specialty steelmaker Firth Sterling, or at any number of other local firms.

Paying tribute to this industrial town's past is now the job of the McKeesport Heritage Center. For more than 16 years, the Center has been collecting historic photographs and memorabilia, amassing (on microfilm) every issue of the *McKeesport Daily News* since 1884, and accumulating local cemetery records and copies of the *Allegheny County Census* from 1790 to 1920.

The Center is home to a mural about steel, displays on life in McKeesport, a scale model of National Tube, a blast furnace replica, and a restored 1832 schoolhouse. Genealogy enthusiasts are encouraged to trace their roots through the Center's scrapbooks, photos, and directories. Since opening its doors, membership has grown from 35 to more than 1,300.

Hungarian Heritage

In southwestern Pennsylvania, "Hungarian" can refer to people from the Magyar ethnic group who speak the Hungarian language. Or people of Slovak background whose families came from Hungarian-speaking parts of Slovakia. Or Hungarian Gypsies. Or people from the many eastern European lands that before World War I were part of the Austro-Hungarian Empire. Most who call themselves Hungarian in this region have ancestors who arrived around 1900 to work in steel and coal. During the Steel Era, so many immigrant laborers came here with passports stamped "Hungarian" that the nickname "hunky" soon applied to mill workers of any ethnic group. A second wave, the "56-ers," came here as refugees following the unsuccessful 1956 Hungarian bid for independence from the Soviet Union. While most of the earlier immigrants were either Protestant (Hungarian Reformed) or Roman Catholic, some were also Hungarian Jews. The largest group of Hungarians settled in Pittsburgh's Hazelwood neighborhood and in the Washington County community of Daisytown. They founded fraternal clubs, beneficial associations, singing societies, and Hungarian Boy Scout troops. In Homestead and Braddock, Gypsy people grew up speaking both Hungarian and their own language, Romani. In the Steel Valley, no Hungarian Gypsy wedding — or funeral — was complete without the soulful music of a violin ensemble. Today there is a **Hungarian Nationality Room** at the University of Pittsburgh and an annual Hungarian Day at **Kennywood Park.** Hungarian Reformed churches are still active in both Hazelwood and Homestead. The **Jozsa Corner Hungarian Restaurant** in Hazelwood features old-world delights — paprikas chicken, goulash, and *palacinky,* and evenings of Hungarian music and dance (Three Rivers Route).

Woodcut by local Hungarian folk artist Alex J. Bodnar

CLAIRTON

U. S. Steel Clairton Coke Works
PA 837 S at Clairton
Outdoor View

For those who worked at the Clairton Coke Works, the smell of rotten eggs (actually, the odor of naphthalene) meant one thing—jobs.

Located on 392 acres along 3.3 miles of the west bank of the Monongahela River, the Clairton Works began coking operations in 1918 and quickly set itself apart from other coke plants by using a radical technology—the by-product coke oven.

This new technology not only produced coke in a more efficient manner, but also enabled the collection and processing of coke-oven gas. Consequently, the Clairton Works is as much a chemical plant as it is a coke plant.

Converting about 6.6 million tons of coal into 4.7 million tons of coke a year, or 13,000 tons of coke per day, the Clairton Works is one of the largest and most environmentally advanced plants in the United States. It produces 55 million gallons of road and roofing tar and 20 million gallons of light oil (a component of plastic) annually. And every day it turns out 45 tons of sulfur, 45 tons of anhydrous ammonia (used in fertilizers and explosives), and 225 million cubic feet of coke-oven gas (to fuel the blast furnace at the U. S. Steel Edgar Thomson Works).

Clairton Works relies on barge transportation for delivery of nearly 18,000 tons of coal a day. Its dock is nearly a mile long. During the winter, the plant keeps a 10-day stockpile of coal in case the rivers freeze.

The Clairton Coke Works from the Monongahela River's north shore

Three sites at the Clairton Works have been designated as wildlife habitats.

Three Rivers Route

MONROEVILLE AREA

From Pittsburgh: Take I-376 E.

Half-Day Tour: Sites 19–21

☎ *George Westinghouse Museum:* Take I-376 E to Forest Hills exit 8A (PA 30). Go 5.5 mi. on PA 30. Left on 5th Ave. (PA 148). Go 1.5 mi. to stoplight. Continue straight 2 blocks into Wilmerding. Left onto Herman Ave. Left onto Commerce St. to Museum on right.
☎ *Sri Venkateswara Temple:* From Museum, return via PA 30 to I-376 E. Take I-376 E Monroeville exit 10B (PA Bus. 22). Stay in left lane. At first stoplight, left on Rodi Rd. (PA 791 N). Immediate right on Old William Penn Hwy.(McCrady Rd.). Go 2 mi. on winding road. Right over narrow bridge on Thompson Run Rd. Go .2 mi. Right on S. McCully Dr. (S. V. Temple Dr.), up hill to Temple. **Croatian Fraternal Union:** From Temple, take Old William Penn Hwy. back to PA Bus. 22 E. Go 1.2 mi. on PA Bus. 22 E. Left on Kingston Dr. to Delaney Dr. CFU building is on corner. **Return to Pittsburgh:** Take I-376 W.

WILMERDING

19

George Westinghouse Museum
412–823–0500
325 Commerce Street, Wilmerding
www.georgewestinghouse.com/museum.html
Mon–Fri, 10AM–4PM; Sat, 11AM–3PM; closed Sundays and holidays
☎ Groups should phone ahead.

above: The first Westinghouse light bulbs were branded "Mazda" lights.

below: The Appliance Room at the museum reminds visitors of the Westinghouse slogan "Every house needs a Westinghouse."

Once upon a time, the George Westinghouse castle served as the offices for the Westinghouse Air Brake Company. Now operated by APICS Educational and Research Foundation, Inc., it has been transformed into a museum housing historical information about the Westinghouse family, as well as memorabilia about Wilmerding and surrounding communities.

George Westinghouse, Jr., will long be remembered as one of the nation's most prolific inventors. Born in 1846 in Central Bridge, New York, George, Jr. began working in his father's shop at a young age and acquired his first patent, for a rotary engine, when he was 19.

A near-collision he saw while traveling by train inspired Westinghouse to develop the air brake in 1866. He then went on to create hundreds of innovations, such as road signals, alternating current, and the first radio station. He even found a way to safely deliver natural gas to homes and industry.

The Westinghouse Museum features an Invention Room where his 361 patents are highlighted, a Room of Achievement with many Westinghouse Company artifacts and photographs, and an Appliance Room.

PENN HILLS

Sri Venkateswara Temple
412–373–3380, ext. 105
1230 South McCully Drive, Penn Hills
www.svtemple.org
Winter: Sun–Th, Sat, 9AM –7:30PM; Fri, 9AM–8:30PM
Summer: Sun–Th, Sat, 9AM –8:30PM; Fri, 9AM–9:30PM
☎ Phone ahead for guided tour.

The Sri Venkateswara Temple has an open-door policy. Its members welcome guests interested in learning about Hinduism and Pittsburgh's South Asian community, exploring the environs of the temple or sampling the cuisine offered in the self-serve cafeteria.

Located in Penn Hills, the S. V. Temple is modeled after the Venkateswara Temple in Tirupati, Andhra Pradesh, India. Completed in the 1980s, it was one of the first Hindu temples built in the United States. More than $925,000 was raised for its construction, primarily from first-generation Indian immigrants longing for a familiar place of worship in their new homeland.

One of the temple's distinguishing features is its two entryways. The side door is used most frequently, while the imposing *Rajagopuram* entrance is reserved for special occasions. Inside, both members and visitors must remove their shoes.

Guests are then asked to follow the Hindu custom of proceeding to the left and exiting from the right. This is done because clockwise circumambulation (to circle on foot as part of a ritual) is held to be favorable in the Hindu religion. In Hinduism, belief and lifestyle are intertwined. For example, physical purity is important for it is believed to mirror mental cleanliness. Consequently, devotees must bathe before coming to the temple. (Visitors, however, are not required to do so.)

above: **Rajagopuram entrance**
below: **Temple members Lakshmi Somayajula (left) and Latha Bhagavatula**

Arranged on two levels, the main temple is a square within a square. The lower level takes visitors around the corridor where the *vahanas* (animal figures) are stored. The upper level, accessible via stairs leading to double glass doors, is the *Mahamandapam* (Great Hall).

While touring the temple, visitors may notice brown paper bags of fruit placed around the Temple. These are gifts to God. Staff member Latha Bhagavatula explains, "When you go to somebody's house, you don't go empty-handed. Same here. Back home in India, people bring their own fruits. But here, we make it convenient."

Six priests perform all rituals at S. V. Temple. On special occasions, additional priests come from other temples — some even from India. The priest acts as a liaison between God and the worshipper, and learns chanting and other skills from a very young age. When a priest is not occupied, he (or anyone else in

Three Rivers Route

Venkateswara, the main deity of the temple

the office) will gladly answer questions from visitors. Self-guided tour booklets also are available.

Sri Venkateswara Temple has a self-serve cafeteria open to everyone. During the week, it offers a standard fare of tamarind rice (rice with spices and nuts) and yogurt rice (rice blended with spices, yogurt, and buttermilk). Snacks like sweet *bhoondi* (made from lentil powder and sugar) and spicy *mixer* (a combination of lentil powder, nuts, and paprika) are also available. On Saturdays, the meals are more varied and elaborate.

Visitors may wonder why the S.V. Temple is so open to non-Hindus. According to Bhagavatula, the answer is simple: Since God is universal, everyone is welcome. "We are proud to be associated with the Pittsburgh community since 1976," says Board Chairman Venkat Venkataraman. Adds Board Secretary Parandham Koduri, "We look forward to a bright future with many more accomplishments in the next generation."

Asian and Middle Eastern Heritages

The steel boom of the late 19th century drew not only Europeans, but also workers from Asia and the Middle East, particularly China and what was then the Ottoman Empire. Chinese laborers were recruited early by the Harmonists to work in the iron mills in Beaver Falls; later Chinese arrivals started small businesses in the steel towns near Pittsburgh. By the early 20th century, Pittsburgh had a small Chinatown.

Lebanese, mostly Maronite Catholics, toiled alongside Europeans in the coal mines and coke patches near Brownsville and in the steel plants in Allegheny County; Syrians, mostly Antiochian Orthodox, worked at mines and mills along the mid-Monongahela River and near Greensburg. Like the larger ethnic industrial communities, they built churches and clubs to maintain their traditional arts, cuisine, language, and customs.

The next waves began to arrive in the 1970s. Some came as students and scholars, responding to the universities' continued expansion after World War II. Some came as professionals — engineers, chemists, architects drawn to the diversifying industries of the region. Others were doctors and technicians attracted by the growth in hospitals and medical research. Still others came as refugees from war-torn homelands. Many ethnic groups were new to the region: Japanese, Korean, Filipino, Asian, Indian, Pakistani, Thai, Vietnamese, Hmong, Palestinian, and Coptic. They arrived as steel was declining, so they missed the millworking and mining experience that had shaped earlier immigrants. They did not form separate enclaves, but spread out primarily in Allegheny County.

The traditions of these ethnic groups can be experienced in a variety of ways. Like their eastern European counterparts, several Lebanese and Syrian churches in the region hold annual festivals, featuring the foods, dances, and music of their groups (Three Rivers Route, Youghiogheny Route, Monongahela Route). The Chinese On Leong Club, dating from the early 20th century, can still be seen in downtown Pittsburgh. **Homewood Cemetery** includes a Chinese section. Other opportunities include sampling the Asian restaurants in Pittsburgh's Oakland, Squirrel Hill, and Lawrenceville neighborhoods; visiting houses of worship such as the **Sri Venkateswara Temple** (Hindu) in Monroeville or the Pittsburgh Islamic Center in Oakland; and attending events such as the Chinese Dragon Boat Festival on the Monongahela River in Pittsburgh. (Three Rivers Route).

A Chinese dragon boat

Pittsburgh Area

MONROEVILLE

㉑ ✠ ♪

Croatian Fraternal Union Museum
412–351–3909
100 Delaney Drive, Monroeville
www.croatianfraternalunion.org
Mon–Th, 8:30am–5pm; Fri, 8:30am–12:30pm

From the outside, the Croatian Fraternal Union (CFU) headquarters looks like any other modern office building. But inside, visitors will discover an outstanding collection of artifacts, costumes, instruments, craftwork, and archives — all evidence of the rich, living heritage of Croatians in the New World.

For the past 100 years, Pittsburgh has been the hub for Croatians throughout North America, and the CFU has served as the driving force for the support and promotion of Croatian cultural traditions. The CFU has started regional Junior and Adult Cultural Federations in the United States and Canada that hold annual public Tamburitza Festivals featuring Croatian folk music and dance. Local lodges in southwestern Pennsylvania and around the country have built centers called "Homes" that sponsor Junior Tamburitza groups and other Croatian cultural activities.

Visitors to the CFU's third-floor museum find exhibits of regional folk costumes, dolls, and embroidery, as well as an ornately carved desk given to the museum by the government of Croatia. Throughout the building are other treasures, such as reversed-glass paintings and line drawings by contemporary Croatian naïve artist Ivan Lackovic-Croata, along with displays of tamburitza instruments and club memorabilia. The CFU produces CDs and videos of Croatian folk arts that are available for sale in the headquarters' gift shop.

top: **Sign for the Consulate of the Republic of Croatia, an honorary office in Pittsburgh**

center: **Stained-glass window depicts the city of Zagreb's emblem.**

left: **Museum display of Croatian costumes and instruments**

Folk cousins of the violin, tamburitza instruments are still handmade by craftworkers in the Pittsburgh area.

Three Rivers Route

OHIO VALLEY

From Pittsburgh: *Take PA 51 N.*

Half-Day Tour: Sites 22–25
Mancini's: *Take PA 51 N. Left on Chartiers Ave. Right on Broadway Ave. Right on 6th St. Mancini's is on left.* **Pierogies Plus:** *From Mancini's, continue on 6th St. Right on Woodward Ave. Right on 5th St. Left on Broadway Ave. Left on Chartiers Ave. Left on Island Ave. (PA 51 N) 3 mi. Pierogies Plus is on right.* **Little Athens of Sewickley:** *Continue on PA 51 N. Right over McKees Rocks Bridge. Left on PA 65 N. Go 8 mi. to Sewickley. Right on Broad St. Left on Beaver St. Go 1 block. Right on Locust Pl. to restaurant.* ☎ **SS. Peter and Paul Church:** *From Little Athens take PA 65 S. Right across West End Bridge to I-279 S to Carnegie exit 2. Bear right at "Y" on Mansfield Blvd. Go 2 blocks. SS. Peter and Paul is on Mansfield at Walnut St.* **Return to Pittsburgh:** *Right on Mansfield Blvd. Right on Chestnut St. Left on Academy St. Follow signs to I-279 N.*

McKEES ROCKS

Mancini's Bakery
412–331–2291
601 Woodward Avenue, McKees Rocks
(entrance on 6th Street off Broadway Street)
www.mancinibread.com
Mon, Wed, Th, Fri, Sun, open 24 hours;
Tues, Sat, 12:30 AM–2 PM

This is what you need to know about a visit to Mancini's. First, the aroma is heavenly. Each loaf is hand-twisted, which means the bakers move like an Indianapolis 500 pit crew to get 10,000 loaves made each day. Next, you need to know that the shop has its original working brick oven from 1924, just to the left of the counter area. Here customers can watch as a baker deftly uses a peel with a seven-foot handle to maneuver the loaves. There is a final challenge...trying to leave Mancini's with only one loaf of their warm, crusty Italian bread under your arm.

BY THE WAY

In 1894, the boroughs of Mansfield and Chartiers merged. Voters named the new town "Carnegie," after Andrew Carnegie. Civic leaders hoped that he would establish a new steel mill in his namesake town. Instead, he gave the town a library and a music hall.

As you cross the McKees Rocks Bridge, you'll see the former Pressed Steel Car Works on your left.

William Matasich bakes bread in the brick oven at Mancini's.

Pittsburgh Area

Pierogies Plus
412–331–2224
342 Island Avenue, McKees Rocks
www.pierogiesplus.com
Mon, 11AM–6PM; Th–Fri, 11AM–7PM

Your Polish grandmother never made this many different kinds of pierogi. Special-order pierogi include mozzarella and provolone, spinach and ricotta, or potato and jalapeno peppers. So, whether it is the traditional potato and cheese, or *lekvar,* or something more exotic you crave, the ladies at Pierogies Plus won't let you down.

Tatyana Plotnikova and Tatyana Shlyakovskaya make pierogi.

S E W I C K L E Y

Little Athens of Sewickley
412–741–1230
518 Locust Place, Sewicley
www.littleathensofsewickley.com
Mon, Tues, Th, 8AM–11PM;
Wed, Fri, Sat, 8AM–2AM; Sun, 8AM–8PM

Sewickley Heights was a summer retreat for Pittsburgh industrialists in the early 20th century.

In the mood for authentic Greek food? Owned and operated by the Kontoulis family for over 30 years, this restaurant features all the favorites, including *spanakopita* (spinach pies), lamb *souvlaki* (shish kebab), flame cheese *saganaki,* and desserts, along with specialties such as a tangy *salonika* hot dip and Greek wines.

Ancient and modern Greece come together at Little Athens of Sewickley.

Three Rivers Route

CARNEGIE

above: Domes are styled after churches in Ukraine

below: Interior icon by parish member Michael Kapeluck

25 ✠ ⋀ Ⓔ

SS. Peter and Paul Ukrainian Orthodox Church
412–279–2111
200 Walnut Street, Carnegie
Mass: Sun, 10AM
☎ Phone ahead for museum or church tour.

Some churches are more than houses of worship — they're also works of art. At SS. Peter and Paul Ukrainian Orthodox Church, the ceilings and walls are canvases for the beautiful iconography of artist Michael Kapeluck. A lifelong member of SS. Peter and Paul, Kapeluck has dedicated his career to "writing" icons, the special religious paintings venerated in the Eastern Orthodox Church.

Artistry is found in other aspects of SS. Peter and Paul as well. For example, each year church members come together to create hundreds of beautiful pysanky — Ukrainian Easter eggs. These colorful eggs are then made available to the public at the annual Pysanky Sale on Palm Sunday. The public is also welcome at the church's Holiday Craft Sale and dinner in November (the menu always features delicious eastern European treats).

SS. Peter and Paul celebrated its centennial anniversary in 2003. To commemorate the occasion, parishioners constructed an exhibit to pay homage to the church's forebears and Ukrainian cultural heritage. The exhibit remains on display in the church's museum.

Ukrainian Heritage

Making pysanky

From a rich Slavic culture in eastern Europe, Ukrainians came to southwestern Pennsylvania in the great wave of immigration during the region's industrialization beginning in the late 19th century. Most were Ukrainian Orthodox Christians, but Ukrainian-speaking Jews came as well. Many Ukrainians found work in steel mills and steel-related factories and foundries, settling in Pittsburgh's South Side neighborhood and in nearby industrial towns such as Carnegie (Three Rivers Route).

They brought with them traditions of dance, embroidered clothing, holiday customs and foods, instrumental music, and religious iconography and architecture, many of which are still practiced here. **SS. Peter and Paul Ukrainian Orthodox Church** in Carnegie is modeled on traditional churches in Ukraine. Easter customs remain important, such as decorating pysanky (intricately dyed Easter eggs), baking paska (butter and egg bread), and taking baskets of traditional foods to be blessed at church, then eaten at Easter Sunday dinner. The Poltava Ukrainian Dance Company, based in Carnegie, was founded in 1964 to perpetuate Ukrainian dance and music traditions and present them to the public at the annual Pittsburgh Folk Festival, at other events in the region, and elsewhere in the United States. This ensemble provides children of Ukrainian background in the Pittsburgh area with a way to learn and carry on the traditions of their ancestors. Other local organizations include the Ridna Shkola of Pittsburgh (Pittsburgh School of Ukrainian Studies).

There are now about 12,000 people of Ukrainian background in the region. Visitors will want to see the Ukrainian cultural exhibits at SS. Peter and Paul Church and stop in at the church's annual Pysanky Sale held on Palm Sunday.

Pittsburgh Area

ALLEGHENY VALLEY

From Pittsburgh: *Follow PA 28 N.*

Half-Day Tour: Sites 26–29
☎ **St. Nicholas Croatian Church:** *Take PA 28 N to Millvale exit 3. At 5-pt. intersection, bear left on Grant Ave. Go 2 blocks. Left on Sheridan St. up hill to "T." Left on Maryland Ave. Church is on left, parking lot on right.* **Chatellier's Bakery:** *Return on Maryland Ave. Right at stop sign (Sheridan). Go 2 blocks. Left on Grant Ave. to stoplight. Right on North Ave. Bakery is on left.* **Blarney Stone Restaurant:** *Continue on North Ave. Right on Lincoln Ave. Right on Ohio St. to stop sign. Left on PA 28 N to Etna exit 4. (Left-hand exit.) From ramp, take Butler St. Go past 4th stoplight to Blarney Stone on right.* **Council of Three Rivers American Indian Center:** *Return on Butler St. to blinking light. Left on PA 28 N ramp. PA 28 N to exit 11. At end of long ramp, left on PA 910 W. Go 4 mi. Left on Saxonburg Blvd. Go .7 mi. At firehouse, right on Charles St. to COTRAIC entrance at end of road.* ***Return to Pittsburgh:*** *PA 910 E to PA 28 S.*

MILLVALE

St. Nicholas Croatian Church
412–821–3438 or 412–231–3892
24 Maryland Avenue, Millvale
www.users.telerama.com~emq/welcom.htm
☎ Phone ahead for tour,
or attend Mass: Sat, 5PM; Sun, 10:30AM

Born in 1900 as the daughter church of St. Nicholas Croatian Catholic on East Ohio Street, St. Nicholas Croatian Church in Millvale has led a sometimes difficult but ultimately rewarding life.

In 1921, the church suffered a devastating fire that gutted its interior. The parishioners, all steelworkers in the nearby mills, immediately started to rebuild. Although structural repairs were completed by the mid-1930s, the walls remained bare.

Father Albert Zagar, the parish priest, heard about a Croatian artist named Maxo Vanka who had recently arrived in eastern Pennsylvania. The priest and the artist agreed that Vanka would have free rein to paint St. Nicholas as long as his work was religious in character. "We wanted to beautify the church," Father Zagar explained. "We wanted murals that would tell the story of this parish, of the people."

In two brief but intense sessions (the first in 1937, the second in 1941), Vanka created darkly powerful murals. His images weave religious themes together with the experiences of the parish's immigrant workers. The stories are told in the context of war, injustice, poverty, and the hope of redemption. (Legend has it that there was even a ghost haunting the project.)

Named to the National Historic Register, St. Nicholas Croatian Church in Millvale is still a vibrant spiritual home to local Croatians, and Vanka's murals continue to be heralded as works of art.

Murals by Maxo Vanka, 1937, 1941:
above: Rededication of St. Nicholas Church
below: The Immigrant Mother Raises Her Sons for Industry

Three Rivers Route

27

Chatellier's Bakery
412–821–8533
213 North Avenue, Millvale
Tues–Fri, 7AM–5PM; Sat, 7AM–2PM

Who would have thought that tucked away in Millvale is one of Pittsburgh's finest French patisseries? The scents of buttery croissants and Breton cake fill the air of this friendly, busy bakery on Millvale's main shopping street.

Long-time employee April Totef takes Raymond Thompson's order.

ETNA

28

Blarney Stone Restaurant
412–781–1666
30 Grant Avenue, Etna
www.blarneystonerestaurant.com
Tues–Fri, 11AM–9PM; Sat, 4PM–MIDNIGHT;
Sun, 10:30AM–2PM brunch, and 4PM–8PM dinner

Stepping into the Blarney Stone is like stepping into one of Dublin's legendary pubs, especially since the restaurant features a lump of the old sod under a piece of Plexiglas® just inside its front door. Visit the Blarney Stone to catch Irish music and dance or to pick up a Galway or Waterford crystal souvenir from their gift shop.

The gift shop features Belleek China with a traditional shamrock pattern.

DORSEYVILLE

Council of Three Rivers American Indian Center
412–782–4457
120 Charles Street, Dorseyville
www.angelfire.com/pa/COTRAIC/
Weekdays, 9AM–5PM

The rockets are gone now, and a wooded hilltop in rural Allegheny County has regained its timeless calm. Once a Cold War missile base, the site is back in the care of people who knew it 20,000 years ago.

When the Council of Three Rivers, a local Native American intertribal organization, acquired the property in the early 1970s, they promptly renamed it "Singing Winds." But the Council's efforts to return the land to peaceful purposes didn't stop there. Buildings once used by the military were reassigned as the Council's American Indian Center and dedicated to promoting the socio-economic development of the Native American community.

Fred Deer witnessed the transformation firsthand, as a member of the Center's advisory council, and as the site's maintenance man. Originally from a Mohawk reservation in Canada, Deer was employed at U.S. Steel's Homestead Works. When the mill shut down in 1986, Deer began devoting his time and energy to the Center.

Ceremonial drum

In fact, his entire family got involved in preserving traditional Native American arts. He was an accomplished wood- and bone-carver. His wife and sister are bead-workers, and together they join other families every September as the Center hosts an intertribal Pow-Wow at Singing Winds. The Pow-Wow draws singers, drummers, and dancers representing native peoples from Cuban Taino to Alaskan Tlingit. Artists display and sell their work at this event, and visitors can enjoy traditional foods like Indian fry-bread.

In addition to the annual Pow-Wow, the Center hosts monthly Native American Community Day gatherings. Guests are welcome to visit the Center, learn more about Native Americans in the region, and listen to the singing winds along the nature trail.

Native American Heritage

People have lived in southwestern Pennsylvania for over 20,000 years — the longest documented human presence in the hemisphere. When Europeans arrived in the 18th century, the Native Americans they encountered were Seneca, Lenape (Delaware), and Shawnee, among others. Allied with the Iroquois, these groups controlled extensive hunting grounds, often situating their villages at river confluences. More Native Americans came into the region, pushed west by European settlement. The French and Indian War and its aftermath at last forced the Native Americans to give up their lands. Many went north to New York; some stayed in the region, intermarrying with white and African-American settlers. Place names such as Kittanning and Aliquippa, Monongahela, Allegheny, Youghiogheny, and Ohio, bear witness to their legacy. Thousands of local residents still claim Native American ancestors.

In the 20th century, the Steel Era attracted new Native American workers to the region. More than 2,500 Native Americans from all over North America carry on traditions including dancing, drumming, beadwork, carving, basketry, and herbal medicine here. Organizations such as the **Council of Three Rivers American Indian Center** and the Thunder Mountain Lenape Nation reinforce native cultural identity. In addition to exhibits at Pittsburgh's **Carnegie Museum** and historical societies in the region, visitors can experience native traditions at the annual Pow-Wow in Dorseyville (Three Rivers Route).

Three Rivers Route

BY THE WAY

The term Golden Triangle first received national attention in 1914 when it appeared in a "Saturday Evening Post" article describing Pittsburgh's downtown.

1. Golden Triangle
2. Strip District and Polish Hill
3. North Side and Troy Hill
4. Bloomfield and Lawrenceville
5. Homewood and Point Breeze
6. Squirrel Hill
7. Oakland
8. Hill District
9. South Side and Mt. Washington

Pittsburgh

If the Three Rivers area was the hundred-year heart of Big Steel, the city of Pittsburgh was its commercial, financial, and educational head. For America and the world, Pittsburgh meant steel.

From its beginnings in the late 18th century, Pittsburgh preferred industry over agriculture, its precious riverfront land yielding to manufacturing and trade. During the 19th century, it was the Iron City, then the Steel City, and the nicknames still resonate today. Its people were known for their willingness to work hard and long, often in dirty and dangerous conditions.

The Point — where the confluence of the Monongahela and Allegheny Rivers form the Ohio — was Pittsburgh's commercial hub. Now called the Golden Triangle, during most of the Steel Era it was a raucous, bustling area dominated by fleets of river barges and mazes of rail freight lines and warehouses.

Along the Monongahela, the South Side was first a center of glassmaking, then home to the giant Jones & Laughlin Steel plant. On the Allegheny side, the Strip District, another early manufacturing area, later became the city's center for wholesale merchants, especially of ethnic foods.

Pittsburgh's steep, wooded hillsides and winding river valleys created self-contained neighborhoods. Several started as separate towns that were later annexed to Pittsburgh. The city's workers crowded into small houses near the industrial plants or occupied homes precariously perched on the slopes. Most people lived life within a block — they walked to work at the plant, walked to church on Sunday, and walked to their shops and clubs. The girl married the fellow next door and they set up housekeeping around the corner from their parents. Children walked to school and no one locked their front doors.

Pittsburgh's riverfront industrial neighborhoods were similar, yet each had its own character. The North Side, originally called Allegheny City, was heavily German. The South Side, originally Birmingham, was a mix of German and eastern European groups. Bloomfield was both Italian and German, while nearby Lawrenceville had many Croatians. Polish Hill was and still is Polish. The Hill District was the port of entry for many newcomers, notably Jews and later African-Americans. Inland neighborhoods such as Oakland and Squirrel Hill began as trolley-car suburbs, but

above: Ironworkers, by John Shryock, 1980s
below: **View of the Point today**

Rivers of Steel Archives

became centers for education and high culture, as well as home to upwardly mobile working families and then post-industrial immigrants.

After World War II, downtown Pittsburgh made a concerted effort to shed its Smoky City image, gradually remaking itself into a showplace of modern architecture with inviting fountains and riverside trails. The neighborhoods have changed too, though several retain distinctive cultures. Pittsburgh has played many cities in films, but its finest role is when it plays itself.

Three Rivers Route

The Golden Triangle

There are few cities in the nation with such a defined downtown as Pittsburgh. Its 255-acre Golden Triangle is bound by Grant Street and the Allegheny and Monongahela Rivers. This compact, pedestrian-friendly area is home to arguably one of the most historically significant tracts of land — the forks of the Ohio River.

Situated in the low land between the two rivers, the site (today's Point State Park), was a focus of the conflict that erupted between England and France. The French and Indian War, as it became known in America, amounted to nothing more or less than a fight for control of this triangle that would some day engender a hardy entrepreneurial spirit.

The Golden Triangle's strategic location within the New World's river system was enviable. As a result, Pittsburgh quickly became a shipbuilding capital and a gateway to the West as pioneers poured through the city and headed down the Ohio River.

The abundance of natural resources — clay, coal, sand, timber, limestone — gave rise to industries designed to meet the growing needs — glass, barrels, rope, and iron — of westward expansion. By the time of the Civil War, Pittsburgh's iron production was thriving and primed to overflow into steelmaking.

But heavy industrialization ultimately took its toll. After World War II, the city's well-earned reputation as a dirty, smoky town led civic leaders to undertake its modernization. Their efforts would serve as the foundation for America's first urban renaissance.

Like everything else in Pittsburgh, the Renaissance began at the Point. Industrial warehouses, train yards, and deteriorating buildings were cleared away to make room for the dedication of Point State Park in 1974. Today, the Golden Triangle's skyscrapers — the Gulf Building, the U. S. Steel Tower, the Frick Building, PPG Place, the former Westinghouse Building, and the former Alcoa Building — memorialize the industries that downtown Pittsburgh spawned.

a PPG Place
b U. S. Steel Tower
c Troy Conley, Rob Tedesco, and Jason Jameson celebrate St. Paddy's Day in Market Square.
d Pittsburgh at noon, 1940s
e Construction of Gateway Center, Pittsburgh's first redevelopment project, 1950s

Photos courtesy of Carnegie Library of Pittsburgh

Pittsburgh Neighborhoods

The Original Power Lunch

Andrew Carnegie, Henry Clay Frick, George Westinghouse, B. F. Jones, and James Laughlin: the Duquesne Club membership read like a who's who of the last turn-of-the-century powerbrokers.

Founded in 1873, the Club charged a $200 initiation fee and $50 a year in dues. Although the club will not disclose its current rates, rumor has it that it adds up to several thousand dollars. It's also rumored that, in an effort to keep business dealings private, verbal agreements are customary in the Club's dining and public rooms.

The once all-male Duquesne Club (women joined in the 1980s) served as a retreat for Henry J. Heinz, founder of the Heinz Company; Eugene W. Pargny, past-president of the American Sheet and Tin Plate Company; Henry Damon Shute, former vice-president in charge of commercial operations at Westinghouse Electric and Manufacturing Company; and William Wallace Blackburn, former vice-president and secretary of Carnegie Steel Company.

In addition, former astronaut and U.S. Senator John Glenn and golfer Arnold Palmer were members. And, in 1921, the Duquesne Club was the setting for the first speech ever broadcast live on radio. Herbert Hoover, then a government official, was the speaker, and KDKA was the station that carried the event.

Noted for its beautiful Garden Patio Room and elegant parties, the Duquesne Club recently bowed to changing times by relaxing its dress code. At least in some rooms at certain times, jackets and ties are no longer required.

f United Steel Workers of America
g The original Alcoa
h Union Trust
i Trinity Cathedral (left) and First Presbyterian (right)
j Haas Mural depicts steel mill interior.

Three Rivers Route

The Golden Triangle

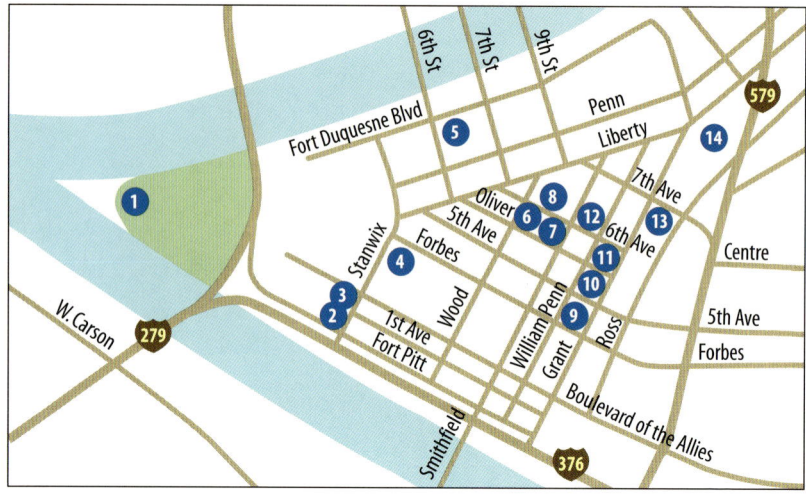

BY THE WAY

Guided walking tours of the Golden Triangle can be arranged through the Pittsburgh History and Landmarks Foundation. Call 412-471-5808.

A stroll through the Golden Triangle, Pittsburgh's commercial hub, is a trip back in time to the Steel Era's center of power and wealth. The buildings themselves tell the story. The U. S. Steel Tower, headquarters of U. S. Steel, is made of Cor-Ten™ steel, a special alloy designed to rust once then never rust again. A few blocks away is the international union headquarters of the United Steelworkers of America, with its distinctive diamond-lattice façade of structural steel. The former Alcoa building is made of aluminum, and the Pittsburgh Plate Glass (PPG) corporate office is a castle of mirrored spires. The elegant William Penn Hotel, which still serves afternoon tea in the Palm Court, was built by Henry Clay Frick in 1916 as a showplace for clients from around the globe. And Frick and Andrew Carnegie were among the first to join the Duquesne Club, where tycoons struck backroom deals. Visitors can even find an outdoor mural about steel-making on Fort Duquesne Boulevard.

Point State Park
101 Commonwealth Place

Westinghouse Building
(now Blattner Brunner)
11 Stanwix Street

United Steelworkers of America
5 Gateway Center
60 Boulevard of the Allies

PPG Place
One PPG Place

Haas Mural
Fort Duquesne Boulevard
between 6th and 7th Streets

First Presbyterian Church
320 6th Avenue

Trinity Cathedral
328 6th Avenue

Duquesne Club
325 6th Avenue

Pittsburgh Neighborhoods

Frick Building
437 Grant Street

Union Trust Building
(now Two Mellon Bank)
512 William Penn Place

Omni William Penn Hotel
412–281–7100
530 William Penn Place
www.omnihotels.com

Alcoa Building
(now Regional Enterprise Tower)
425 6th Avenue

U. S. Steel Tower
600 Grant Street

Penn Station
(now The Pennsylvanian)
1100 Liberty Avenue

City of Bridges

Pittsburgh has more than 1,100 bridges. Several cross the city's three rivers; some span hollows between the hills; and many are built over roadways, railways, and even other bridges. Varied in shape, size, and construction — suspension, truss, and cantilever among others — most were engineered with structural steel and cables produced in local mills. They take their names from the thoroughfares they extend (the 9th Street Bridge, the Smithfield Street Bridge, the Liberty Bridge), the neighborhoods they touch (the Highland Park Bridge), or their role in industry (the Hot Metal Bridge and the Fort Wayne Railroad Bridge). Some bridges have been renamed to honor notable individuals in the city's history. The Sixth Street Bridge, which spans the Allegheny near the Pittsburgh Pirates' home field, PNC Park, is now called the Roberto Clemente Bridge in tribute to the team's renowned right fielder. On game days, the city closes this bridge to cars, turning it into a spacious promenade for fans strolling between the downtown Cultural District and the ballpark.

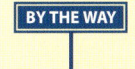

Pittsburgh has more bridges than any other city in the world except Venice, Italy.

a **Hot Metal Bridge**
b **Smithfield Street Bridge**
c **Roberto Clemente Bridge,** one of three sister bridges

Three Rivers Route

The Strip District and Polish Hill

The Strip District is a 300-acre expanse between Liberty Avenue and the Allegheny River. Flat and easy to build on, it was the location of the city's earliest foundries. It was in the Strip that George Westinghouse and Charles Martin Hall first produced their revolutionary inventions — air brakes and aluminum. And it was here that Thomas Armstrong cornered the world market on cork.

Around 1800, Irish Catholic immigrants settled in the Strip, attracted by the promise of jobs. In 1808, the first non-Protestant church — St. Patrick's — was built. The Strip would later become home to communities of German, Polish, and Slovak immigrants. They would be drawn to long, brick row houses close to industry and jobs. Today, much of the Strip's housing has been ground away by industry, but several churches built by immigrants have survived. The most visible is St. Stanislaus Kostka Church (1892). Situated on Smallman Street, it features rich frescoes depicting biblical and Polish history.

Even before St. Stanislaus Kostka was constructed, there was a significant community of Poles living and working in the Strip. During the 1880s, the Poles began moving up the 139 acres of steep slope above the district. They called this neighborhood *Polskie Gory* or Polish Hill. Here, a generation of Polish workers built the majestic Immaculate Heart of Mary Church (1906).

The Strip District is now known less for industry and more for gastronomical opportunities. The seeds of that change were

a

b

c

d

a **Shopping stops in the Strip**
b **The faithful climb St. Patrick's steps on their knees**
c **Immaculate Heart of Mary church interior**
d **St. Stanislaus Kostka**

Pittsburgh Neighborhoods

sown nearly a century ago when, in 1906, the Pennsylvania Railroad tracks were ripped out of downtown Pittsburgh and the railroad relocated its food sheds to the Strip. The heart of the Strip — 17th to 21st Streets along Penn Avenue — became an impromptu marketplace. Shoppers bustling in and out of ethnic food stores, bakeries, fancy restaurants, bars, and all-night sandwich shops — such as Pittsburgh's most famous, Primanti Brothers — make the Strip one of the liveliest neighborhoods in the city.

e **Society for Contemporary Craft interior**

f **Carol Pascuzzi and Gretchen Toma sell cheese at Pennsylvania Macaroni Company.**

g **Sights and scents of the Strip**

The magic of La Prima Espresso: the right machine, the right blend of beans, (properly ground), and the right barista to do the brewing.

Sip in the Strip

Coffee: you love it, you hate it; it's good for you, it's bad for you; it's soothing, it's stimulating; it's exotic, it's familiar. For Sam Patti, owner of La Prima Espresso Company, it's business as usual.

But that wasn't always the case. Some 15 years ago, when Patti first set up shop in the Strip District, cappuccinos and lattes seemed like strange brews to most Pittsburghers. "We opened on a Saturday in October," he recalls, "and we sold one espresso that entire day."

Fortunately, Patti was more interested in creating a buzz around his wholesale coffee-bean and espresso-machine business than in serving individual cups of java.

Still, La Prima has become a café in the truest European sense of the word. It's a destination, a place where people come to talk and exchange ideas (often in Italian), enjoy fresh pastries at the adjacent Piccolo Forno, and, of course, sip coffee. On any given Saturday, there might even be an accordion or violin player amid the crowd of shoppers and gawkers.

According to Patti, the neighborhood is a bazaar, a marketplace where small, local purveyors can sell their wares and people from across the economic spectrum can afford to buy them. The Strip District, he says, "is about community, family, and food."

Three Rivers Route

 The Strip District and Polish Hill

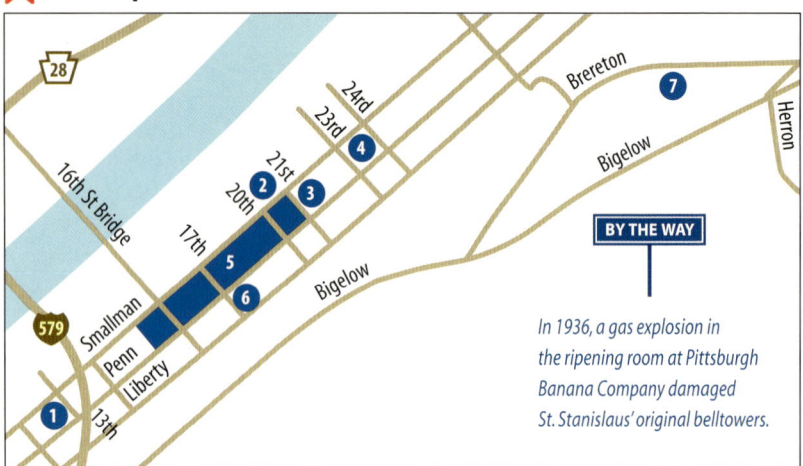

In 1936, a gas explosion in the ripening room at Pittsburgh Banana Company damaged St. Stanislaus' original belltowers.

Senator John Heinz History Center

To learn about Pittsburgh's past, make a visit to the Heinz History Center, perhaps followed by a stop at the Society for Contemporary Craft to see current work by local artists. Take a leisurely morning walk through the Strip District along Penn Avenue, the city's wholesale market area. You'll see St. Patrick's Church and St. Stanislaus Kostka Church, whose names speak of the longstanding presence of Irish and Polish workers. Farther up Penn Avenue try Ceili dancing at Mullaney's Harp and Fiddle, an Irish pub. A short drive leads to Polish Hill, where queenly Immaculate Heart of Mary Church reigns over the neighborhood.

Senator John Heinz Pittsburgh Regional History Center
412–454–6000
1212 Smallman Street
www.pghhistory.org
Daily, 10AM–5PM
Library & Archives, Tues–Sat, 10AM–5PM
Adults: $6; Seniors and students: $4.50; Children 6–18: $3

Society for Contemporary Craft
412–261–7003
2100 Smallman Street
www.contemporarycraft.org
Tues–Sat, 9AM–5PM; Sun & Mon, closed
Admission: Free

St. Stanislaus Kostka Church
412–471–4767
57 21st Street
Mass: Sat Vigil, 4PM; Sun, 9AM, 11AM; Mon & Fri, 7:15AM; Wed, 7PM

Mullaney's Harp and Fiddle
412–642–6622
2329 Penn Avenue
www.harpandfiddle.com
Sun, 4PM–MIDNIGHT; Mon, 11:30AM–10PM;
Tues, 11:30AM–MIDNIGHT; Wed & Th, 11:30AM–1AM;
Fri & Sat, 11:30AM–2AM

Penn Avenue Wholesalers
Penn Avenue from 15th to 21st Street
Mon–Sat, 7AM–3PM (varies by store)

St. Patrick's Church
412–471–4767
1711 Liberty Avenue
Mass: Tues & Th, 12:10PM

Immaculate Heart of Mary Church
412–621–5170
3048 Brereton Street
Mass: Sat Vigil, 6PM; Sun, 9AM, 11AM;
Mon–Sat, 8AM; 1st Sat, 9AM

Polish Heritage

People of Polish background live all over southwestern Pennsylvania. There were Polish steelworkers in Homestead and McKeesport, Polish coke workers in Fayette County. Pittsburgh even has a Polish Hill, and there are Polish communities in other Pittsburgh neighborhoods as well, including Lawrenceville and the South Side. The Polish language has given the region its most widely used spellings of eastern European *pierogi* (filled dumpling) and *kielbasa* (sausage). Polish families were among the first settlers in the Pittsburgh area, but most Poles came to the region during the steel-led industrial expansion of the late 19th century. By 1910, Poles and Slovaks made up 33 percent of the coal-mining workforce in Allegheny, Fayette, and Westmoreland Counties. By 1920, Pittsburgh had the largest community of Poles in Pennsylvania. Many from peasant stock in the Old Country, Polish immigrants came to be known as some of the hardest workers in the region's mills and mines. Coal patches and milltowns often had a Polish Catholic parish, and a Polish National Alliance or Polish Falcons club lodge. The Falcons' national headquarters is still in the Pittsburgh area, and there has been a Polish Arts League in the region since the 1940s. Visitors can attend the annual Polish Day at **Kennywood Park;** enjoy Polish food, music, and dance at the Pittsburgh Folk Festival; tour the **Polish Nationality Room** at the University of Pittsburgh (Three Rivers Route); discover **St. Maximilian Kolbe Shrine** in tiny Footedale (Monongahela Route); and savor Polish *paczki* (doughnuts) before Lent at Good Samaritan Church in Ambridge (Ohio-Beaver Route).

Barbara Bomba, Flo Denicola, and Patty Frauenholz celebrate Christmas at Immaculate Heart of Mary Church.

Irish Heritage

Irish eyes. The luck of the Irish. Getting your Irish up. These expressions show the Irish stamp on American cultural life. Irish Catholics began arriving in southwestern Pennsylvania in large numbers in the 1840s, pushed by the devastating potato famine in their homeland and pulled by the promise of work building canals and railroads in the New World. Immigration continued during the Steel Era, with Irishmen finding jobs as miners and mill workers, municipal police, and firefighters. And the Irish are still coming for work in construction, or as professionals in medicine, technology, and other fields. There are now more than 380,000 people of Irish background in southwestern Pennsylvania, two-thirds of whom live in Allegheny County.

Because the Irish did not form distinct ethnic neighborhoods, their pervasive cultural influence has been diffused. Many of the area's first Catholic parishes were established by Irish worshippers. Pittsburgh's Saint Patrick's Day Parade, now one of the largest in the United States, was first held in 1869. The early immigrants founded fraternal clubs such as the Ancient Order of Hibernians and the Daughters of Erin, which helped them continue Celtic traditions. In the 1960s, Irish newcomers started the Irish Centre of Pittsburgh, which holds folk arts classes and cultural events. There is an **Irish Nationality Room** at the University of Pittsburgh. The area now boasts a dozen or more Irish organizations, not only fraternal societies, but also Irish pubs such as **Mullaney's Harp and Fiddle**, performing groups, schools of Irish dance, a Gaelic Arts Society, even a Gaelic Football Club and an Irish Rowing Club. Visitors will find that Saint Patrick's Day has grown in importance, as well — the celebration now lasts for two weeks in March, with events all over the region.

Irish dancing at Mullaney's

Three Rivers Route

North Side and Troy Hill

Once the epicenter of life and business along the Ohio and Allegheny Rivers, Allegheny City was annexed to Pittsburgh in 1907 and renamed the North Side. According to many historians, that was the beginning of the end for this once-thriving community.

The final blow was dealt between 1946 and 1970. That's when the North Side's older homes, schools, churches and synagogues, and commercial and industrial buildings were demolished as part of the city's Renaissance I initiative.

Although first settled by the English — the Scots, Irish, Germans, Croatians, Slovaks, Ukrainians, Greeks, Italians, Poles, Lithuanians, and, later, African-Americans all followed. Among the famous people associated with the North Side are composer Stephen Foster, who worked there; writer Gertrude Stein and choreographer Martha Graham, who were both born in the area; and painters Mary Cassatt and Henry O. Tanner, who both lived there.

Looking to preserve the best of the North Side, a small group of developers and individuals began renovating the neighborhood's beautiful Victorian homes in the 1970s. In addition, many communities formed preservation and citizens' organizations, such as the Mexican War Streets Society and the Allegheny West Civic Council.

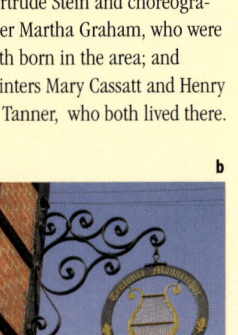

Today, the North Side encompasses Spring Garden/The Flats, Spring Hill/City View, East Allegheny, North Shore, Allegheny Center, Central Northside/Mexican War Streets, Allegheny West, Manchester, Chateau, Woods Run, and Troy Hill.

Situated high above the Allegheny River, Troy Hill in particular offers a breathtaking view of Pittsburgh. With narrow streets and closely set homes, Troy Hill boasts a large German population.

Troy Hill's points of interest include the Chapel of St. Anthony, built in 1880 and organized by Father Suibertus Goddfried Mollinger. Now known as the Most Holy Name of Jesus Parish, the church houses the world's largest collection of saints' relics (with the exception of the Vatican's).

Also in Troy Hill is the oldest firehouse in Pittsburgh — and the only one to ever have a bell. Called *Die Glocke Sarah* (The Sarah Bell), the bell was dedicated in 1989 in honor of those who worked to preserve the firehouse, ghosts and all. Rumor has it that long-dead firemen still meet in the firehouse to play cards, just like they did when they were living. In the Voegtly Evangelical Church Cemetery rests a granite memorial dedicated in 1995 to the region's career and volunteer firefighters. Finally, the former H. J. Heinz Company (now Del Monte) factory, once famous for its ketchup and pickles, can be found at the base of Troy Hill.

a **Troy Hill Fire Station**
b **Teutonia Männerchor**
c **Voetly Cemetery headstone**
d **The Priory Inn**

Pittsburgh Neighborhoods

Fifteen Minutes and Still Counting

Andy Warhol has enjoyed more than his allotted 15 minutes of fame. Even now, years after his death, he remains a pop culture icon. Not bad for this Pittsburgh son of Slovak immigrant workers.

Born Andrew Warhola, the Andy we've come to know and love (or hate) studied art and design at Carnegie Tech (now Carnegie Mellon University). With his diploma in hand, he left for New York City and never looked back.

By the 1960s, his images of Campbell's Soup cans (tin-covered steel) and Brillo soap pad boxes (steel-wool soap pads) were fast becoming the essence of hip. Some 30 years later, The Andy Warhol Museum, one of the most comprehensive single-artist showcases in the world, opened on Pittsburgh's North Side.

Today, Andy's brother Paul Warhola still owns a local scrap-metal business, and Andy himself rests in peace in Bethel Park.

e St. Anthony's Chapel
f Bruce Wagenhoffer and Joe Brandt eat lunch at Penn Brewery.
g *Brillo Box,* Andy Warhol, 1964
h Alecia Shipman pulls up a pot with Sharif Bey's guidance at Manchester Craftsmen's Guild.
i View of the new Alcoa Building on the North Shore

BY THE WAY

The pull-tab on a can was developed by Alcoa and first used by Iron City Brewery in 1962.

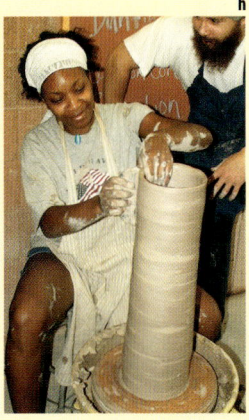

51

Three Rivers Route

⭐ North Side and Troy Hill

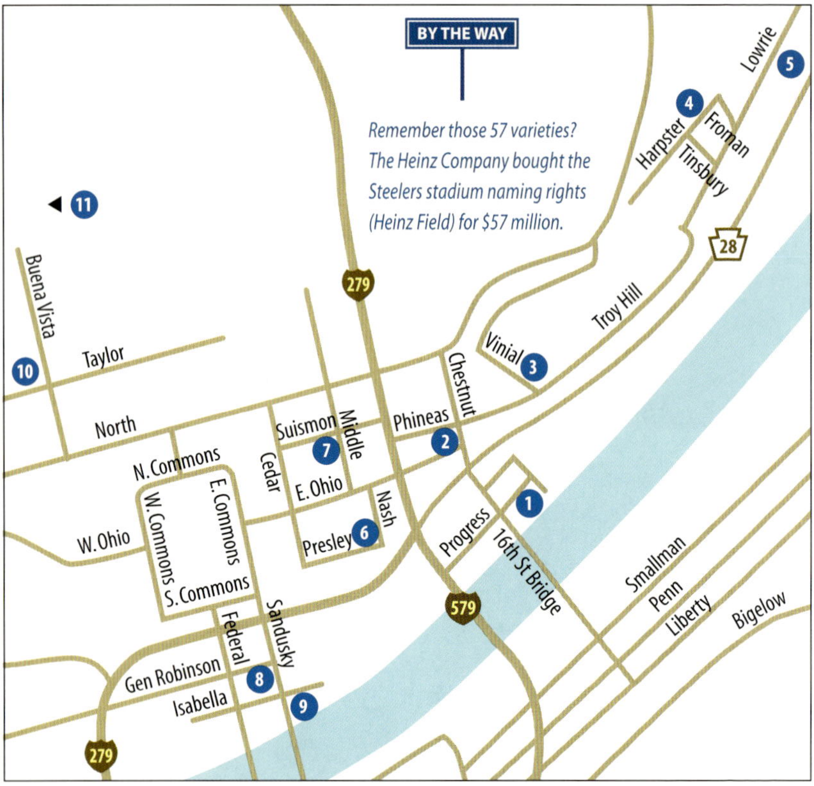

BY THE WAY

Remember those 57 varieties? The Heinz Company bought the Steelers stadium naming rights (Heinz Field) for $57 million.

German heritage permeates the North Side: food and beer at Max's Allegheny Tavern and the Pennsylvania Brewing Company; song at the Teutonia Männerchor; and religion at St. Anthony's Chapel. The Priory, now a European-style inn, once housed German Benedictine monks. Other sites speak of industrial heritage: the former H. J. Heinz plant and the undulating architecture of the new Alcoa building. Easily accessible are the Warhol Museum (Pittsburgher Andy Warhol's Carpatho-Rusyn family name was "Warhola") and the Manchester Craftsmen's Guild, known for jazz concerts, gallery exhibits, Hmong folk arts display, and its innovative Bidwell Training Center.

① 🏭
H. J. Heinz Company Plant (now Del Monte)
1062 Progress Street
www.heinz.com

② ✠
Teutonia Männerchor
412–231–9141
857 Phineas Street
Members only

③ ✠ Ⓔ
Pennsylvania Brewing Company
412–237–9402
800 Vinial Street
www.pennbrew.com
Mon–Sat, 11AM–11PM

④ ✠ ⋏
St. Anthony's Chapel
412–323–9504
1704 Harpster Street
Tues, Th, Sat, 1–4PM; Sun, 12:30–4PM
Tours: Sun, 1PM, 2PM, and 3PM

Pittsburgh Neighborhoods

5
Voegtly Cemetery
1955 Lowrie Street
Open until dark

6
The Priory–A City Inn
412–231–3338
614 Presley Street
www.thepriory.com

7
Max's Allegheny Tavern
412–231–1899
537 Suismon Street
www.maxsalleghenytavern.com
Mon–Th, 11AM–11PM; Fri–Sat, 11AM–12PM; Sun, 9:30AM–10PM
Reservations recommended for groups of 5 or more

8
Warhol Museum
412–237–8300
117 Sandusky Street
www.warhol.org
Sun, Tue, Wed, Th, Sat, 10AM–5PM; Fri, 10AM–10PM
Adults: $10; Seniors 55+: $7; Children 3–18 and students, $6;
Members of Carnegie Museums: Free; Fri, 5–10PM: half price

9
Alcoa Building
201 Isabella Street

10
Wilson's Bar-B-Q
412–322–7427
700 North Taylor Avenue
Mon–Sat, 12AM–10PM

11
Manchester Craftsmen's Guild
412–322–1773
1815 Metropolitan Street
www.manchesterguild.org
Gallery hours: Mon, Wed, Th, Fri, 9AM–5PM; Tues, 9AM–9PM
For classes, jazz performances, and directions,
visit the Guild's web site.

Courtesy of the Pittsburgh Steelers

Here We Go, Steelers!

In the beginning — 1933 — the city's first professional football team was known as the Pittsburgh Pirates. It wasn't until 1938 when, in an effort to pay tribute to the region's steel heritage and generate more fan support, owner Art Rooney decided to change the name. The rest, as they say, is Steelers history.

The fifth-oldest franchise in the NFL, the Pittsburgh Steelers is the only team to sport a corporate-inspired logo. The three diamonds — yellow for coal, orange for ore, and blue for steel scrap — were created by the U. S. Steel Corporation.

When the Steelmark logo, as it's called, made its debut, the players were still wearing gold helmets, and there was some concern about the clash of colors. Hedging their bets, the powers that be suggested affixing the diamonds to the right side only.

As the Steelers started winning with more frequency, the helmets turned black. The emblem, however, remained where it was, making the Steelers the only NFL team to have a one-sided logo.

The Steelers' new home — Heinz Field — marks another Pittsburgh corporate connection.

Pittsburgh is the only city in which all the major sports teams wear black and gold.

Three Rivers Route

Bloomfield and Lawrenceville

The name Bloomfield is said to have originated when George Washington wrote in his journal about traveling through "a field of many blooms." Most of the flowers may be gone, but the neighborhood continues to blossom.

Annexed to Pittsburgh in 1868, Bloomfield's earliest residents were farmers, many of German descent. Now nicknamed "Pittsburgh's Little Italy" because of its large Italian and Italian-American population, Bloomfield is primarily a working-class neighborhood. Tailors, shoemakers, florists, barbershops, butcher shops, and Italian groceries and restaurants line Liberty Avenue, its main thoroughfare.

When the steel mills were running, many of Bloomfield's residents had jobs at the Edgar Thomson Works, Mesta Machine, and J&L Steel. The different types of housing that evolved are still visible. There are small row houses built in the late 1800s for the mill workers, and larger, more elaborate homes that were designed for the white-collar professionals and managers. Today, homes are often kept in the family, passed down from generation to generation.

Bloomfield's two Catholic churches feature prominently in the neighborhood. St. Joseph's Church was built in 1872 by German immigrants, while the Italians built Immaculate Conception. These churches became one parish in 2001.

Lawrenceville was founded in 1814 up the Allegheny River from Pittsburgh on land owned by William B. Foster, father of composer Stephen C. Foster. Foster named the new community for Captain James Lawrence, a naval officer in the War of 1812. At its heart was the Arsenal, an iron foundry that produced military hardware. As Pittsburgh grew, so did Lawrenceville. Irish and German iron and glass workers moved in from Pittsburgh's Strip District, founding churches such as Saint Mary's on 46th Street in 1853 and St. John's Evangelical Lutheran in 1859. The post–Civil War industrial expansion attracted new workers such as Poles and Croatians, especially after Pittsburgh annexed the community in 1868, and a forge, later called Heppenstall, was built in 1903. During the 20th century, African-Americans also established a presence.

Like Bloomfield, Lawrenceville has maintained a European flavor, with small row homes closely set along narrow streets. Church still forms the mainstay of community life. The African-American congregations sponsor gospel choirs. St. Mary's parishioners make Polish *pierogi* for sale on Fridays during Lent. There is even an active German singing society.

a **Sandy Falcione bakes biscotti at Donatelli's.**
b **The Bloomfield Bridge Tavern**
c **St. Joseph Catholic Church**
d **Church Brew Works interior**

Pittsburgh Neighborhoods

The Ties that Bind

According to August (Augie) Carlino, Sr., Bloomfield is built on a foundation of heritage (Italian), family (extended), religion (Catholic), politics (Democratic), and hard work (mostly blue collar).

Carlino should know. He's spent his 70-plus years in this neighborhood. Like many residents, he followed the example set by his parents. His mother and father grew up across the street from one another. "Fourth and fifth generations of families stay here in Bloomfield," Carlino says. "Somehow, from somewhere, everyone in Bloomfield is related."

His grandfather worked in the mills and his father became a stonemason who had a hand in creating two Pittsburgh landmarks: the statues of Honus Wagner (now at PNC Park) and Christopher Columbus (in Schenley Park).

Carlino learned to speak Italian and to appreciate the value of hard work from his family. He attended Schenley High School where he played football. After serving in the military, he became a construction coordinator and Democratic Party Ward Chair for Bloomfield, a position he's held since 1970.

Carlino and his wife, Amelia (Milly), met at a big-band dance in 1953. "Dancing," Carlino says, "took people out of the neighborhood to places like McKeesport and McKees Rocks." Milly was originally from the South Side. After Carlino courted her for three years, the couple married in 1956 and made their home in Bloomfield. They have two children and four grandchildren.

"Our children's generation is really the first to move away," Carlino says. Despite that trend, he's convinced that Bloomfield will remain a tight-knit community. "Believe it or not," Carlino says, "this is the hub of the city of Pittsburgh. I see it staying strong and predominantly Italian."

f Entering Bloomfield from the Bloomfield Bridge

g Leslie Kaplan works in the flame shop at the Pittsburgh Glass Center.

h Doughboy Square, World War I memorial in Lawrenceville

i Allegheny Cemetery entrance

Three Rivers Route

 Bloomfield and Lawrenceville

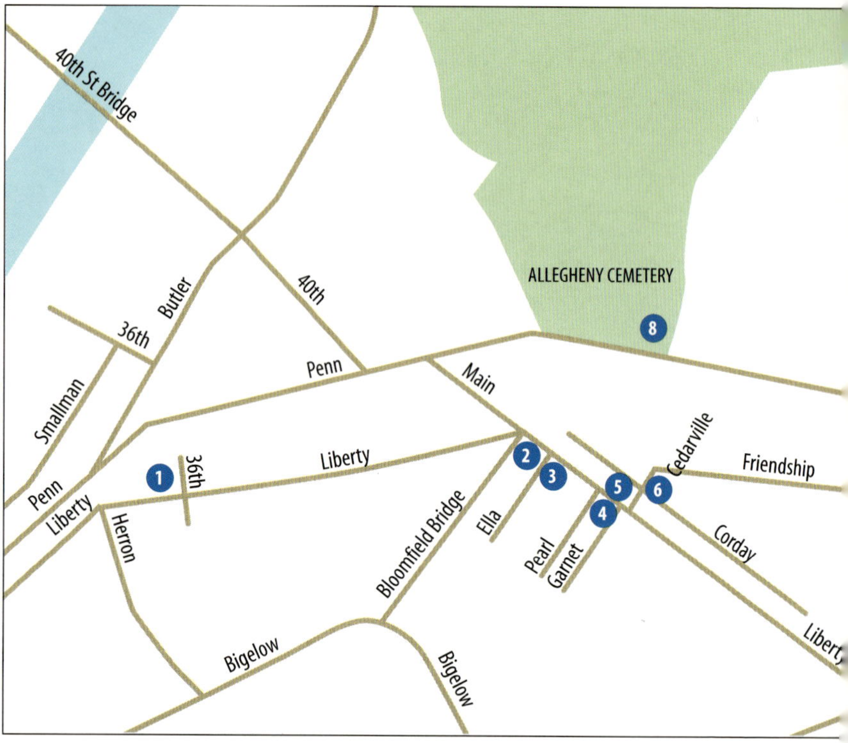

Driving up Liberty Avenue, visitors can savor Lawrenceville's cultural past with locally brewed German- and British-style beer and ale at the Church Brew Works, a brewpub housed in what was originally St. John the Baptist Church. The church was built around 1900 to serve the expanding population of Irish workers employed in the Strip District's steel plants. In Bloomfield, Liberty Avenue takes on a Mediterranean cast, lined with Italian groceries and restaurants. The sassy Bloomfield Bridge Tavern calls itself "The Best Polish Restaurant in Little Italy." Originally German, stately St. Joseph's Church in Bloomfield is now the center of a parish that incorporates both Italian and German congregants. Along Penn Avenue, the Pittsburgh Glass Center welcomes observers as artisans carry on one of the city's oldest industrial pursuits. A place for a quiet stroll is Allegheny Cemetery, the final resting place not only of Irish workers and Pittsburgh industrialists, but also of Stephen Collins Foster, a Lawrenceville native whose father, William B. Foster, founded Lawrenceville in 1814.

**① **
Church Brew Works
412–688–8200
3525 Liberty Avenue
www.churchbrew.com
Mon–Th, 11:30AM–11:45PM
Fri & Sat, 11:30AM–1:00AM; Sun, 12PM–10PM

**② **
Bloomfield Bridge Tavern
412–682–8611
4412 Liberty Avenue, Pittsburgh
Tues–Sat, 4PM–1AM; Kitchen closes at MIDNIGHT
Must be 21

Pittsburgh Neighborhoods

Captain James Lawrence, Lawrenceville's namesake, was captain of the Chesapeake in the War of 1812. His motto, "Don't Give Up the Ship," is part of the neighborhood's official seal.

a Italian olive oil
b Polish menu
c Italian cheeses and sausages

The Ateleta Club

Many of Bloomfield's Italian immigrants hailed from Ateleta. This southern Italian village (in Greek, *ateleta* means "free of taxes") was founded in 1810 by Gioacchino Murat, a French leader and friend of Napoleon Bonaparte. In a noble gesture, Murat gave the town to the people, but, by 1910, the people of Ateleta were starving. As a result, many chose to leave their beloved village for a better life in America.

Still, there's no place like home, so, in 1924, Bloomfield's population of Ateleta natives joined together to form the Societa' di Beneficenza Ateleta "for beneficial and protective purposes." Decades later, the Ateleta Club's ranks had grown large enough to fill an entire building. Complete with a meeting hall, bar, and recreation facilities, the Club opened its headquarters on Cedarville Street in 1941.

But times changed. By 1999, the group sold its building to the Lower Bloomfield Unity Council with the understanding that it could still hold meetings there. However, only a handful of members remain.

❸
Del's Bar and Restaurant
412–683–1448
4428 Liberty Avenue
www.delsrest.com
Sun, 1–10 PM; Mon–Th, 11:30 AM–11 PM
Fri & Sat, 11:30 AM–MIDNIGHT

❹
St. Joseph's Roman Catholic Church
412–682–2354, 412–682–5353
4712 Liberty Avenue
Sat Vigil, 5 PM; Sun Mass, 7:30 AM; 10:30 AM; 6:30 PM
Mon–Sat Mass, 11:30 AM

❺
Donatelli's Italian Food Center
412–682–1406
4711 Liberty Avenue
Mon–Sat, 8 AM–6 PM; Sun, 8 AM–1:30 PM

❻
Groceria Italiana
412–681–1227
237 Cedarville Road
Mon–Sat, 9 AM–6 PM; Sun, 10 AM–2 PM

❼
Pittsburgh Glass Center
412–365–2145
5472 Penn Avenue
www.pittsburghglasscenter.org
Mon, Fri, Sat, 10 AM–4 PM; Tues, Wed, Th, 10 AM–7 PM
or by appointment

❽
Allegheny Cemetery
412–682–1624
Entrances at:
4715 Penn Avenue and 4734 Butler Street
www.alleghenycemetery.com
June–Aug: 7 AM–7 PM; Sept–Apr: 7 AM–5:30 PM
May: 7 AM–8 PM

Three Rivers Route

Homewood and Point Breeze

In its heyday, Homewood was where you would find some of the region's most notable industrialists like Carnegie, Frick, Westinghouse, and Heinz. The neighborhood's earliest residents were of British, German, and Irish descent. African-Americans, many of whom worked for the wealthy aristocrats in the area, made their homes on the north and south sides of the railroad tracks.

But as the working middle class grew, so did its need for housing. As a result, African-Americans, as well as Italian, German, and Irish immigrants, also started to call Homewood home. By the 1950s, many working-class African-Americans continued to move into the area, while white middle- and upper-class residents left the city for the suburbs. A decade later, another large influx of African-Americans, those forced to leave the Hill District to make way for the construction of the Civic Arena (now the Mellon Arena), arrived in Homewood.

Churches became centers of social activity, and cultural life flourished. Community choral groups like the Treble Clef Club, Raymond Walls' Intercultural Choir, and the Cardwell Dawson Choir were popular. In 1941, Mary Cardwell Dawson founded the National Negro Opera Company, a Pittsburgh institution until 1960.

The death of Martin Luther King, Jr., in the 1960s traumatized the community, and it has never completely recovered. Today, people are working to revitalize Homewood through churches, service agencies, and cultural organizations such as the Afro-American Music Institute, founded in 1982.

Homewood points of interest include the Homewood Branch of the Carnegie Library, the last library built by Andrew Carnegie, which opened in March 1911, and the Trolley Station Oral History Center housed in the Pittsburgh Coliseum building.

Point Breeze was originally part of South Homewood until residents decided to rename their community in the 1950s. Its earliest homes belonged to wealthy industrialists and professionals.

After trolleys came into the neighborhood in the 1800s, one of the first planned suburban developments in the nation took root in North Point Breeze. To this day, the area's homes have a diverse array of architectural styles, including Civil War row houses, Victorian gingerbread houses, and 1920s villas.

Point Breeze's main attraction is the Frick Art and Historical Center, which features the Frick Art Museum, the Car and Carriage Museum, a concert hall, Clayton (the restored estate of Pittsburgh industrialist Henry Clay Frick), a playhouse, and a greenhouse. In Homewood Cemetery, visitors will find the final resting places of members of the Frick, Heinz, Benedum, and Mellon families. Visitors can also enjoy Frick Park, which includes a nature reserve, hiking trails, and tennis and basketball courts.

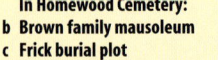

a Homewood Library interior

In Homewood Cemetery:
b Brown family mausoleum
c Frick burial plot
d Asian headstone

Pittsburgh Neighborhoods

e Heritage Umbrellas: project by the Trolley Station Oral History Center, the Senior Citizen Home, and Crescent Grade School displayed at the Trolley Station

f Chair made by London Fitzgerald, Reizenstein Middle School student. The project was a collaboration of the Society for Contemporary Craft, Gregory Warmack (Mr. Imagination), and the Trolley Station Oral History Center.

g Frick Art Museum

h Entrance to Frick Park

The Trolley Station Rides Again

Homewood's past, present, and future intersect at the Greater Pittsburgh Coliseum Complex, and that's the way proprietor John Brewer likes it. In the beginning, however, the decision to take over a landmark that had seen better days wasn't high on his list of things to do. "I never dreamed of owning this facility," Brewer says. "That's just the way it worked out."

This Frankstown Avenue building had many lives. Dating back to the early 1900s, it was a trolley station, a Port Authority garage, and a skating rink. By the time Brewer assumed responsibility for the structure in 1989, it was little more than a "black hole."

It took Brewer nearly 10 years to renovate the complex into its current configuration — which includes a 14,000-square-foot ballroom, an upscale club and catering service (Ramseys II), a recording studio, and the Trolley Station Oral History Center.

Dedicated to preserving the traditions and history that define the African-American community, the Center is now home to a collection of Charles "Teenie" Harris photographs. Harris was the principal photographer for the *Pittsburgh Courier* from 1936 to 1975. In addition, the Center displays artwork and features a Westinghouse High School hall of fame. The ballroom serves as a gathering place for community fundraising events, reunions, and cabarets.

According to Brewer, who grew up in Homewood, the Coliseum Complex is an important part of his neighborhood — past, present, and future.

Three Rivers Route

 Homewood and Point Breeze

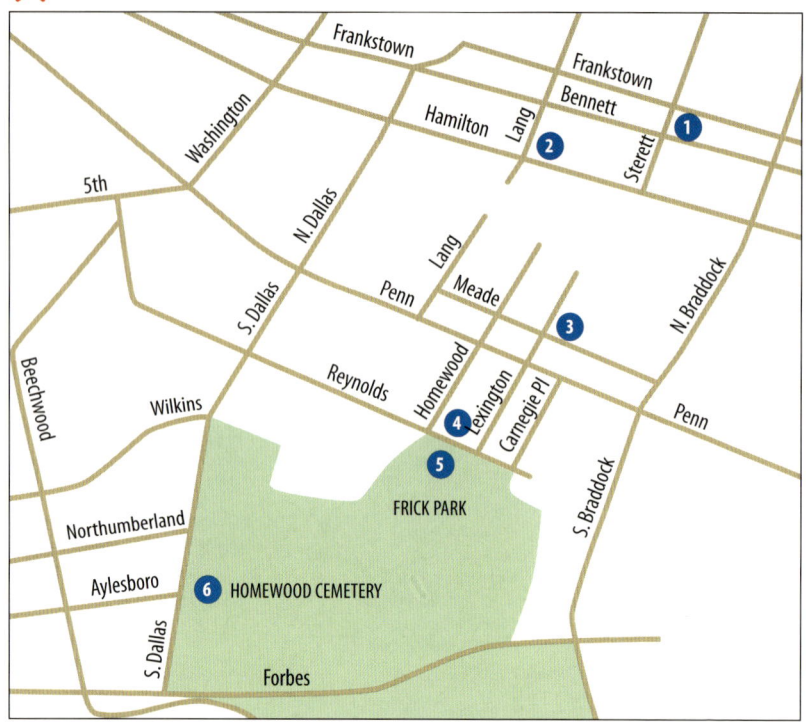

BY THE WAY

To appreciate the extent of Frick Park, try this route: Enter at Homewood and Reynolds, and take the trail down to Lower Frick Park. Angle left. You can follow this trail past Regent Square all the way to Nine Mile Run in Squirrel Hill.

The 19th-century identity of Homewood–Point Breeze as the country retreat of Pittsburgh's wealthy entrepreneurs can be experienced at Clayton, the mansion where the Henry Clay Frick family lived; Frick Park, the vast nature reserve donated to Pittsburgh by Frick's daughter; the Carnegie Library of Homewood, built by Homewood resident Andrew Carnegie to serve the needs of his fellow industrialists; and Homewood Cemetery, where the Fricks, the Mellons, the Scaifes, and other Steel Era leading lights are neighbors for eternity. In the 20th century, Homewood–Point Breeze became one of Pittsburgh's important African-American communities. The Trolley Station Oral History Center focuses on local African-American heritage through its documentary efforts and its displays of historic photographs.

Trolley Station Oral History Center
412–371–3445
Pittsburgh Coliseum
7310 Frankstown Avenue
☎ Phone ahead

Carnegie Library, Homewood Branch
412–731–3080
7101 Hamilton Avenue
www.clpgh.org
Mon, 11AM–7PM; Tue, 10AM–5PM; Wed, 11AM–7PM;
Th, 10AM–5PM; Sat, 10AM–5PM; Fri & Sun, closed

Construction Junction
412–243–5025
North Lexington Avenue and Meade Street
www.constructionjunction.org
Mon, Tue, Th, Fri, 8AM–5PM; Wed, 8AM–7PM;
Sat, 9AM–5PM; Sun, 11AM–4PM

Pittsburgh Neighborhoods

Frick Art and Historical Center

At the turn of the century, Point Breeze was the preferred address for many of Pittsburgh's rich and famous industrialists. Today the Fricks' family home, Clayton, endures as one of the finest examples of a Victorian mansion from that era.

Henry Clay Frick and his new bride, Adelaide Howard, purchased Clayton in 1882. At the time, it was an 11-room home, but local architect Frederick J. Osterling would transform it into a 23-room chateau-style mansion.

For the next 22 years, the Fricks would entertain presidents and raise their family at Clayton. When they moved to New York in 1905, it was as if they had simply gone to tea. They left behind an astonishing collection of artifacts that today makes Clayton one of the most complete museum homes in the country. From highchairs and children's books to family photos and sterling flatware, Clayton provides an intimate glimpse into the life of the Frick family a century ago.

Clayton is located on the grounds of the Frick Art and Historical Center, a 5-acre complex of historical buildings, museums, and gardens. In addition to Clayton, there's the Frick Art Museum, which houses Helen Clay Frick's personal collection of fine and decorative arts (porcelains, bronzes, rare examples of 17th- and 18th-century furniture and the works of Old Masters); and the Car and Carriage Museum, which displays more than 20 vintage automobiles (Henry Clay Frick's 1914 Rolls Royce Silver Ghost touring car and Howard Heinz's 1898 Panhard, reputed to be the first car in Pittsburgh).

But a trip to the Frick Art and Historical Center doesn't have to be all about mansions or vintage automobiles. Visitors may want to take a moment to stop and smell the roses at the greenhouse that has supplied Clayton with fresh flowers since 1897 or sit on the patio of the Frick Café that has twice been voted the best place for lunch in the city.

a Clayton, the Frick family home
b Headstone from the pet cemetery at Clayton
c Antique car built by Penn Motor Car company, once located in Point Breeze

Frick Art and Historical Center (Clayton)
412–371–0606
7227 Reynolds Street
www.frickart.org
Tues–Sat, 10am–5pm; Sun, 12am–6pm; closed Mon
Clayton: Adults: $10; seniors, students, children: $8
Reservations recommended for Clayton
Café Lunch: Tues–Sat, 11am–5pm; Sun, 11am–6pm
Café Tea: Tues–Sat, 3pm–5pm; Sun, 3pm–6pm

Frick Park
412–422–6550
Homewood Avenue and Reynolds Street

Homewood Cemetery
412–421–1822
1599 South Dallas Avenue
homewoodcemetery.org
Gates open daily, 8:30am–dark (5pm in winter)

Three Rivers Route

Squirrel Hill

Named for the black squirrels that made this area a favorite Native American hunting ground, Squirrel Hill remained somewhat isolated even as wealthy industrialists and merchants like Andrew Carnegie, Henry Clay Frick, and the Mellons began building their estates in surrounding communities.

It wasn't until streetcars started running along Fifth Avenue and the Squirrel Hill Development Company opened for business in 1890 that Squirrel Hill was seen as prime real estate. Soon roads were being paved and modest-sized houses were being constructed for middle- and working-class families. By 1930, most of the available land was already claimed.

During this boom time, Squirrel Hill evolved into two distinct sections. There was "north of Forbes," where the wealthier Scots-Irish and German-Jewish residents settled, and southern Squirrel Hill, the area middle- and working-class eastern European Jews, Irish, Italian, and Germans called home. Squirrel Hill was attracting new residents from nearby communities like the Hill District and Oakland but that changed after World War II. While other ethnic groups were relocating from Pittsburgh out to the suburbs, Jews from outlying milltowns and mine patches began moving into Squirrel Hill. This growth and consolidation accelerated in the 1980s and 1990s with an influx of Russian-speaking Jewish immigrants and an upswing in Orthodox Judaism.

Signs of Jewish identity can be found throughout the area. For example, synagogues representing the full spectrum of Jewish belief—from the Ultra-Orthodox to Reconstructionism and everything in between (Shaare Torah, Orthodox; Beth Shalom, Conservative; and Temple Sinai, Reformed)—are concentrated within just a few blocks of Forbes and Murray Avenues. Along Murray, visitors will find two landmark establishments: Murray Avenue Kosher and Pinskers Books and Judaica—for many, the essence of Squirrel Hill. Inside the stores, the basics of Jewish life—from menorahs to kosher wines—are available.

a **Rabbi Dovber Marcus holds a menorah at Pinskers Judaica.**
b **Inbal Ami displays challah baked at Rolladin's.**

The *Eruv*

The Jewish Sabbath begins every Friday at sundown. It's a time for quiet reflection and prayer, a time when work is strictly forbidden. For many Orthodox Jews, carrying anything—umbrellas, prayer books, even babies—out of doors is considered work.

However, according to the Talmud (the book of Jewish civil and ceremonial law dating back to the 5th century), Jews may carry objects on the Sabbath if they remain in an enclosed area. That could mean a house, a specific site offset by natural boundaries, or a walled city, like Jerusalem.

In the spirit of that last example, the Squirrel Hill Orthodox community (like other communities throughout the world) built its own symbolic wall called an *eruv*. Nowadays, this age-old notion is realized in very modern terms. Telephone lines and other wires delineate most of the wall, while fences and ravines make up the rest.

Now, some 20 years after its debut, Squirrel Hill's *eruv* still requires care. Volunteers are on call to repair damage from acts of God or vandalism. Encompassing most of Squirrel Hill, the *eruv* was not designed as a barrier, but rather as a means of bringing people together.

Pittsburgh Neighborhoods

An Extended Family

Sheila Chamovitz keeps an eye on things in her Squirrel Hill neighborhood. As a documentarian and longtime resident of this East End community, it goes with the territory.

Sheila was a newlywed and a relatively new filmmaker when she first settled in Squirrel Hill in 1969. Although she grew up in a Jewish household in nearby Stanton Heights, she admits to experiencing a bit of culture shock upon her arrival.

"I was startled to see all these Jewish things happening outside my door," Sheila recalls. "The whole idea of being so exposed about your Jewishness was really surprising to me."

Nowadays, Forbes and Murray Avenues reflect Squirrel Hill's sensibilities. Near their intersection is the Jewish Community Center (JCC), which boasts a clock with Hebrew numbers, and houses the Jewish Museum of Pittsburgh. "Up street" along Forbes are dress shops, gift stores, and a Carnegie Library of Pittsburgh branch, while a walk down Murray reveals a number of kosher eateries, as well as an array of ethnic restaurants and groceries featuring Asian and Italian cuisine. Everywhere in Squirrel Hill — the shops, the library, the 61C Cafe, the delis, the Giant Eagle grocery store — is a place of gathering, a place to find friends and family.

d **Jewish Community Center**
e **Beth Shalom Synagogue directory**
f **Bulk rice from Young's Oriental**
g **Murray Avenue Kosher sign**
h **Pasta from La Cucina Flegrea**
i **Hanukkah dreidels**

Through the years, she began feeling more at home. The neighborhood was like a house, warm and welcoming, and Murray Avenue, with its kosher butchers, bakeries, and delis, was the dining room. "It had a real sense of extended family," she says. "And I loved it."

Still, Sheila says, most people would be surprised to learn that Squirrel Hill's current population is far more diverse than it appears at first glance. "Statistically," she says, "Squirrel Hill is less than 30 percent Jewish, but because there's such a critical mass of Jews in one place, it feels and is identified as the Jewish community — and the corner of Forbes and Murray is its heartbeat."

Three Rivers Route

 Squirrel Hill

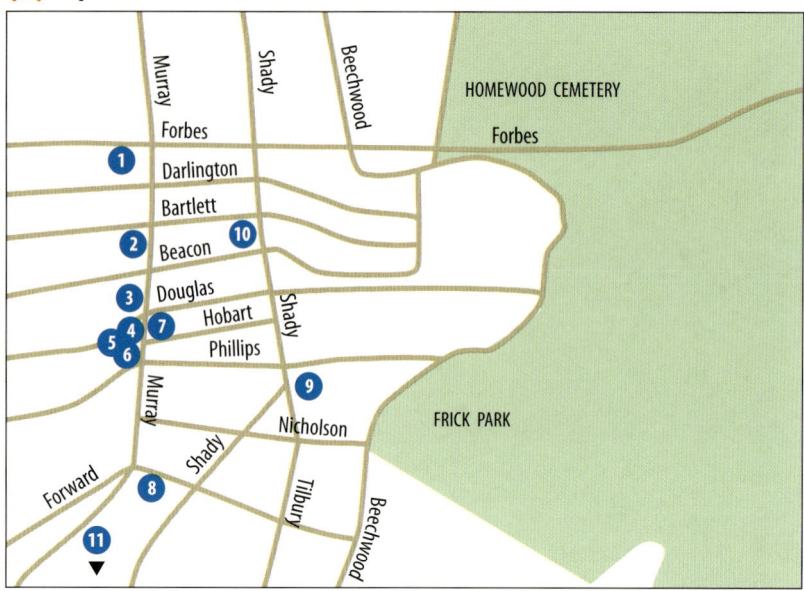

BY THE WAY

The first synagogue in southwestern Pennsylvania was Rodef Shalom, established in Pittsburgh in 1854.

Two neighborhood promenades, Murray Avenue and Forbes Avenue, define Squirrel Hill. Near their junction is the Jewish Museum at the Jewish Community Center (JCC). A few blocks away, Murray Avenue Kosher, Pinskers Judaica, and other kosher markets and restaurants serve Squirrel Hill, as do synagogues of all sizes and denominations, such as Beth Shalom (Conservative) and Poale Zedeck (Orthodox), scattered within easy walking distance. But reflecting Squirrel Hill's increasingly cosmopolitan character, Murray and Forbes Avenues are also home to multi-ethnic businesses, such as family-owned regional Italian restaurants, and Chinese, Vietnamese, Indian, and Middle Eastern establishments. *Side trip:* Josza Corner Hungarian Restaurant.

Jewish Museum at the JCC
412–521–8010
5738 Forbes Avenue
www.jccpgh.org
Mon–Th, 6:15AM–10PM; Fri, 6:15AM–6PM;
Sat, 1PM–7PM; Sun, 7:45AM–6PM

Murray Avenue Kosher
412–421–1015
1916 Murray Avenue
Sun–Th, 8AM–6PM; Fri, 8AM–3PM

Pinskers Judaica
412–421–3033
2028 Murray Avenue
Mon–Wed, 10AM–6PM; Th, 10AM–8PM;
Fri, 10AM–3PM (2PM in winter); Sun, 10AM–5PM

La Cucina Flegrea
412–521–2082
2114 Murray Avenue
Mon–Sat, 5AM–10PM

Rolladin Bakery
412–521–5555
2120 Murray Avenue
Sun–Th, 7AM–7PM; Fri, 7AM–4PM

Mineo's Pizza House
412–521–2053
2128 Murray Avenue
www.mineospizza.com
Sun–Th, 11AM–1AM; Fri–Sat, 11AM–2AM

Pittsburgh Neighborhoods

Jewish Heritage

Squirrel Hill resident Doris Dyen views an exhibit on immigration at the Jewish Community Center.

Latkes frying on Hanukkah? Lights kindled on Shabbat? Jewish traditions are alive and well in southwestern Pennsylvania. All four branches of Judaism flourish in the region: Orthodox, Conservative, Reform, and Reconstructionist. Most of the main Jewish institutions are now headquartered in Pittsburgh's Squirrel Hill neighborhood (Three Rivers Route), but Jews live, work, play, and worship throughout the region. Members of both a religion and an ethnic group, Jews have been an integral part of southwestern Pennsylvania life since the late 18th century. Many came as merchants, selling their wares as itinerant peddlers or starting small businesses. During the Steel Era, Jewish shops offered coke patch residents a welcome alternative to the company store, and provided basic foods and dry goods to mill workers' families. Well-known department stores, such as Kaufmann's, grew from these beginnings. In the larger regional towns, Jews established synagogues, some of which — in Ambridge, Uniontown, and Washington, for example — are still active. In Pittsburgh, the main Jewish port of entry in the early 20th century was the Hill District. From there Jews relocated east to Oakland, then to Squirrel Hill. They spoke German, Romanian, Polish, Hungarian, Lithuanian, Russian, and, of course, Yiddish, founding synagogues based on their countries of origin. They started hospitals, social service agencies, schools, and civic clubs. The late 20th century saw a new influx of Russian-speaking immigrants and Hebrew-speaking Israelis. There are now gallery exhibits on Jewish life and public events such as the annual Israel Day parade, in addition to the yearly round of holiday rituals. Today, more than 45,000 Jews live in the region, some adhering strictly to Jewish law, others less so, yet all are part of "klal Yisrael," the Jewish people.

Kazansky's
412–521–4555
2201 Murray Avenue
www.kazanskysdeli.com
Mon–Fri, 10am–10pm; Sat & Sun, 8am–10pm

Young's Oriental Grocery Store
412–422–0559
5813 Forward Avenue
Mon–Sat, 10am–7pm

Poale Zedeck Synagogue
412–421–9786
6318 Phillips Avenue
www.poalezedeck.org
☎ Phone ahead

Beth Shalom Synagogue
412–421–2288
5915 Beacon Street
www.bethshalompgh.org
☎ Phone ahead

Side trip:

Jozsa Corner Hungarian Restaurant
412–422–1886
4800–4804 2nd Avenue
Mon–Fri, 11am–6pm
Directions: Take Murray Avenue through Greenfield to "T". Right on Hazelwood Ave. to next "T". Left on 2nd Ave. to restaurant on corner.

Three Rivers Route

Oakland — Cathedrals of Culture

Almost from the beginning, Pittsburgh's Oakland neighborhood was associated with leisure, culture, and education. Until the 1860s, Oakland was a separate community, primarily the domain of wealthy English, Scots-Irish, and German landowners, merchants, and prominent industrialists. At first, many built summer residences there, then — after the Great Fire of 1845 in downtown Pittsburgh — permanent homes. The name Oakland may come from Oakland Farm, a luxurious estate established in 1806 by English immigrant James Chadwick.

From the Civil War onward, there were really two Oaklands. With the advent of horse-drawn then electrically powered public streetcars, central Oakland, though still home to many of the city's elite, became a popular middle-class suburb of Pittsburgh. The area drew upwardly mobile immigrants, including many Irish and Jews looking to escape the Hill District's crowded tenements. South Oakland, however, was a working-class stronghold oriented toward the iron and steel plants that lined the Monongahela River along Second Avenue. The period 1860 to 1900 was South Oakland's "Iron Age," with many skilled craftsmen and artisans. From 1892 to the 1960s, steel held sway, and unskilled workers, especially Italians, came to dominate the neighborhood.

The turn of the 20th century saw unprecedented construction in central Oakland, as prosperous industrialists decided to create a "Civic Center" for Pittsburgh, a cultural showplace for the city's high society. Mary Croghan Schenley, the whiskey heiress, gave the city 300 acres to form Schenley Park and sold land to build the elegant Schenley Hotel (now the University of Pittsburgh's student union), which housed rich and famous visitors coming to Pittsburgh. The Phipps family built a horticultural conservatory nearby. Andrew Carnegie constructed his Carnegie Institute, focusing on what he considered man's highest pursuits: art, literature, science, and music.

This new cultural core of Pittsburgh soon included the Carnegie Technical Institute (now Carnegie Mellon University) and the University of Pittsburgh. Other industrialists also contributed cultural edifices, such as Heinz Chapel, the Cathedral of Learning, and the Stephen Foster Memorial on the University of Pittsburgh campus. Many private clubs,

a **Heinz Chapel**
b **Temple Rodef Shalom**
c **Holy Spirit Byzantine Catholic Church**
d **Schenley Park Visitors Center**
e **Phipps Conservatory**

Pittsburgh Neighborhoods

such as the Pittsburgh Athletic Association, moved to Oakland. To the cultural institutions were added major medical institutions, including many of the city's hospitals. Sports were represented by Forbes Field, home of the Pittsburgh Pirates. Many religious denominations made Oakland their center as well. The Pittsburgh Roman Catholic Diocese built St. Paul Cathedral on prestigious Fifth Avenue in Oakland in 1906 and located its Central Catholic High School nearby. In 1923, St. Nicholas Greek Orthodox Church was founded on Forbes Avenue, later becoming that denomination's cathedral. The Jewish community built Rodef Shalom Temple, an architectural masterpiece, on Fifth Avenue in Oakland, as well as the city's only Jewish hospital, Montefiore.

After World War II, the concentration of universities and colleges in Oakland became both a magnet for returning soldiers from every cultural group in the region wishing to complete their educations and begin new civilian lives, and a direct port of entry for new immigrant students from all over the world: Syria-Lebanon, Thailand, Taiwan, India, and Latin America. The universities expanded, taking over buildings previously owned by the industrial elite. Older houses were made into apartments, and new apartment housing was built, attracting not only students but others, such as African-Americans from the Hill District, who could not afford to own or were prevented from owning, their own homes.

At the turn of the 21st century, Oakland is still the educational center of Pittsburgh. Its diversity of cultural groups is reflected in the city's most varied selection of ethnic restaurants.

f *Industry Mural* by John White Alexander at the Carnegie Museum

g *Foreground:* Hammershlag Hall, Carnegie Mellon University
   Background: Cathedral of Learning, University of Pittsburgh

h *Cooper Mural*, University Center, Carnegie Mellon University

i *Two Kings Mural* by Mikalojus Kastantas Ciurlionis, Lithuanian Room, Nationality Rooms, University of Pittsburgh

Three Rivers Route

 **Oakland**

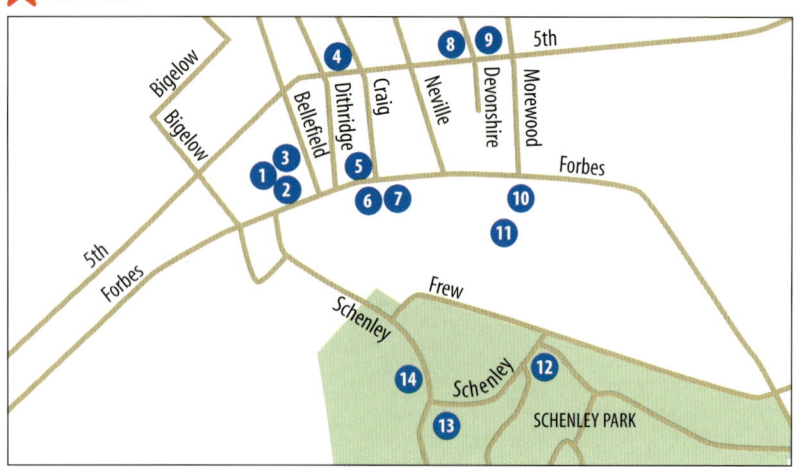

BY THE WAY

At Andrew Carnegie's urging, Forbes Field, the world's first all-steel and concrete baseball stadium was built in 1909. Look for its home plate, embedded in the first floor of the University of Pittsburgh's Wesley W. Posvar Hall, and the brass plaque in the sidewalk outside, where Bill Mazeroski's 9th-inning homer left the park to win the 1960 World Series for the Pittsburgh Pirates.

Oakland is organized around Forbes and Fifth Avenues. The Carnegie Institute and the sites within the University of Pittsburgh and Carnegie Mellon University (CMU) campuses are most accessible on foot. These include the Carnegie Institute's Industry Murals and the Carnegie Mellon University Cooper Mural, the Heinz Chapel (modeled on French Gothic churches), and the Nationality Rooms within the Cathedral of Learning building (each room decorated to reflect the cultural traditions of a different ethnic group in the region). Just off Forbes Avenue are the Phipps Conservatory and Schenley Park, both created by wealthy industrial families as places for city residents to connect with nature. Along both Fifth and Forbes are Roman and Byzantine Catholic, Greek Orthodox, and Jewish houses of worship, known for their architecture, their annual cultural events, and, at Rodef Shalom Temple, an unusual botanical garden that features plants named in the Bible.

University of Pittsburgh
Nationality Rooms
412–624–6000
Cathedral of Learning (5th Ave entrance)
First Floor
www.pitt.edu/~natrooms
Mon–Fri, 9AM–2:30PM; Sat, 9:30AM–2:30PM; Sun, 11AM–2:30PM
Adults: $3; Seniors over 60: $2;
Youth ages 8–18: 50 cents

Stephen Foster Memorial
412–624–4100
Forbes Avenue and Bigelow Boulevard
www.pitt.edu/~amerimus/museum.htm
Mon–Fri, 9AM–4PM; tours by appointment

Heinz Chapel
412–624–4157
Bellefield Avenue (Between Forbes and Fifth)
www.discover.pitt.edu/chapel
R.C. Mass: Sun, 11:30AM; Mon–Fri, 12PM (Sept–April)
Compline Service: Sun, 8:30PM (Sept–April)

St. Paul Roman Catholic Cathedral
412–621–4951
5th Avenue at Craig Street
www.catholic-church.org/st.paulcathedralpgh
Mass: Sun, 6:30AM, 8AM, 10AM, 12AM (choir), 6PM
Mon–Sat, 6:45AM, 8:15AM, 12:05PM, 6PM

St. Nicholas Greek Orthodox Cathedral
412–682–3866
419 S. Dithridge Street
www.stnickspgh.org
Othros/Matins: Sun, 8:30AM
Mass: Sun, 9:30AM

Pittsburgh Neighborhoods

Andrew Carnegie

Andrew Carnegie was a living contradiction. Born in Dunfermline, Scotland, Carnegie and his family left their home for America in 1848. A weaver by trade, Carnegie's father struggled to survive, for Dunfermline's once thriving linen industry had fallen on hard times.

Just 13 years old when he arrived in the States, Andrew Carnegie took on a series of jobs — as a bobbin boy in a cotton mill in Allegheny City on Pittsburgh's North Side, as a messenger for the Pittsburgh Telegraph Office, and as a secretary at the Pennsylvania Railroad.

But, ultimately, Carnegie found himself in the right place, southwestern Pennsylvania, at the right time — the dawn of the Gilded Age. Realizing the potential of a burgeoning steel industry, Carnegie amassed a fortune by age 33. But, he was never at ease with his wealth or his role in society. Although he wrote that it was the responsibility of the rich to "benefit the welfare of the community," he broke the unions at his mills and slashed his workers' wages.

When he sold the Carnegie Steel Company to J. P. Morgan in 1901, he pocketed a cool $250 million. But by the time he died 18 years later, he had built nearly 3,000 libraries throughout the world and had given away more than $350 million.

"Dippy" (*Diplodocus carnegii*) greets visitors at the Carnegie Museums.

Carnegie Museums of Pittsburgh
412–622–3131
4400 Forbes Avenue
www.carnegiemuseums.org
Sun, NOON–5PM; Tues–Sat, 10AM–5PM; closed Mon
Adults: $10; Seniors: $7
Youth ages 3–18 and students $6
Members and non-member children under 3: Free
John White Alexander Industry Murals
Second floor stairwell, Natural History Museum
Carnegie Music Hall
By event only

Holy Spirit Byzantine Catholic Church
412–687–1220
4815 5th Avenue, Pittsburgh
☎ Phone ahead or attend Mass: Sun, 10AM

Rodef Shalom Biblical Botanical Garden
412–621–6566
Rodef Shalom Temple
4905 5th Avenue
www.rodefshalom.org
June 1–Sept 15: Sun–Th, 10AM–2PM; Sat, NOON–1PM;
Wed evening, 7–9PM (June–Aug)
Admission: Free

Carnegie Mellon University
412–268–2000
5032 Forbes Avenue
www.cmu.edu
Cooper Mural
University Center, 2nd Floor
Daily: 8AM–MIDNIGHT (Hours vary when school is out)
Hornbostel Buildings
Throughout campus

Westinghouse Memorial
Schenley Park, on Schenley Drive near West Circuit Road (Outdoors)

Schenley Park Visitor's Center
412–687–1800
One Schenley Drive
pittsburghparks.org
Daily, 9:30AM–5PM (Seasonal changes)

Phipps Conservatory & Botanical Gardens
412–622–6914
One Schenley Park
www.phipps.conservatory.org
Tue–Sun, 9AM–5PM; Fri, 9AM–9PM
Adults: $6; Seniors 60+: $5;
Youth ages 2–12: $3; Students with ID: $4

Three Rivers Route

The Hill District

In the early 19th century, British and German settlers built estates and farms in the Hill District. When banker Thomas Mellon bought farmland on the slopes nearest the city, he subdivided the land into smaller plots and sold them to businesses. Irish laborers came in droves to the area. Then, business tycoon John Herron bought land adjoining his estate in Minersville. The property was rich in coal, which he used to fuel his lumber, brick, and other businesses. Soon he was building rows of tenement houses for his workers. Between 1850 and 1870, the Hill District bustled as railroads connected the "downtown" area with outlying communities. Irish, German, and southeast European Catholics came to work and live in the area.

After the Civil War, Scots-Irish, Irish, Germans, Greeks, Poles, Syrians, Lebanese, Italians, German and Russian Jews, Romanians, Russians, Slovaks, Armenians, African-Americans, and a few Chinese comprised the ethnic and racial background of the Hill. By the 1880s, Slavs, Italians, and Jews made up the majority of the population.

By 1900, the Hill was predominantly a blue-collar residential neighborhood where almost all of Pittsburgh's Jews (c. 40,000) were located. By the mid-1920s, Jews began to move from their Lower Hill homes to the Upper Hill, and eventually to other neighborhoods like Squirrel Hill and Oakland. African-Americans from southern states and Italian immigrants began moving into the Lower Hill. By 1930, African-Americans comprised more than half of the Hill District's population.

Businesses, including cigar-rolling factories, print shops, doctors' offices, beauty shops, dry cleaners, furniture stores, movie theaters, and hotels, thrived. The Hill District also boasted one of the most culturally rich arts communities in Pittsburgh. The Crawford Grill hosted performances by many jazz greats. The *Pittsburgh Courier,* a nationally acclaimed African-American newspaper, originated in the Hill District and remains in circulation. The Pittsburgh Crawfords, a Negro League baseball team that would win the 1936 championship, originated at McKelvey School.

Unfortunately, this prosperity did not last. In 1955, the federal government approved a plan to clear 105 acres of land for public buildings, displacing many people. When the Civic Arena was constructed at the corner of Wylie and Fullerton Streets, even more people were forced to move and businesses closed. The riots that followed the assassination of Martin Luther King, Jr. caused devastation as well. Soon, many African-Americans who could afford to move left the Hill District.

Today, residents are attempting to revitalize their community. Organizations like the YMCA, the Hill House Association, and local church groups sponsor programs. The Hill District Project Area Committee raised public and private funds to commemorate Freedom Corner — the intersection of Centre Avenue and Crawford Street where many civil rights demonstrations were held.

a St. Benedict the Moor steeple
b St. Benedict the Moor interior

Pittsburgh Neighborhoods

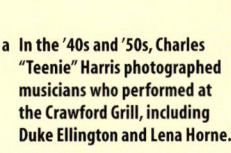

Dancing in the Streets

Henry Belcher was born the son of a sharecropper. In 1926, he and his family left the South in search of a better life. They settled in the Hill District, where the 11-year-old Belcher discovered a new world.

When he wasn't running errands or selling newspapers, Belcher was learning to tap dance. His teachers were other kids, and his stage was any street corner.

"It was a fad then," he says. "Everyone would dance." It wasn't long before Belcher and his buddies decided to take their show on the road. They called their style of dance "rhythm hoofin' " and it carried them to clubs and theaters throughout the country.

"It was quite an adventure," he says. But by the 1950s, Belcher grew weary of the road. So, he returned to Pittsburgh, got married, and hung up his tap shoes. Since then, however, the self-proclaimed "Dancin' Demon" has been persuaded to strut his stuff and share his knowledge and skills with young people.

But times are different. "Not too many kids are interested in tap," the 89-year-old says. "It's all about hip-hop." And the Hill District is different as well. "It was a poor neighborhood, but wonderful," Belcher recalls. "It was open all night and you could find everything there."

Although Belcher found his share of fame, his dancing days didn't necessarily bring him a fortune. "We never did make any money," he says. "But we earned a million dollars' worth of experience."

a In the '40s and '50s, Charles "Teenie" Harris photographed musicians who performed at the Crawford Grill, including Duke Ellington and Lena Horne.

b The Dancin' Demons

c The image, *Spiritual Form* by Carlos F. Peterson, graces a re-dedicated Freedom Corner.

d A 1976 march protesting unfair hiring of blacks for construction jobs began at Freedom Corner. Leading the march were: Mike Desmond, Reverend Jimmy Joe Robinson, Nate Smith, and Byrd Brown.

Three Rivers Route

The Hill District

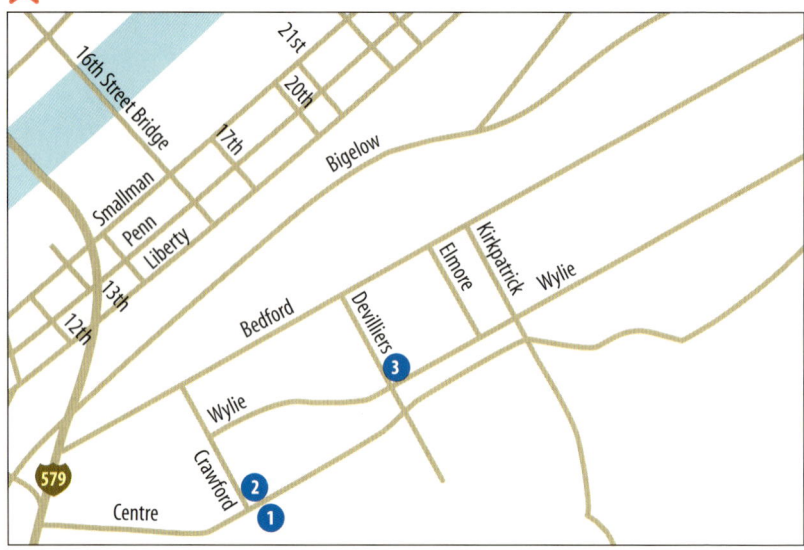

BY THE WAY

Around 1900 there were over 100 factories in the Hill District making cigars from Pennsylvania tobacco. Jewish immigrant families stripped tobacco leaves at home at night, then took them the next day to be rolled into fat "stogies." The workers were unionized and paid by the cigar.

Once a teeming immigrant neighborhood, the Hill District evolved into Pittsburgh's showplace for African-American heritage. At the junction of Centre and Crawford Avenues, Freedom Corner is the jump-off point for parades and social-action marches, and St. Benedict the Moor Church blends Catholic practice with African and African-American art and custom (there's a gospel mass every Sunday). Along Wylie Avenue, Ebenezer Baptist Church hosted many gospel concerts,* and the original Crawford Grill was Pittsburgh's jazz mecca in the early 20th century.

Freedom Corner
Centre Avenue and Crawford Street, Pittsburgh
www.freedomcorner.org
Outdoors

St. Benedict the Moor Catholic Church
412–281–3141
91 Crawford Street, Pittsburgh
www.thesafety.net/~benedict
☎ Phone ahead or attend Mass:
Sat, 4PM; Sun, 9AM, NOON

Ebenezer Baptist Church
412–281–6583
2001 Wylie Avenue, Pittsburgh
www.ebcbaptist.org
*Destroyed by fire March 13, 2004

Courtesy of Carnegie Museum of Art, Pittsburgh: Charles "Teenie" Harris Photo Archive

top: The Crawford Grill circa 1945
bottom: Wylie Avenue circa 1945

Pittsburgh Neighborhoods

African-American Heritage

They are one of the oldest ethnic groups in the region and one of the newest. One of the most widely dispersed and most concentrated. One of the most visible and one of the least well known. African-Americans have been a vital force in southwestern Pennsylvania for more than 200 years. They came as servants, slaves, and freemen among the first settlers in the region, working the charcoal-fired iron furnaces in Fayette County and keeping house for the wealthy in Pittsburgh. In the mid-19th century, before the Civil War, they continued to come, often via the Underground Railroad. Some went on further north, but many stayed to make new lives here. From the 1870s and 1880s on, the lack of jobs in the South and the rise of steel in southwestern Pennsylvania, drew more African-Americans, part of the Great Northern Migration that continued into the 1920s.

Most of these newcomers settled in Pittsburgh's Hill District and in the mill and foundry towns that lined the region's rivers. The men worked mostly the "hot jobs" in the plants, often with little hope of advancement or union support, but it was a living. The women kept the home together and raised the children, sometimes also working in "private duty" as housekeepers, as well as caring for a father or husband injured on the job or too ill to work. After World War II, urban renewal caused great upheaval: many African-Americans in Pittsburgh's Hill District were relocated to the Mon Valley milltowns, while others moved to Pittsburgh's Homewood neighborhood, and on into Wilkinsburg and the eastern suburbs. Since the late 20th century, there has been another small influx of newcomers, this time students and professionals from the Caribbean and Africa.

From the Drums Came All That Jazz, quilt by Tina Brewer, 1995

Each group in turn has contributed its own customs and traditions to African-American identity in the region. In the early 19th century, Pittsburgh African-American journalist Martin Delany fueled the nation's abolitionist movement, while local African-Americans' stories fired the imagination of Pittsburgh songwriter Stephen C. Foster, who sympathized with their yearning for equality. African-Americans founded Baptist and African Methodist Episcopal (AME) churches in the region, where "lining" hymns and call-and-response spirituals were fervently sung. The women made quilts to keep their families warm and cooked dishes with flavors of the South. During the region's industrial boom, a few African-Americans became businessmen: Cumberland "Cum" Posey of Homestead owned coal barges and used the money he made to start the Homestead Grays baseball team, a mainstay of the Negro League. Pittsburgh's Hill District in the 1920s and 1930s saw the flowering of jazz and the founding of the National Negro Opera Company.

Church-related and other traditions still help African-Americans maintain a sense of continuity. Sacred songs, from old-time spirituals to the newest gospel choir anthems, express community cohesion. Domestic folk arts flourish with organizations such as the African-American Heritage Quilters. And, since the 1970s, new immigrants have added African music, dance, and clothing styles, and Caribbean steel-pan music and fried plantains to the African-American cultural mix. Visitors to the region today can discover the places where jazz was created, see the **African Heritage Nationality Room** at the University of Pittsburgh and exhibits on African-American culture at the **Heinz History Center**, and experience local traditions firsthand, such as gospel masses, tap dancing, drum-and-dance ensembles, steel-pan concerts, and barbecued ribs (Three Rivers Route).

Three Rivers Route

South Side and Mt. Washington

The South Side has been home to 19th-century immigrants and 21st-century counter-culturalists, steel mills and coffee shops, domed cathedrals and crowded bars. But in pre-Revolutionary War times, this three-mile expanse was simply full of promise. At least that's what Major John Ormsby saw when he arrived in 1763 to lay claim to the tract of land running along the south shore of the Monongahela River given to him by England's King George III.

The property was divided into the four boroughs — South Pittsburgh, Birmingham, East Birmingham, and Ormsby — that would eventually make up the South Side Flats. (The area between the river and the train tracks has come to be known as the Flats, while, not surprisingly, the South Side Slopes got its moniker from the adjoining hills.

a Flags at George Cupples Stadium (formerly South Stadium)
b Duquesne Incline
c Grand Concourse restaurant, Station Square
d Bessemer converter, Station Square
e St. John the Baptist Ukrainian Catholic Church
f Oliver Bath House

However, it wasn't until after the major's death that his son-in-law, Dr. Nathaniel Bedford, took on the role of surveyor, naming streets after his relatives (Sarah, Jane, Mary, and Josephine). He saved the christening of Carson Street for a seafaring friend and Bedford Square for himself. In 1872, the boroughs were officially annexed to the City of Pittsburgh.

As the area continued to grow and build a reputation as a hub for glassmaking, it started attracting immigrants, first German, English, Irish, and Scottish workers. Then with the advent of steel production — in the form of the 100-plus-acre Jones & Laughlin plant — a new wave of eastern European immigrants arrived. Although these Slovaks, Ukrainians, Poles, Croatians, Serbians, and Lithuanians came here to work, they soon began constructing their own schools, churches, and places to live.

Pittsburgh Neighborhoods

Hip, Trendy, and Cool

Beth Marcello is more than a South Side resident; she's an advocate for city living in general and her neighborhood in particular. For the past 10-plus years, Marcello has made the South Side Slopes (the hillside area known for its steep, narrow, meandering streets and steps) her home. During much of that decade she has also served in various capacities, including president, for the South Side Local Development Company.

But as the glass and steel industries slowly disappeared from the landscape, the neighborhood was left to redefine its place in the world.

Recognizing a need to become proactive rather than reactive, the South Side Local Development Company (SSLDC), a community-based nonprofit organization, was formed in 1982. Three years later, the group successfully sponsored the East Carson Business District as the country's first participant in the National Trust for Historic Preservation's Main Street Program. By 1996, the business area had earned the National Trust's Great American Main Street Award.

The SSLDC is also responsible for organizing the Historic South Side House Tour and the annual South Side Summer Street Spectacular.

Other neighborhood attractions include: the South Side Works, a redevelopment project in the process of transforming the former LTV site (which was the former J&L site) into commercial and residential properties; and the South Side Market House of 1891, restored after a 1915 fire, now a community center.

Why has she volunteered so much time to her community? "The easy answer," Marcello replies, "is that someone has to do it. But very early on I got urban living in my blood. I really believe in it."

Prominent on her long list of favorite South Side things are the intangibles, like the energy, the vitality, and the diversity of the neighborhood. Marcello also likes the fact that she can walk to the post office or bank, to the Riverfront Trail, and to her favorite restaurants (Bruschetta's, City Grill, Dish, Nakama, and the 17th Street Café) and nightspots (Club Café, Mario's, and the Blue Note) around Carson Street, also known as the Flats.

"There's always someplace new to go," she says. "The South Side has become a hip, trendy, cool place to be." Still, Marcello adds, many of the ethnic traditions that defined the neighborhood — church bingo, pierogi making, and babushka-clad women sweeping sidewalks — remain an important part of the community's identity.

g *Foreground:* Riverfront Park
  Background: Birmingham Bridge
h South Side Market House
i Jerome Jocuns serves dessert at Old Europe Restaurant.
j *Steelworkers' Monument* by James O'Toole

Three Rivers Route

South Side and Mt. Washington

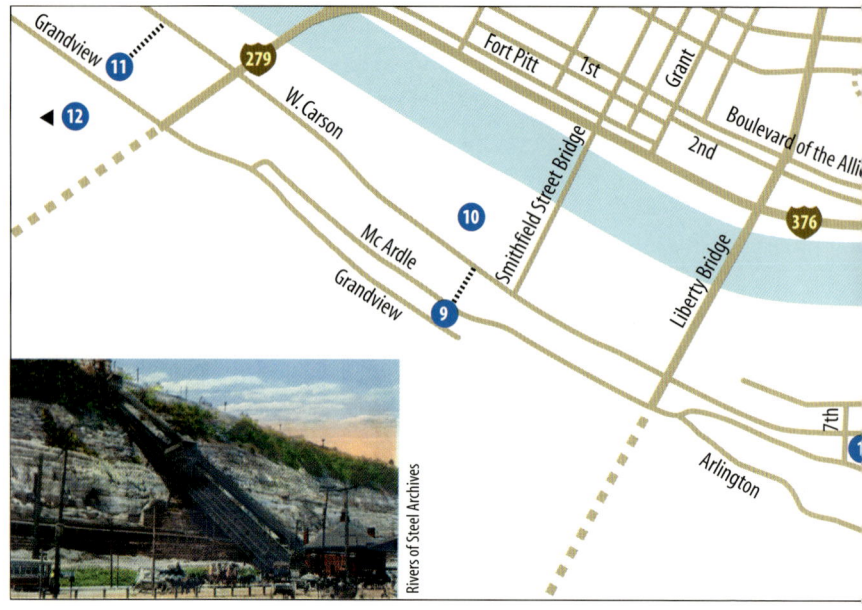

The Monongahela Incline, circa 1915

Pittsburgh's hillside steps are often refered to as "paper streets" because they show up on maps as streets, but confound unsuspecting motorists.

A drive along Carson Street is a drive through South Side's industrial past and its trendy present. Station Square, once a rail depot, now houses the fine Grand Concourse restaurant and a courtyard featuring a 20-foot-high Bessemer steel converter. Still in use, the Oliver Bath House was built for employees of the Oliver Iron and Steel Company. The Hot Metal Bridge, actually two bridges, was part of the Jones & Laughlin Steel Company's South Side Works, carrying raw materials and molten steel across the river; peaceful Riverfront Park was originally part of J&L as well. Ethnic and community life are represented by the Old Europe Restaurant, featuring eastern European specialties, and local landmarks such as St. John Ukrainian Church, the South Side Market House, and St. Michael's Church, where the passion play, *Veronica's Veil*, is performed during Lent. The Monongahela and Duquesne Inclines, built in the 19th century to carry down coal mined from the hillside, now carry people up to Mt. Washington's Grandview Avenue promenade; and the West End Overlook offers a spectacular view of Pittsburgh's Point.

St. John Ukrainian Catholic Church
412–481–5022
109 South 7th Street
☎ Phone ahead

Abruzzi's
412–431–4511
52 South 10th Street
Mon–Th, 11:30am–10pm; Fri, 11:30am–11pm
Sat, 4–11pm; Sun, 4–9pm

Oliver Bath House
412–488–8380
38 South 10th Street
Mon–Fri, 9am–9pm; Sat, 10am–9pm; Sun, 11am–9pm

South Side Market House
412–488–8390
15 Bedford Square, Pittsburgh

Pittsburgh Neighborhoods

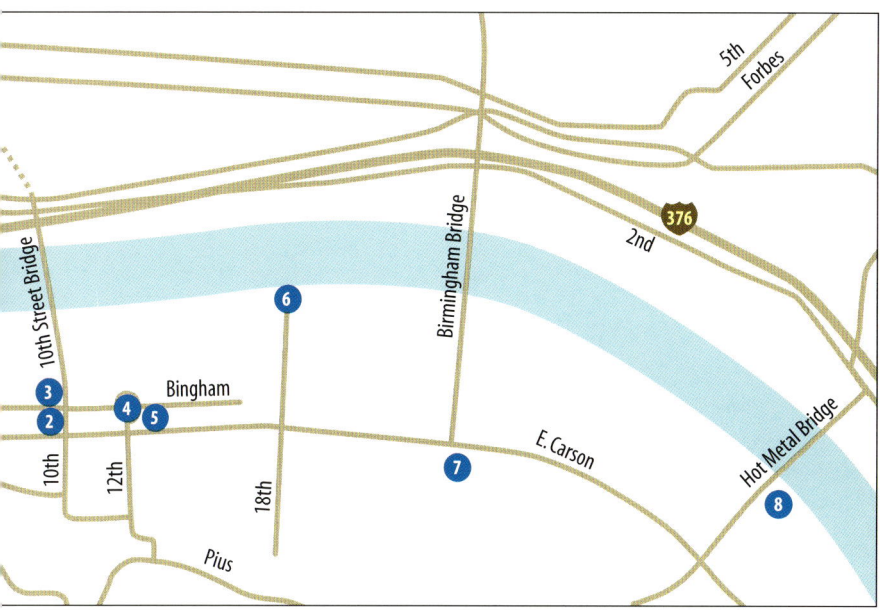

5 ✠
Old Europe Restaurant
412–488–1700
1209–1211 East Carson Street, Pittsburgh
Tue–Sat, 5–11PM; Sun, 4–11PM

6 ✠ Ⓔ
Riverfront Park/Boat Landing
18th Street on the Monongahela River

7 ✠ ☕
Mallorca Restaurant
412–488–1818
2228 East Carson Street
www.mallorcarestaurant.com
Mon–Th, 11:30AM–10:30PM;
Fri & Sat, 11:30AM–11:30PM; Sun, NOON–10PM

8 🏭
Steelworkers' Monument
By James O'Toole
Outdoors near the Hot Metal Bridge

9 ✠ 🏭
Monongahela Incline
412–422–2000
Grandview Avenue and Wyoming Avenue
www.portauthority.org/ride/pglncline.asp
Mon–Sat, 5:30–MIDNIGHT
Adult: $1.75; Children and disabled: $.85

10 🏭 ∧ ☕
Station Square
1–800–859–8959
Smithfield Street Bridge and Carson Street
www.stationsquare.com
Mon–Th, 11:30AM–10:30PM;
Fri–Sat, 11:30AM–11:30PM; Sun, NOON–10PM

11 ✠ 🏭
Duquesne Incline
412–381–1665
1220 Grandview Avenue
trfn.clpgh.org/incline
Mon–Sat, 5:30–12:45PM; Sun, 7–12:45AM
Adult: $1.75; Children (6–11): $.85

12 🍃
West End–Elliott Overlook
Rue Grande Vue, Elliott
Outdoors
*Directions: Carson St. to West End Circle.
Go through underpass. Bear right .5 mi.
up hill on Steuben St. Right on Chartiers Ave.
to stoplight. Right on Lorenz Ave. up hill to
"T." Right on Rue Grande Vue into Overlook.*

Three Rivers Route

E   EVENTS CALENDAR

For specific dates and times of events see: **www.riversofsteel.com**

Events that occur in several months are abbreviated with an *. See Recurring Events for full contact information.

Recurring Events

Regional Heritage
Rivers of Steel National Heritage Area
412–464–4020
The Bost Building
623 E. Eighth Avenue, Homestead
Changing exhibits and events on regional cultural and industrial traditions

Gospel Mass
St. Benedict the Moor Church
412–281–3141
91 Crawford Street, Pittsburgh
Every Sunday at noon

Hungarian Nights
Jozsa Corner Restaurant
412–422–1886
4800 2nd Avenue, Pittsburgh
Every 2nd Friday: Call for reservations.
Hungarian food, music, and dancing.

Irish Dancing
Mullaney's Harp and Fiddle
412–642–6622
2329 Penn Avenue, Pittsburgh
Every Tuesday evening

Jewish Heritage
United Jewish Federation
412–992–5243
Squirrel Hill, Pittsburgh
www.ujf.net
Changing events on Jewish traditions

Environmental Events
Nine Mile Run Watershed Association
412–371–8779
1400 S. Braddock Avenue, Pittsburgh
www.ninemilerun.org

*Nationality Days**
Kennywood Park
412–461–0500
4800 Kennywood Boulevard, West Mifflin
www.kennywood.com
June–Labor Day

*First Fridays at the Frick**
Frick Art and Historical Center
412–371–0606
7227 Reynolds Street, Pittsburgh
www.frickart.org
Free outdoor concerts
June–September

*Soup Sega**
Bulgarian-Macedonian National Educational and Cultural Center
412–461–6188
449 West 8th Avenue, West Homestead
September–May: Saturday mornings

January

*Soup Sega

February

Soul Food Luncheon & African Market
YWCA of McKeesport
412–664–7146
410 9th Avenue, McKeesport

Heart of Glass
Pittsburgh Glass Center
412–365–2145
5472 Penn Avenue, Pittsburgh
Mid-February

*Soup Sega

March

Saint Patrick's Day Parade
724–379–6600
Downtown Pittsburgh
www.pittsburghirish.org/parade
Early March

Veronica's Veil Passion Play
St. Michael Church Auditorium
412–431–5550
44 Pius Street
trfn.clpgh.org/vvp
March–April (Lent)

*Soup Sega

April

Pysanky Easter Egg Sale
SS. Peter and Paul Ukrainian Orthodox Greek Catholic Church
412–276–9718
220 Mansfield Boulevard, Carnegie
Palm Sunday

*Soup Sega

May

Calliope Annual Benefit Concert
Calliope: The Pittsburgh Folk Music Society
412–432–0333
10 Bedford Square, Pittsburgh
www.calliopehouse.org

Greek Food Festival
St. Nicholas Greek Orthodox Cathedral
412–682–3866
419 S. Dithridge Street, Pittsburgh
Early May

Pittsburgh Folk Festival
Station Square
412–243–6856
Station Square, Pittsburgh
Memorial Day Weekend

*Soup Sega

June

Three Rivers Art Festival
Point State Park
412–281–8723
www.artsfestival.net
Early June

*Nationality Days
*First Fridays at the Frick

July

*Nationality Days
*First Fridays at the Frick

August

Shadyside Arts Festival
412–621–8481
Penn and Fifth Avenues, Pittsburgh
www.shadysideartsfestival.com
Early August

International Village
412–675–5020 x60
Renziehausen Park, McKeesport
3rd weekend

Ypapanti Greek Food Festival
Presentation of Christ Church
412–824–9188
1575 Electric Avenue, Pittsburgh
3rd weekend
www.greekburgh.com

Greek Food Festival
Holy Trinity Greek Orthodox Church
412–321–9282
302 West North Avenue, Pittsburgh
www.holytrinitypgh.org/festival
Late August, early September

*Nationality Days
*First Fridays at the Frick

September

Homegrown Crafts Fair/
Allegheny County Rib Cook-Off
Mon-Yough Riverfront Entertainment and Cultural Council
412–678–1727
South Park Fairgrounds, Library
Labor Day weekend

Festa Italiana
412–261–2811
Chevrolet Amphitheater, Station Square, Pittsburgh
Labor Day weekend

Pittsburgh Irish Festival
412–422–1113
Chevrolet Amphitheater, Station Square, Pittsburgh
www.pghirishfest.org

Dragon Boats Race
Three Rivers Rowing Association
412–231–8772
South Side Riverside Park, Pittsburgh
www.pittsburghdragonboatfestival.org

American Indian Pow-wow
Council of Three Rivers American Indian Center
412–782–4457
120 Charles Street, Dorseyville

Oktoberfest
Pennsylvania Brewing Company
412–237–9402
800 Vinial Street, Pittsburgh
Last two weekends

*Nationality Days
*First Fridays at the Frick
*Soup Sega

October

Mavuno African-American Visual and Performing Arts Festival
Sweetwater Center for the Arts
412–741–4405
200 Broad Street, Sewickley

*Soup Sega

November

*Soup Sega

December

First Night Pittsburgh
412–201–7380
Downtown Pittsburgh
New Year's Eve
Ethnic and other cultural events

*Soup Sega

Ohio-Beaver Route

Thunder of Protest

Southwestern Pennsylvania's people are known for cherished values and their deeply held beliefs. Nowhere is this more evident than in the industrial valleys of the Ohio and Beaver Rivers. For more than 200 years, communities here have shown a willingness to take a stand, even to support unpopular positions.

above: **Steelworkers picket near the Tunnel, 1936–37.**

opposite page: **Blast Furnace Plant, J&L Aliquippa Works, early 1960s**

For hundreds of years, the Ohio-Beaver riverfronts were a Native American trading area. During its first century of European settlement, the region was strongly affected by the Harmony Society, German Protestant religious dissidents who were also successful industrial entrepreneurs.

Arriving shortly after 1800, the Harmonists founded or furthered many of the larger communities in the Ohio and Beaver valleys. Centered in Economy, now the Old Economy state historic site in Ambridge, their industrial pursuits included some of southwestern Pennsylvania's earliest iron foundries and rolling mills.

Due in large part to the Harmonists' early ventures, iron production prompted the growth of a string of towns along the Beaver River, including Beaver Falls, New Brighton, and Fallston. The Harmonists' warehouses and shipping interests propelled Rochester and Bridgewater to commercial importance.

But the Harmonists were equally well-known for their strong and unconventional views on social organization, which included celibacy and communal living. The Harmonists divided during the 19th century over the issue of marriage. A small group broke away from the main settlement at Economy and built their own towns on the other side of the Ohio in Bridgewater and Monaca.

In the Ohio-Beaver area's second century of development, iron and steel held sway. The town of Ambridge, started by the American Bridge Company on property purchased from the Harmonists, became a center for iron and steel manufacturing. Across the river, the Jones & Laughlin Steel Company (J&L) built southwestern Pennsylvania's largest basic steel mill complex, the Aliquippa Works, in 1900. New locks and dams were constructed on the Ohio, and barge-building facilities and vast railroad yards sprang up in response to the upsurge in industry. Thousands of immigrants from eastern and southern Europe, along with African-Americans from the southern states, poured into the Ohio-Beaver area to work in the new Aliquippa and Ambridge mills. The communal and egalitarian ideals of the Harmonists gave way to a society in which management "cake-eaters" lived in gracious homes in Beaver, far from the cramped milltown workers' quarters.

Like most steel producers, J&L tried to keep production high and costs low. Worried about labor unrest, the company kept a tight rein over its facilities and workforce. And there was reason for worry. From the late 1880s on, steel workers in southwestern Pennsylvania grew resentful of the poor working conditions and the harsh methods used by company owners to maintain control.

The companies strongly resisted workers' efforts to unionize. In Aliquippa, J&L was particularly noted for its repressive measures, which included requiring its workers to live in company-built neighborhoods segregated by ethnicity, with round-the-clock surveillance by company police and strictly enforced curfews. Things came to a head in 1937 at Aliquippa's famous Tunnel, when dissident workers challenged J&L's policies and — aided by U.S. Supreme Court rulings — changed the course of history for the American steel workers.

Visitors to the Ohio-Beaver area today will enjoy its parks and river views, delight in its ethnic churches and restaurants, and warm to the down-to-earth friendliness of its people. But if they listen closely, they also will hear the echo of the "thunder of protest" that shaped the area's gritty, no-nonsense character.

Ohio-Beaver Route

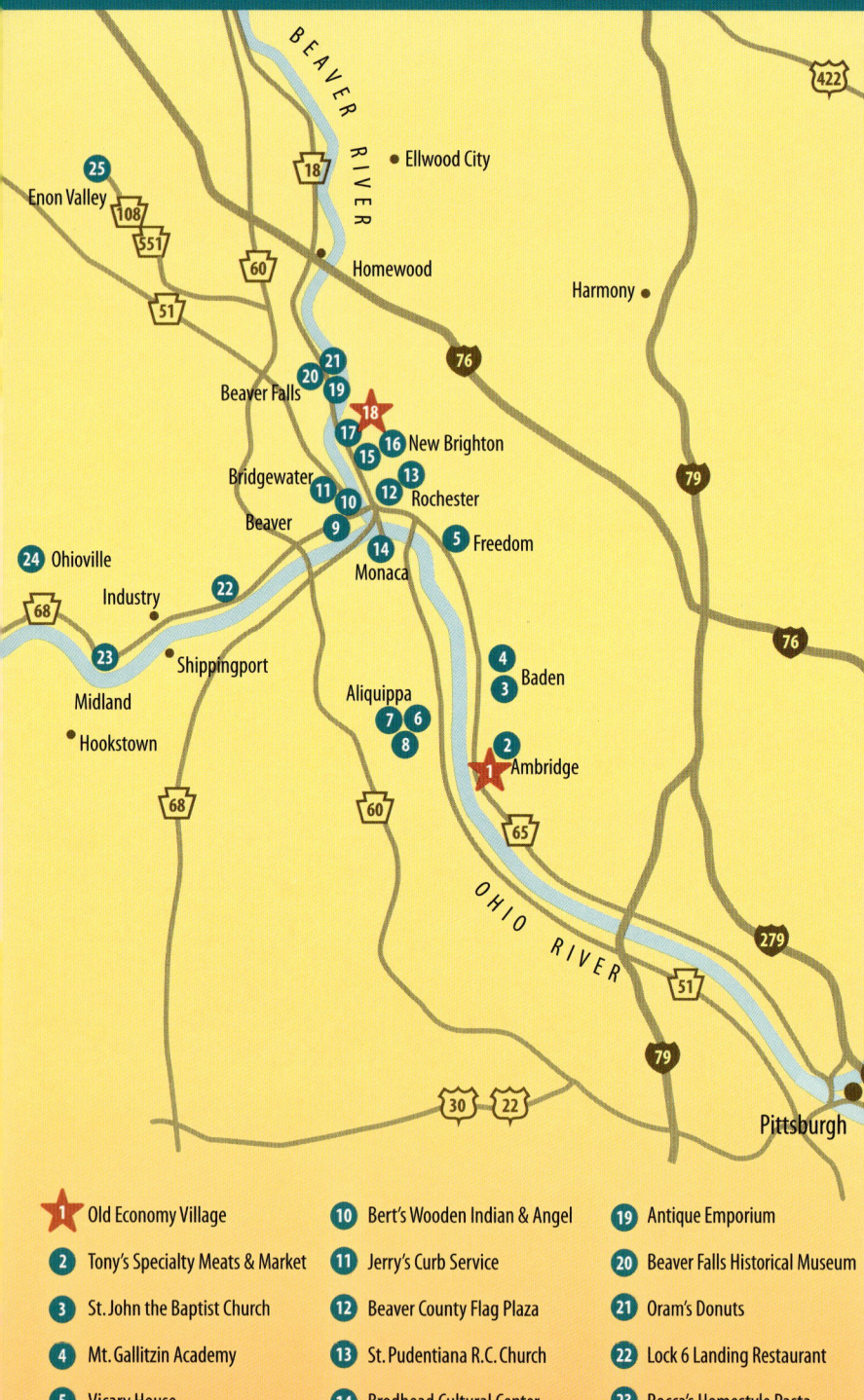

1. Old Economy Village
2. Tony's Specialty Meats & Market
3. St. John the Baptist Church
4. Mt. Gallitzin Academy
5. Vicary House
6. The Tunnel & Shrine
7. B. F. Jones Memorial Library
8. Lebanese Club
9. Beaver Area Historical Museum
10. Bert's Wooden Indian & Angel
11. Jerry's Curb Service
12. Beaver County Flag Plaza
13. St. Pudentiana R.C. Church
14. Brodhead Cultural Center
15. Christ Episcopal Church
16. Rosalind Candy Castle
17. Bricker's Restaurant
18. Merrick Free Art Gallery
19. Antique Emporium
20. Beaver Falls Historical Museum
21. Oram's Donuts
22. Lock 6 Landing Restaurant
23. Rocca's Homestyle Pasta
24. GCU St. Nicholas Chapel
25. SNPJ Recreation Center

Northwest from Pittsburgh

AMBRIDGE AREA

From Pittsburgh: *Take PA 65 N to Ambridge.*

One-Day Tour: Sites 1–5
Old Economy: *From PA 65 N, right on 13th St. Left on Church St.*
Lunch at Tony's Specialty Meats: *Continue on 13th St. Right on Merchant St. Left on 14th St. Go 2 blocks. Left on Duss Ave. Go 1.1 mi. Tony's is on left. Or lunch on Fridays at* ***St. John the Baptist Church:*** *Stay on Duss Ave. (becomes State) 1.4 mi. Left on Linmore Ave. St. John's is on right.* ***Mt. Gallitzin Academy:*** *Return to State. Left on State (merges into PA 65 N). Go .3 mi. Mt. Gallitzin is on right.* ***Vicary House:*** *Stay on PA 65 N to Freedom exit. Straight on 3rd Ave. Right on Harvey's Run Rd. Vicary House is on left.* ***Return to Pittsburgh:*** *PA 65 S.*

AMBRIDGE

Old Economy Village
724–266–4500
270 16th Street, Ambridge
www.oldeconomyvillage.org
Tues–Sat, 9am–5pm; Sun, noon–5pm
Adults: $7; Seniors and AAA: $6; Youth 6–17: $5

SYMBOLS
★ Must-See Site
● Point of Interest Site
🏭 Industry
✳ Folklife
🍃 Nature
⋀ Art & Architecture
☕ Food
🛍 Shopping
Ⓔ Events Calendar
☎ Phone Ahead

The quiet of Old Economy Village is interrupted by the rush of nearby 21st-century traffic. The buildings stand full of everyday objects, as if the occupants might yet return. The clock on the church steeple shows no minute hand. Minutes, after all, seemed insignificant when the promise of Heaven on Earth was so near.

Old Economy exists today much as it did back in 1824. Founded by the Harmony Society, the town served as a place to work hard, live devoutly, and wait patiently. But things didn't exactly turn out as Father George Rapp envisioned. Believing that man could live in harmony with his fellow man as well as with God, Rapp set out to prepare his followers for the second coming of Christ.

Seeking religious freedom, the Harmonists fled their native Germany in 1804. Settling first in Butler County, Pa., then moving west to the state of Indiana, they eventually traveled back to Pennsylvania and put down roots. Calling their home along the Ohio River "Oekonomie," the Harmonists began to thrive. At one time, 800 members lived communally, sharing the joys and hardships equally. Together, they built their church, a meeting house, and homes. They cleared the land to plant and harvest crops. They built shops for the blacksmiths, tanners, and cabinetmakers among them. They powered textile mills with steam engines. And, they sold their products throughout the world.

St. John's Lutheran Church

The Harmony Society

I think it probable, from what I have heard from the older members, that when they were comfortably settled at Economy, the Harmony Society was for some years in its most flourishing condition. All had come on together from Indiana; and all were satisfied with the beauty of the new home. Those who had suffered from malarious fevers here rapidly recovered. The vicinity to Pittsburgh, and cheap water communication, encouraged them in manufacturing... They erected woolen and cotton mills, a gristmill and sawmill; they planted orchards and vineyards; they began the culture of silk, and with such success that soon the Sunday dress of men as well as women was of silk, grown, reeled, spun, and woven by themselves.
— Charles Nordhoff. *The Communistic Societies of the United States; from Personal Visit and Observation*, 1875.

Ohio-Beaver Route

Seven Principles of the Harmony Society

1. Community property
2. Abstinence
3. Priestliness

These three are most important. Further,

4. Advance the honor of God and the welfare of man, or which is the same, love God above all and thy neighbor as thyself.
5. Make up all sufferings still due.
6. The old Adam and his works must disappear.
7. Prepare yourselves for the future coming of the Lord, so that when He comes you need not be shocked. That is its main goal, point and foundation.

Docents in period costumes give living-history tours.

But, despite their economic good fortune, the Harmonists would not survive much beyond the turn of the century. By the 1830s, a third of their members left to follow another self-proclaimed prophet. In 1847, Father Rapp died without ever having witnessed the event he lived for. With storekeeper Romelius Langenbaker (a.k.a. Mr. Baker) taking over the reins from Father Rapp, the Harmonists recognized investment opportunities. Buying into railroads and oil wells, the society infused the region's burgeoning industries with early working capital. But in the end, it was the Harmonists' celibacy that sealed their fate. By 1905, they were no more.

The Blacksmith's Shop and Granary

Although many of the community's holdings were sold to the American Bridge Company (that's where Ambridge got its name), the Harmonists' story, accomplishments, and ideals, have been preserved in Old Economy Village. The Commonwealth of Pennsylvania took over the site in 1916, and today it's maintained by the Pennsylvania Historical and Museum Commission. Encompassing six acres, this National Historic Landmark features 17 authentic Harmonist buildings (circa 1824–1830), gardens, and streets, along with more than 16,000 artifacts.

Guided tours take visitors through the life and times of the Harmonists. Visitors can see the Museum Building and Feast Hall where society members would gather for holidays and anniversaries; the Print Shop where the oldest flat-bed press in America still stands; the Community Kitchen; the Cabinet Shop; the Granary, the Wine Cellar; the relatively grand residence of George Rapp; and the more modest Baker House. The gardens, too, have been restored to their 1829 splendor. With tulips, dahlias, and fruit trees blooming, they reflect the Harmonists' sensibilities.

Programs, workshops, and festivals celebrating German heritage and traditions — the foundation of the Harmonist society — take place throughout the year. Surrounded by Ambridge's National Register Historic District, Old Economy is at home in the modern world.

The Feast Hall in the late 1800s

German Heritage

Germans were among the first non-English-speaking immigrants to settle in southwestern Pennsylvania, beginning in the mid-18th century. Early German Protestant groups came seeking religious freedom. These included the Harmonists, who founded what is now known as **Old Economy** (Ohio-Beaver Route), the Mennonites, and the Amish.

German Catholics also settled in the region. **St. Vincent's Archabbey,** started in the mid-19th century by a German Benedictine order in Latrobe (Youghiogheny Route), still operates a monastery and maintains its own gristmill.

Later, German glassmakers, metalworkers, and mechanics became the backbone of industrial craftwork in the region's burgeoning iron and steel industry.

Henry Clay Frick, owner of hundreds of coke ovens and famous as Andrew Carnegie's hard-nosed partner during the Homestead Steel Strike in 1892, was of German background. Visitors can trace Frick's life story at his birthplace, now the **West Overton Museums** in (Youghiogheny Route) and at **Clayton,** the mansion he built in Pittsburgh at the height of his career (Three Rivers Route). In the 20th century, German-speaking immigration continued, including the arrival of the Bruderhof, a utopian Protestant group expelled by the Nazis in the 1930s. A Bruderhof community remains today near Farmington (Youghiogheny Route).

Most people in what are now Pittsburgh's South Side and North Side spoke German well after the Civil War. **St. Anthony Catholic Church** in the North Side neighborhood of Troy Hill, famous for its relics, the **Teutonia Männerchor** building along the Allegheny River, and the **German Nationality Room** at the University of Pittsburgh (Three Rivers Route), bear witness to the importance of German traditions.

Members of the Pittsburgh Teutonia Männerchor may rent a peg on which to hang beer steins for $12.00 a year.

Although few place names in the region represent German settlement, the influence of German culture is still felt in subtle ways, such as the custom of making and eating sauerkraut at New Year's celebrations, and in public events like community Oktoberfest celebrations. Restaurants such as **Max's Allegheny Tavern** and the **Penn Brewery** on Pittsburgh's North Side (Three Rivers Route) or the **Kleiner Deutschmann** in Springdale (Alle-Kiski Route) offer visitors a chance to sample German cuisine.

O, Children, fraktur by Marta Urban, 2001. The art of *fraktur* (handwritten baptism and marriage certificates) was a German tradition in this area until the mid-19th century. Local artists have revived this folkcraft.

Renee Ruggiero of the Alpen Schuhplattler, a German folk dance ensemble based at the Teutonia Männerchor

Ohio-Beaver Route

Ambridge — A Town of Ethnic Churches

Ambridge has had an interesting and varied history. Growing from the quiet home of one of the world's best-known utopian communities into a booming industrial center with all of the comforts of a big city, Ambridge has had its share of prosperity and decline.

In 1804, the Harmony Society, a group of German immigrants led by George Rapp, founded a settlement they called "Economy," on land that would later become known as Ambridge. Frustrated with the religious and social climate of his hometown in Germany, Rapp wanted to start a utopian society where his followers could live communally and be self-sufficient. Although initially prosperous, the Harmonists were not destined to last.

Beginning in 1894, the Harmony Society sold land to several companies. In 1904, the American Bridge Company built a facility there, and started a new town named "Ambridge." American Bridge would become one of the largest steel prefabrication plants in the world. The new plant needed laborers and drew immigrant workers of many ethnic backgrounds to Ambridge, ready to start new lives in America.

Often, each ethnic group lived in its own neighborhood. At first sight, it is nearly impossible to distinguish one ethnic area from another, because the housing was built by contractors, rather than the immigrants themselves. But ethnic distinctions are apparent in the churches and social organizations. And although ethnic neighborhoods persisted, people in Ambridge recall that the different nationalities maintained friendly relations.

clockwise from top:
Altar of Holy Ghost Russian Orthodox Church; Domes of Holy Ghost Russian Orthodox Church; Façade of St. John the Baptist Orthodox Church; Holy Trinity Greek Orthodox Church; Doors of SS. Peter and Paul Ukrainian Catholic Church

As more people moved into town to work for American Bridge and other companies, Ambridge expanded. Within 15 years, the population had doubled to 12,730. A 1930 tally showed that Poles made up the largest foreign-born population, followed by immigrants from Italy, Czechoslovakia, Yugoslavia, Russia, Greece, Scotland, Austria, Germany, Romania, and England. There was also an African-American population. More than 20 ethnic organizations catered to these communities!

Religious affiliation also shows the diversity of ethnic groups in Ambridge. In 1974, the town had 24 worship sites. The oldest, St. John Lutheran Church of Old Economy, was started by the Harmony Society and still exists today. Young people who had been Lutherans in Germany but wanted to use English in their services created Zion's First Evangelical Church. At the Ambridge Assembly of God, members could attend either a Ukrainian or an English service. When immigrants from Austria-Hungary and Galicia came to Ambridge, they started the Russian Orthodox Church of the Holy Ghost. The congregation of the Holy Trinity Greek Orthodox Church came from Greece, while that of St. John's Greek Catholic Church came from the eastern tip of Slovakia. The Divine Redeemer Church's members were Slovak Roman Catholics, while those of St. Stanislaus Church were Polish Roman Catholics. Christ the King Church served the Italian Catholic population, and Croats attended Holy Trinity Roman Catholic Church. There is even a Coptic Orthodox church, St. Mary's, founded by Christians from Egypt and Ethiopia. Ambridge locals, though, will tell you that they often simply went to the church closest to their home.

Ambridge's population enjoys sharing its heritage. Old Economy is well-maintained and draws many visitors year-round. Ambridge celebrates its ethnic diversity with two annual festivals: Nationality Days in the spring and Good Samaritan Parish Ethnic Days in the fall.

BY THE WAY

Rumor has it that Ambridge had the most bars and churches per square mile of any milltown in America.

top: **Window of Holy Ghost Russian Orthodox Church**
bottom: **Altar of St. Vladimir Ukrainian Orthodox Church**

Ohio-Beaver Route

❷ Tony's Specialty Meats & Market
724–266–8669
2919 Duss Avenue, Ambridge
Mon–Sat, 10AM–6PM

At Tony's Specialty Meats & Market, tasting is believing. "I can tell you about it until I'm blue in the face," says Ellen Rich, who with her husband, Tony Rich, and her son-in-law, Tony Joseph, is the proprietor of this Ambridge establishment, "but until you try it …"

Although customers can try Tony's beef, chicken, pork, lamb, veal, and fish in select grocery stores throughout the region, the faithful travel from surrounding counties to buy directly from the source.

The market is an unlikely neighbor in this industrial part of town. A machine shop in a former life, the building was transformed just two years ago into Tony Rich's vision of a traditional, family-run Italian delicatessen. Offering all the favorites — sausages, salami, capicola, and a variety of cheeses — the store also features a mural depicting both Tony Rich and Tony Joseph standing front and center.

But it's behind the scenes where the magic — a scientific process called vacuum tumbling — takes place. Once Tony Rich discovered this German technique, he decided to bring it home to western Pennsylvania. Tony's Market now houses three tumblers. Each can handle up to 500 pounds of meat. After the meat is sealed inside, rotating cylinders gently pick it up and drop it back down in a special marinade. The secret to the sauce, the Tonys say, is that no oils and fats are used, only spices and water.

The tumbling allows the beef, chicken, or other meat to evenly absorb the marinade. The result: "very plump, very moist, very tender meat," Tony Rich says. Word has it that the Delmonico steaks, pulled pork, and jalapeno-cheese hotdogs are extraordinary.

Tony Rich's appreciation of meat may have come from his days in his father's slaughterhouse, but his understanding of the formula for success is something he taught himself. According to Ellen, "He's a natural."

Nationality Days in Ambridge

The annual Nationality Days celebration began in Ambridge in 1965. Every year, booths displaying diverse ethnic foods and crafts are assembled on Merchant Street between 5th and 8th Streets. Spectators can also visit the Nationality Days stage to view various types of entertainment. Sponsored by the Ambridge Chamber of Commerce, the festival draws up to 100,000 visitors each year.

Nationality Days originated as a way to display and share Ambridge's diverse ethnic heritage. Churches or ethnic organizations recruit volunteers to sell foods that include gyros (lamb-filled pitas), Southern fried chicken, lasagna, stuffed cabbage, sweet potato pie, and baklava. The entertainment changes each year. In the early years, tamburitzan groups, a Scottish bagpipe corps, Italian folk dancers, and spirtual singers performed. Now attendees can expect to see Polish folk art and pysanky (Ukrainian egg-decorating), or listen to Native American storytelling, klezmer music, gospel music, German oom-pah bands, and Italian mandolin players, in addition to many other types of entertainment.

Ambridge got its name from the American Bridge Company. Now headquartered in Coraopolis, Pa., American Bridge erected New York's Chrysler Building in 1929 and Chicago's John Hancock Building in 1970.

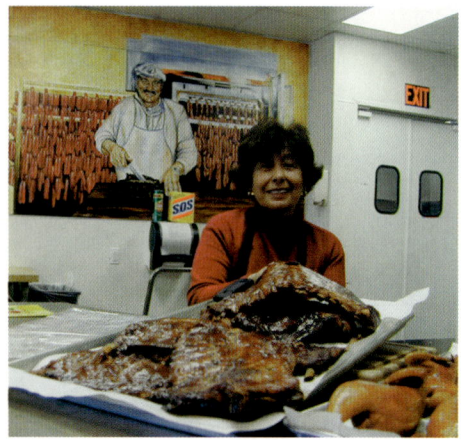

Shirley Klak displays mouth-watering ribs at Tony's.

BADEN

St. John the Baptist Catholic Church
724–869–2280

377 Linmore Avenue, Baden
Fridays (1st Fri in Oct–Last Fri in April), 10AM–4PM
Sit down for lunch or carry out pierogi (order in the morning).

The caps that the "pierogi ladies" wear are red, the color of the Polish flag.

Mafalda (a.k.a. Muffy) Cappabianco was pressed into service more than 30 years ago when the pastor of St. John the Baptist Church called on her to head a new venture — the pierogi kitchen. "I never did anything like that before," Muffy recalls. "It was a first for everybody."

Father Aranowski realized his church could raise extra funds by selling homemade pierogi. "But more than that," Muffy says, "he also saw that, by working together, members of the parish would feel a greater sense of community."

His vision remains true today. With Muffy still at the helm, some 60 church volunteers gather every Friday from the beginning of October through the end of April to make and sell some of the best pierogi in town. At $4 per dozen, it's a tough deal to beat.

Preparations begin on Wednesday when a half-dozen people peel 150 pounds of onions and strain 60 pounds of cottage cheese. Thursday a few good men wash, cut, and boil 350 pounds of potatoes, add sharp cheese to the mix, and get kraut and prunes ready.

On Friday, Muffy's production line shifts into gear at 5:30 a.m. The dough is prepared, the circles cut out, and the fillings dropped in and pinched closed. The pierogi are boiled, cooked, and served. By 4 p.m., all the plates have been cleared, the pots washed, and the 500-plus pierogi sold.

Ellen Napoleon and Mafalda Cappabianco, pierogi ladies at St. John's

Mt. Gallitzin Academy
724–869–2505

1016 West State Street, Baden
www.stjoseph-baden.org/MGA/default.asp
Pathways on the grounds are open throughout the year.

As you drive on PA 65 N from Ambridge to Baden, you'll see on the right the Koppel Steel Corporation, which produces seamless tubular products.

In 1904, the Sisters of St. Joseph started St. Joseph's Hospital in Pittsburgh to serve workers, and Mt. Gallitzin Academy in Baden to educate girls.

Enjoy a peaceful stroll along the prayer walk and peace labyrinth at Mt. Gallitzin Academy.

Ohio-Beaver Route

FREEDOM

Vicary House
724–775–1848
1235 3rd Avenue, Freedom
Mon–Fri, 10AM–2PM
Donations are appreciated.

They say old soldiers never die; they just fade away. What about old sea captains? William Vicary, for one, chose to retire along the shores of the Ohio River in what is now Freedom, Pa.

Born and raised in Philadelphia, Vicary began his seafaring career in 1788 at the age of 17. Later, he commanded merchant ships bound for China, Australia, and the East Indies. In 1806, Captain Vicary and his bride, Anna Maria Gossler of Columbia, Pa., decided to make a home on dry land. They moved to Sewickley Bottoms in 1821, becoming friends with Father George Rapp and other Harmonists in nearby Economy.

Soon the Captain purchased 604 acres for $5,304 and started to build his house of sandstone blocks quarried on the property. Like many New England merchants and shipbuilders, Vicary built his house in the Federal style, with a square floor plan, columns, and large windows. The house was an anomaly in western Pennsylvania, where Victorian structures reigned.

The house stayed in the Vicary family until 1911, when the Captain's granddaughter, Anna Harvey, moved to Los Angeles. By the early 1970s, progress in the form of Route 65 threatened to destroy the house. Thanks to the efforts of the Beaver County Historical Research & Landmarks Foundation and concerned citizens, the Vicary House was saved. In 1974, it was put on the National Register of Historical Places, and in 1998, it became the Foundation's official headquarters.

"Restoration work continues," says Vicary House Executive Director Brenda Applegate. "Our plan is to take the house back to the 1820s." In the meantime, high school students are invited to spend a day in the 1800s, churning butter, doing laundry, cooking meals, and helping with restoration projects. The Vicary House holds historical craft demonstrations and holiday festivals, and offers guided tours of the house and gardens.

The Beaver County Historical Research & Landmarks Foundation is located in Vicary House.

BY THE WAY

Freedom was founded by the followers of Bernard Müller, who broke away from the Harmony Society. They named their town in celebration of their freedom from the Harmonists, who ironically had emigrated from Germany in search of religious freedom.

Conway Yards, one of the nation's largest automated classification switching yards in the 1960s, can be seen from Vicary House's front porch.

Northwest from Pittsburgh

Greek Heritage

Taste the mouth-watering gyros (lamb-filled pitas) and *spanakopita* (spinach and feta cheese in filo dough). Watch the dancers in traditional costumes. Listen to the mesmerizing music. No, you don't have to buy a plane ticket to Greece. Come to southwestern Pennsylvania.

Greeks came to America for many of the same reasons that other immigrants came. They heard of the enormous wealth that could be made, and bravely ventured into this unknown land. Often men left their families behind until they had earned enough to send for them. But no matter how strongly the Greeks love America, their hearts will always be in Greece. This sentiment is evident in southwestern Pennsylvania's Greek-American communities, where people diligently save their money to visit the homeland as often as possible.

Why, then, have so many Greek-Americans chosen to remain in southwestern Pennsylvania? The answers aren't always romantic. When a wife came from the old country to join her husband and start a family, the couple often discovered that they were unable to afford to transport themselves and their children back to Greece. Sometimes men were hurt or killed in the mills, mines, or other industries, preventing families from returning. Others were deterred by Greece's turmoil during the Greek Civil War (1946–49) or the devastation that followed.

Greek weaving pattern from the island of Crete

Although many Greeks have their sights on the old country, they have flourished in southwestern Pennsylvania. Prominent communities in the region include those in Ambridge (Beaver County), Canonsburg (Washington County), and Oakland (Pittsburgh), among others. Churches are markers of identity, where Greek-Americans meet to worship, eat, dance, play music, and socialize. Greek food festivals are numerous and very well attended by Greeks and non-Greeks alike, featuring not only tantalizing treats but also traditional music, dance, and crafts. Local restaurants such as **Little Athens of Sewickley** (Three Rivers Route) have Greek nights for dancing, singing, and feasting. And, Greeks are traditionally involved in the restaurant business, serving the food of their own culture, as well as American-style delicacies.

To experience Greek culture at its finest, visit southwestern Pennsylvania.

above: Detail of jacket and shoes from the Evzone costume, the Greek national uniform

below: Mark Augoustidis and Carrie Betchunis, members of the Grecian Odyssey Dancers of East Pittsburgh, dance the *kalamatiano*.

Courtesy of Mary Doreza

Ohio-Beaver Route

Aliquippa

Aliquippa was founded in 1901. The town was named for Queen Allequippa, leader of the Seneca tribe in the mid-18th century. Her people's campsites and villages, strung along southwestern Pennsylvania's rivers, include one near the site of present-day Aliquippa. The town was associated right from the beginning with the Jones & Laughlin (J&L) Steel Company. J&L, expanding from its original plant on Pittsburgh's South Side, built steel works along seven miles of Ohio riverfront in Beaver County.

Aliquippa became one of the region's largest company towns. J&L built houses for the workers, arranged in neighborhoods called "plans," and J&L management controlled all decisions about which plans workers could live in. The workers were segregated by ethnic background: Italians were assigned to one plan, Croatians to another. Through company-enforced curfews, J&L kept workers from socializing with those of other ethnic groups and plans.

This train depot now houses the offices of J&L Structural Steel Inc.

All this was done to prevent workers from organizing protests against company policies. Known as a leader among the "little steel" companies, J&L was adamantly anti-union. During the labor struggles of the mid-1930s, "**the Tunnel**," a railroad underpass that led from the town into the mill, became the site of several battles between workers and company militia. The struggle prompted the U.S. Supreme Court's validation of the Wagner Act, which legitimized workers' rights to organize and led to the founding of the United Steel Workers of America.

After World War II, J&L, like the "Big Steel" corporations, began to decline, finally selling most of its operations in the mid-1980s to LTV Corporation, which soon closed most of the plants. Some steel is still made in Aliquippa: J&L Structural Steel operates a small mill on the original plant site.

After seeing the workers' monument at the Tunnel, visitors may stop along Franklin Avenue at the **B. F. Jones Library**, built by the daughter of the co-founder of J&L, to learn more about the labor heritage of Aliquippa. Those who wish to may drive through one of the housing plans to see the extraordinary scale of J&L's vision of company control.

Aliquippa's many cultural groups, now private owners of their homes, have built new ethnic clubs and restaurants to keep their traditions alive — the Lebanese and Croatians, especially. A special treat for visitors is the annual Festa di San Rocco in August, a saints'-day celebration sponsored by Aliquippa's Italian community featuring local Italian band music, food, and a parade.

Worker housing in Plan 12 circa 1920

Union pins from the 1930s

ALIQUIPPA

From Pittsburgh: Take PA 65 N to Ambridge. To cross Ambridge-Aliquippa Bridge, go right on 8th Ave. Left on Church St. Left on 11th St. Cross bridge. After bridge, right on PA 51 N.

Half-Day Tour: Sites 6–8
The Tunnel & Shrine: Follow PA 51 N (Constitution Blvd.). Bear right at "Y" on Station St. past J&L Structural Steel Offices on right, to "T." Shrine is ahead. Tunnel is on right. **B. F. Jones Library:** Left on Franklin Ave. Go .6 mi. to Library on left. **Lebanese Club:** Stay on Franklin Ave. Go .6 mi. Left on Kennedy Blvd. Go 1.5 mi. to Raccoon St. Lebanese Club is on right just past Croatian Club. **Return to Pittsburgh:** Continue on Kennedy Blvd. to PA 60 S (Beaver Expwy).

What's left of J&L? In Aliquippa, you'll see the former 14-inch steel mill, the former tin mill, and the new offices of J&L Structural Steel.

6 The Tunnel & Shrine
Constitution Boulevard and Franklin Avenue, Aliquippa

It was built in 1910 to provide a passageway under the Pittsburgh & Lake Erie Railroad tracks into the J&L Steel Company's Aliquippa Works. Nearly three decades later, the Tunnel became a direct link to history.

Employing some 15,000 workers, the J&L mill was a force to be reckoned with, and the days of reckoning started on May 12, 1937. Just a month earlier, the U.S. Supreme Court ruled that employers must bargain in good faith with union representatives. The verdict was hailed as "the greatest legal victory in American working class history."

Immediately following the decision, negotiations between the Steel Workers' Organizing Committee (SWOC) and J&L began in earnest, but a resolution was nowhere in sight. On the night of May 12, 1937, the union voted to strike — and the Tunnel quickly became the staging ground. By the 11 p.m. shift change, thousands of workers had gathered in and around the Tunnel. As May 13 dawned, only a few hundred workers remained in the mill. The rank and file, including many women workers, were still holding the line in the Tunnel. The possibility of serious violence was imminent.

News of the strike spread. On May 14, Pennsylvania Governor George Earle arrived on the scene. After touring the Aliquippa Works, he urged the parties to negotiate a peaceful settlement. Later that day, J&L agreed to recognize union elections, and a new contract was signed.

Although life and work along the Ohio River no longer revolve around the J&L Aliquippa Works, the Tunnel still stands as a passageway to the past.

The Tunnel in 1937 (top) and today

Wagner Act monument and workers' shrine

Ohio-Beaver Route

BY THE WAY

The Laughlin Library in Ambridge is named after Alexander Laughlin, Jr., not James Laughlin of the Jones & Laughlin Steel Co.

⑦
B. F. Jones Memorial Library
724–375–2900
663 Franklin Avenue, Aliquippa
www.aliquippa.lib.pa.us
Mon–Th, 8:30AM–8:15PM; Fri, 8:30AM–6PM; Sat, 9:30AM–5PM

Benjamin Franklin Jones, Sr., would probably be surprised at how things turned out. After all, the one building left standing that still bears his name is not the steel mill he helped to found, but rather the Aliquippa library.

During its heyday — the 1930s and 1940s — Aliquippa was a thriving community, thanks almost entirely to the Jones & Laughlin Steel Company. As the longest plant in the world, J&L stretched some seven miles down the Ohio River. It produced 3 million tons of raw steel per year and employed 15,000 people.

But by the mid-1980s, the once-mighty mill was forced to shut down its last blast furnace. For local residents, this marked the first time in nearly 80 years that it wasn't raining soot. Nowadays, this small river town is struggling simply to stay afloat. And nowhere is that more evident than in the central business district. But the B. F. Jones Memorial Library remains an oasis on Franklin Avenue.

When the idea of building a library in honor of her father was presented to Elisabeth Horne in 1926 — more than a decade after the steel industrialist's death — she saw it as an opportunity to serve the educational and cultural needs of the white-collar managers and immigrant laborers who settled in Aliquippa. So Horne offered to pay for the library's construction and initial furnishings and procured a promise from the borough to continue funding and operating it.

For three years, Horne worked with the Pittsburgh-based architectural firm of Bartholomew & Smith to create a one-story, 15,000-square-foot facility. Designed in a restrained Italian-Renaissance style, the library's exterior is made of gray Indiana limestone.

Stepping inside, visitors are greeted by a larger-than-life bronze statue of the building's namesake. The interior features solid mahogany and brass doors, decorative wrought-iron screens by Oscar Bach, and marble wall medallions. Today, the library is listed on both the Pennsylvania and National Registers of Historic Places.

The library's shelves are stocked with historic photographs of Aliquippa, the J&L mill, and the residential "plans" built by the company to accommodate segregated ethnic groups, as well as 80,000-plus books, books-on-tape, CDs, videos, and DVDs. Still striving to serve the needs of the community, the library also offers computer classes and children's activities.

Labor Speak

arbitration *resolution of a dispute by a third and neutral party.*

blacklist *a list of names to be discriminated against, either in employment or patronage.*

boycott *refusal to deal with, buy, supply, or handle products of a business to exert pressure in a labor dispute.*

lockout *the shutting down of a workplace by the employer to pressure the workers into accepting the employer's terms.*

scab *a worker who refuses to strike, or who takes the place of a striking worker.*

union shop *a workplace in which all workers whom the union is legally required to represent must pay union dues or a service fee.*

wildcat strike *a labor strike without the authorization of the union representing the strikers.*

Northwest from Pittsburgh

Lebanese Club
724-375-8335
815 Raccoon Street, Aliquippa
Fri, 4–11PM; Sat, 4–10PM; Sun, 2–7PM

Where there's food, there are usually friends. And where there are friends, there is usually a community. Some 50 years ago, the Lebanese Club in Aliquippa was founded to foster that sense of community. "When you walk into the place," says Mike Fayad, Lebanese Club president, "you're not walking in as a stranger."

Although the 57-year-old Fayad grew up in the neighborhood, he was the first in his family to join the Club. That was 30 years ago. The Club remains an oasis of authentic ethnic cuisine. Every weekend, the women who man the kitchen come armed with recipes dating back generations — and the meals they prepare are nothing short of delicious. "The restaurant is run by the older Lebanese women," Fayad says. "The younger generation doesn't feel like cooking."

Fayad recommends the grape leaves, kibee, and, of course, the shish kebab.

June Sarkis and Marcella Cavoulas prepare traditional Lebanese lamb and stuffed grape leaves.

Station Street Reunion

The black and white photographs of high school football players and young men looking handsome in their new Army uniforms stood as silent witnesses to a time — and place — long since past.

The time was the 1930s and 1940s, and the place was Aliquippa. Back then, the Jones & Laughlin Steel mill not only fueled the town's thriving business district, but also built planned communities for the families of its workers. These communities became home to the Italian, Greek, Russian, Serbian, Croatian, Irish, and Polish immigrants (to name just a few of the nationalities) who came to the region in search of better lives.

In the fall of 2001, some of the children of those immigrants, now in their 60s, 70s, and 80s, gathered at an Aliquippa restaurant for the eighth Station Street (and Highland Avenue, Kiehl Street, Elm Alley, and the Wye) reunion. The first one was held in 1972 and boasted 300 attendees. The 2001 version brought 170 guests — including the Andrewses, Dukovichs, Ferezans, Kakious, Kleins, Mendicinos, and Vafeases — together.

"My parents owned the grocery store on Station Street," says Morris Klein, now a grandfather himself. "The three of us, my mother, younger sister, and I, came over from Romania in the late 1920s. I was just 3. My father was already here working at Sam Roth's clothing store in Aliquippa.

"We opened Klein's Confectionary and Grocery Store in 1935 or '36. We lived above the store, and everyone — my parents, my sister, my brother, and me — worked there. We would stay open until midnight for the J&L shift workers. It was all book trade or credit.

"I left when I was 18 to go into the service. After the war, I went to Edinboro University and never lived in Aliquippa again. My wife and I settled in Pittsburgh where we raised our two kids and I worked as an electrical estimator. I never wanted to carry on the family store. It closed in the '60s when they tore down most of the houses to build Constitution Boulevard.

"I think my parents would be surprised to see all these people here at the reunion. None of us really keep in touch anymore, so it's nice to say hello and find out what's happened to everyone.

"I hope our children will continue the tradition, but I'm not so sure."

— Barbara Klein, excerpt from article for the *Pittsburgh Post-Gazette*, Sept. 11, 2001.

Ohio-Beaver Route

Mouth of the Beaver River

Looking into the mouth of the Beaver River

Where the Beaver River meets the Ohio, there are four communities with separate personalities, but shared experiences: Beaver and Bridgewater on the western shore, Rochester on the eastern shore, and Monaca across the Ohio to the south.

"Imagine a rolling, wooded English landscape, with the softest of blue skies, dotted at three-mile intervals by fat, quiet villages…" So wrote British author and poet laureate Rudyard Kipling in the 1890s, describing the town of **Beaver**. The site was known to Native Americans for more than 3,000 years. In the 1770s, George Washington explored the area, pronouncing it "a fine body of land." Following the Treaty of Fort McIntosh in 1785, the Beaver Reserve was established, including the site of the fort along present-day River Road.

The community of Beaver was laid out in 1791, and in 1800 the town was designated as the county seat for Beaver County. With its wide streets, public parks, and courthouse, Beaver became an oasis of gentility during the county's rough-and-tumble years of industrial expansion through the 19th century.

The town was home to many of the county's mill managers, lawyers, and other white-collar professionals, primarily of Scots-Irish, English, and some German descent. Visitors today can learn about the town's history at the Beaver Historical Museum, walk along historic River Road, where Fort McIntosh was located and where some of the town's oldest houses still stand. The courthouse square in the center of town is still a broad public park, bordered by stately Victorian-era residences.

Located next to Beaver, **Bridgewater** has an altogether different character. Where Beaver reflects old-family connections, Bridgewater welcomes newcomers. Where Beaver is refined-and-proper, Bridgewater is let-your-hair-down. Where Beaver is a white-collar community, Bridgewater grew as a blue-collar town. The site originally was a river ford on the Tuscarawas Trail, and by 1725 a Delaware Indian village. Still later, the site was known as Stone's Point, a favorite stopping place for steamboats and immigrants heading west. Bridgewater Borough, named for a city in England, was incorporated in 1835, and by then had become a freight-loading hub for canal and river barges.

As early as 1803, there were freight warehouses built by the Harmony Society to serve their growing industries in Economy on the other side of the Ohio River. The town soon included several iron foundries and other industries, such as barge repair. In addition to German, English, and Scots-Irish immigrants, the town of Bridgewater had one of the area's earliest African-American communities.

above: **Victorian homes line River Road in Beaver.**
below: **Beaver's Courthouse Square**

As a low-lying river town, Bridgewater has been buffeted by floods through the years, but has also benefited as a bridge connector to Rochester. Today, Bridgewater offers a variety of activities. After exploring the town's compact business district, with its craft shops and restaurants on Bridge Street, or sampling produce at the weekly farmers' market, visitors might enjoy strolling along scenic Riverside Park or stepping back into the 1950s for a burger at Jerry's Curb Service.

Northwest from Pittsburgh

Flatiron building in Rochester

As you cross the bridge (PA 18/65 N) into Beaver Falls, you'll see the former Babcock & Wilcox steel tube plant on the right.

Rochester's doughnut in the sky

Across the Beaver River from Bridgewater, **Rochester** is the commercial hub of the county. First settled just before 1800, Rochester was incorporated as a borough in 1849.

The town was born of canal and river traffic, spurred by completion of the Beaver Division Canal in 1834. When the railroad arrived, Rochester flourished, being situated at the junction of two mainlines of the Pennsylvania Railroad system. The railroads attracted industry, and, by the late 19th century, Rochester was a center for glassmaking as well as river-related trade, augmented by construction of the Girard Locks.

Manufacturing declined during the 20th century, and Rochester is now primarily residential. During the summer, many festivals and concerts take place at its Riverfront Park. One of the largest events is the annual River Regatta. Rochester is the future home of the Beaver Industrial Heritage Museum.

Monaca's history, like Bridgewater's, was also intertwined with that of the Harmony Society. The town began as a tract of land owned first by Ephraim Blaine and then by Francis Helveti, described as a Polish nobleman. When Helveti's sheep-raising venture failed, the property was sold to one of his creditors, Father George Rapp of the Harmony Society.

In 1822, the Harmony Society sold the property to Stephen Phillips, who started a boat-building business. One of Phillips' boats later brought Harmony Society members back from their Indiana settlement to their final home at Economy.

In 1834, several Harmonists seceded from the main village at Economy and decided to move across the river. They bought land from Phillips to found a town they called Phillipsburg, incorporated in 1840. By 1876, Phillipsburg had 600 residents, two hotels, a German Lutheran church, and a reputation as a good site for manufacturing. In 1877, the Pittsburgh & Lake Erie Railroad was built through town, prompting the growth of glassware-making and other industries.

In 1892, the borough was renamed Monaca, an Indian name from the French and Indian War. Monaca, which had a brick public school as early as 1852, is today home to the Pennsylvania State University's Beaver Campus.

This bridge's name changes each year depending on which town's high school football team wins the final game of the season.

Courtesy of Lucy Schaly for the Beaver County Times

Ohio-Beaver Route

BEAVER AREA

From Pittsburgh: Take PA 65 N to PA 68 W (becomes 3rd St.) into Beaver.

Half-Day Tour: Sites 9–14
Beaver Historical Museum: Left immediately after railroad viaduct onto River Rd. Museum is 2nd depot on left. **Bert's Wooden Indian and Angel:** Right on River Rd. Go 1 block. Left on 2nd St. Right on Beaver Ave. Cross 3rd St. Go to 2nd stop sign. Right on 5th St. Go 1 block. Left on Sharon Rd. Right on Leopard Ln. Bert's is on left. **Jerry's Curb Service:** Continue on Leopard Ln. Cross PA 51. Go 1 block. Left on Mulberry St. Go 1 block. Right on Canal St. Go 2 stop signs. Left on Riverside Dr. Jerry's is .6 mi. on left. **Beaver County Flag Plaza (in Riverfront Park):** From Jerry's, right on Riverside Dr. Right on Leopard Ln. to stoplight. Left on PA 51 S. Cross PA 51 bridge. Stay in right lane. Take immediate 2nd right marked PA 68/51 N/18 S. Straight to 2nd stoplight. Right at sign for Riverfront Park/Flag Plaza. Follow ramp to "T." Left to Park .4 mi.
☎ **St. Pudentiana:** Return to ramp. Straight at stoplight on New York Ave. Right on Adams St. Left on Virginia Ave. Go 8 mi. Left on Harrison St. Church is on left. ☎ **Brodhead Cultural Center (events only):** Right on Harrison St. Right on Virginia Ave. Right on Adams St. (PA 68 S). Left on PA 18 S through Monaca 1.6 mi. Left on Old Brodhead Rd .6 mi. Brodhead Cultural Center is on right (just past Penn State entrance). **Return to Pittsburgh:** Right on Old Brodhead Rd. to PA 60 S to Pittsburgh.

The Curtiss-Wright plant, built in 1941 in Beaver, received three "E" Awards for production, producing thousands of airplane propellers for fighters and bombers. The site was sold in 1947 to Westinghouse and became the center of its Standard Control Division. The site is north of the Beaver Cemetery.

BEAVER

Beaver Area Historical Museum
724–775–7174
1 River Road Extension, Beaver
Summer and Fall: Wed and Sat, 10AM–3:30PM

In a land called Beaver, it seems only fitting that the local museum would pay tribute to this furry mammal. The Beaver Area Historical Museum agrees, so a solitary stuffed beaver figures prominently in its displays. Noted for its paddle-like tail and industrious incisors, the beaver is the second-largest rodent in the world, measuring up to 4 feet and weighing up to 95 pounds. (Just in case you were wondering, the capybara of South America is the largest.) Although the Museum's beaver is anonymous, he (or she) represents a long and storied past. The earliest settlers and Indians hunted and traded beavers. In fact, they nearly hunted the animal into extinction.

Of course, the tale of the Beaver area extends beyond its namesake. And in telling that story, the Museum packs a lot of information into a relatively small space. The building is a former freight station for the Pittsburgh & Lake Erie (P&LE) Railroad. The 90-year-old station stood vacant from the 1960s until 1996 when the Borough of Beaver turned the property over to the Beaver Area Heritage Foundation. Two years and $350,000 later, the transformation was complete. The building features insulation, new windows, and total climate control, while original features like the oak flooring in the main room, exterior lighting fixtures, and the outdoor water fountain were carefully preserved.

Cast-iron drinking fountain outside the Beaver Area Historical Museum

Northwest from Pittsburgh

left: Interior view of the museum
below: Coal barges pass beneath the P&LE railroad bridge.

A 40-foot-long mural portraying two centuries of events and people holds center stage (although the beaver might want to dispute that claim). The mural traces the development of one of the first known Indian villages (Sawkunk, meaning "mouth of the stream") in the 1700s and continues through World War II when the Curtiss-Wright corporation built an airplane-propeller plant in Vanport. Some of the faces in the crowd include the Delaware Indian leader Tamaqui (a.k.a. King Beaver), the 18th-century General Lachlan McIntosh, U.S. Senator Abner Lacock, coal merchant John F. Dravo, Dr. Ruth Wilson, and Mayor Robert P. Linn (the longest-serving mayor in the country).

Next door, the Museum is constructing an authentic log house with timber said to have been salvaged from Fort McIntosh. Practically in its backyard looms the P&LE's 1,787-foot cantilever bridge. Opened to railroad traffic in 1910, and still in operation, the bridge spans 769 feet across the Ohio River.

A corps of 50 to 60 volunteers keeps the Beaver Area Heritage Foundation and Historical Museum running.

BRIDGEWATER

Bert's Wooden Indian & Wooden Angel Restaurants
724–774–7992
308 Leopard Lane, Beaver
Tues–Th, 11am–10pm; Fri–Sat, 11am–midnight; Sun, 11am–9pm

Bert's Wooden Indian was opened by Bert and Julia Sebastian in 1948. They started out serving just "Bert's Bar B. Q.s," hand-cut fries, mugs of root beer, sundaes, and ice cream floats. A lot of people helped them along the way, especially Bert's sisters, Virginia and Annie, and Julia's sister, Frances. In 1968, they expanded and opened the Wooden Angel.

Constucted in 1910 for $1,500,000, Beaver's P&LE Railroad Bridge was the longest suspension truss cantilevered bridge in the world.

This colorful wooden Indian welcomes diners as they enter Bert's Wooden Indian Restaurant.

Ohio-Beaver Route

11

Jerry's Curb Service
724–774–4727
1521 Riverside Drive, West Bridgewater
Year-round: Sun–Th, 10:30AM–MIDNIGHT; Fri–Sat, 10:30AM–1AM

Back in and turn on your lights to place your order for Jerry's famous hand-cut fries or a root-beer milkshake at this '50s-era drive-in restaurant. Jerry Reed, a young army vet, opened Jerry's Curb Service, the first car-hop restaurant in the area, in 1947.

Look for the Beaver County Industrial Museum, planned to open in Rochester in 2005. The museum will highlight the steel and glass industries of Beaver County.

ROCHESTER

12

Beaver County Flag Plaza
Riverfront Park, Rochester

On Veteran's Day 2000, the community spirit of Rochester Borough reached new heights with the raising of a 30-by-60-foot U.S. flag. Flying from a 120-foot-tall pole, Old Glory serves as the centerpiece of the Beaver County Flag Plaza.

Located along the bank of the Ohio River, the plaza's half-acre also features flags from our nation's past (for example, the 13 stars representing the original colonies). There are granite panels engraved with flag facts as well as the names of the county commissioners, borough officials, and private citizens who donated their time, talent, and money to bring the plaza to life. The granite work was done by local Italian stonemasons who saw the Plaza as their expression of civic pride.

Northwest from Pittsburgh

13

St. Pudentiana Roman Catholic Church
724–775–0801
Harrison Street and California Avenue, Rochester
☎ Phone ahead or attend Mass: Tues, Th, Sun, 8AM

Named for a minor 2nd-century saint, this small church is a labor of love, built in 1926 by Italian immigrant artisans. Parishioners supported the church by donating rings and other family jewelry.

MONACA

14

Brodhead Cultural Center
724–773–3816
Penn State Beaver Campus, Old Brodhead Road, Monaca
www.br.psu.edu/bcc
☎ Phone ahead or check web site calendar.

The summer calendar is always full with the best in local bluegrass, barbershop, and ethnic dance ensembles at this outdoor cultural center (open for events only).

Aaron Skrbin, Kara Turkovich, Kristina Braovac, and Chris Burcin of the Duquesne University Tamburitzans perform songs and dances of Eastern Europe at the Brodhead Cultural Center.

Photo © Graule Studios

Beaver Falls' hometown boy, Joe Namath

Football

Maybe it can be traced to the old country where athletic achievements were a source of ethnic and community pride. Maybe it dates back to the days of mill-sponsored youth leagues and tough competition. Or, maybe it's the water. Whatever the cause, the results are hard to argue with.

There are few places on Earth that produce as many professional football players as western Pennsylvania. The short list reads like a Hall of Fame roll call: there's Johnny Unitas (Pittsburgh), Joe Namath (Beaver Falls), Mike Ditka (Carnegie), Tony Dorsett (Aliquippa), Dan Marino (Pittsburgh), Joe Montana (New Eagle), and Jim Kelley (East Brady).

And football continues to be one of the region's consuming pastimes, especially when Monaca and Rochester high schools square off. Every October, this gridiron contest marks the end of the regular season and the beginning of another year's worth of bragging rights.

Still, there's more at stake here than school spirit. Separated by a bridge over the Ohio River, these long-time Beaver County rivals play for the right to call that bridge their own. Literally. The final score of their annual encounter determines whether this expanse will be known as the Monaca-Rochester Bridge or the Rochester-Monaca Bridge for the next 365 days (366 if it's a leap year).

101

Ohio-Beaver Route

NEW BRIGHTON AREA

From Pittsburgh: *Take PA 65 N to PA 18 N to New Brighton. PA 18 N becomes 3rd Ave.*

One-Day Tour: Sites 15–21
☎ **Christ Episcopal Church:** *On 3rd Ave. between 12th and 13th Sts.* **Rosalind Candy Castle:** *Turn around on 3rd Ave. Left on 13th St. to 5th Ave. Candy Castle is on corner.* **Brickers Restaurant:** *Return to 3rd Ave. Go right. Brickers is on corner of 3rd Ave. and 8th St.* **Merrick Free Art Gallery:** *Left on 3rd Ave. Left on 11th St. to 5th Ave. Merrick is on corner.* **Antique Emporium:** *Left on 5th Ave. Left on 8th St. Right on 3rd Ave. (PA 18/65 N). Follow PA 18/65 N into Beaver Falls (becomes 7th Ave.). Emporium is on right.* **Beaver Falls Historical Society/Museum:** *Stay on 7th Ave. Museum is on left in Beaver Falls Library basement.* **Oram's:** *Stay on 7th Ave. Oram's is on right.* ***Return to Pittsburgh:*** *PA 18 S to PA 65 S.*

NEW BRIGHTON

Christ Episcopal Church
724-847-3760
1217 3rd Avenue, New Brighton
Open every day
☎ Phone ahead for church tour

The rough stone exterior contrasts with the graceful arches inside Christ Episcopal Church.

It's been said that when a door shuts, a window opens. As the region's steel mills began to close down in the 1980s, many churches responded by opening their hearts. New Brighton's Christ Episcopal Church opened its kitchen to visitors.

By 1985, the once-prosperous Ohio-Beaver region was awash in unemployment. That same year, Christ Episcopal's parish secretary, Dorothy Hazen, learned about a government program designed to help religious organizations establish soup kitchens. With her church's blessing, she filled out the paperwork and was soon notified that a $10,000 grant from the Federal Emergency Management Agency (FEMA) was on its way. After securing additional funding from the diocese, the Beaver Valley Episcopal Outreach — more commonly known as the soup kitchen — started cooking.

Nearly 20 years and more than 340,000 meals later, the kitchen still serves the community, and Hazen continues to serve as director. With a corps of six to 15 volunteers, the kitchen is open Tuesdays and Wednesdays from 11 a.m. to 2 p.m. According to Hazen, everybody is welcome.

Dorothy Hazen and helpers Mabel and Paul Henn prepare lunch.

Northwest from Pittsburgh

Rosalind Candy Castle
724–843–1144
1301 5th Avenue, New Brighton
www.rosalindcandy.com
Mon–Fri, 8:30am–6pm; Sat, 10am–6pm

In 1914, Greek immigrant Gust Zachos opened a restaurant and candy store in Freedom. Several decades later, the Rosalind Candy Castle moved to New Brighton. Elizabeth Crudden, who worked in the shop after school during the 1940s, later purchased the business. The Crudden family still owns and operates the Candy Castle using Zachos' original recipes.

Patty Irwin (right) hands Nancy Radcliff a box of Rosalind's chocolates.

Bricker's Restaurant
724–843–9852
8th Street and 3rd Avenue, New Brighton
Mon-Fri, 7am–7pm; Sat, 7am–3pm

It's true that there's no such thing as a free lunch, but a nickel lunch isn't bad. Back in the 1980s, when the steel mills started spewing hundreds of unemployed workers onto the streets, Dick Bricker decided to do something to help his neighbors.

As the owner of Bricker's Restaurant, he began offering the now-famous 5-cent lunch. For an entire year (1982–1983), a nickel would buy such filling fare as macaroni and cheese or rigatoni. Prices have gone up a bit since then, but other traditions continue.

Bricker's father opened the restaurant in 1952 as an Isaly's franchise. A decade later, Dick and his mother moved the business to its present location — a former union hall on the corner of 8th Street and 3rd Avenue. The restaurant is still family-owned and -operated, but now it's Bricker's daughters who stand behind the counter.

Second-generation owner Linda Gravener

Ohio-Beaver Route

Merrick Free Art Gallery
724–846–1130
1100 5th Avenue, New Brighton
Tues–Sat, 10AM–4:30PM; Sun, 1PM–4PM
Admission: Free

Edward Dempster Merrick was born of a certain time and circumstance. The time was the mid-1800s and the circumstance was a successful family business.

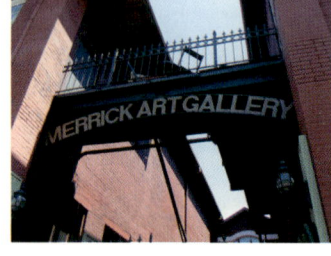

After serving in the Civil War and exploring the still-wild West, Dempster (as future generations affectionately called him) did what was expected. He returned home to New Brighton, and joined his brothers, Charles, Frederick, and Franklin, in running the Standard Horse Nail Company. But, it was the unexpected that ultimately defined his life and legacy. "He wasn't allowed to pursue art as a child," says Merrick Art Gallery Director Cynthia Kundar. As he approached his 50th birthday, Dempster decided to make his dreams a reality.

Dempster began buying paintings, particularly those of the Hudson River School, and creating his own works. In 1880, he founded the Merrick Free Art Gallery and Public Library. For the next 30-plus years, the simple red brick building, a former railroad station, served as his home, his studio, and his muse.

"He was considered to be very eccentric," Kundar says.

The Gallery, complete with its collection of more than 200 paintings, stands today. However, Dempster's own paintings are gone. Legend has it that after his death in 1911, his canvases were unceremoniously tossed into a bonfire — only the frames were spared. Despite the fact that Dempster's work was never fully appreciated, he took the plight of the struggling artist much to heart. His instructions specified that the Gallery was to be kept open, free to the public, a safe haven for local artists.

In addition, he stipulated that one trustee, always a blood relation, would watch over the facility. From 1959 to 2002, that individual was Robert Silas Merrick, Sr.

Sunlit stairs lead to galleries lined with paintings.

BY THE WAY

The Hudson River School was the first coherent school of American art, active from 1825 to 1870. Artists of the school painted landscapes of the Hudson River Valley and surrounding New England in a romantic, realistic style.

Robert also happened to head the Standard Horse Nail Company. Together, Robert and his wife, Eva Mae Merrick, saw the Gallery through difficult times. According to Eva Mae, the Gallery had fallen into a 50-year period of neglect. To revitalize Dempster's dream, the two Merricks established a conservation program for the paintings, installed electricity, replaced the heating system, and hired a director.

Franklin Merrick, Dempster's youngest brother

Like its founder, the Gallery's collection remains eclectic. And chances are that's not going to change as another Merrick (Ted) begins his stint as trustee. Although no longer home to the library (it moved in 1984), the Gallery continues to house books, rocks and minerals, a permanent collection of 19th-century paintings, and a piano that Stephen Foster was said to have played when it graced the Merrick House Hotel during the 1850s.

The Gallery also hosts the Beaver Valley Artists Annual Show, takes in tour groups and school classes, and offers a beautiful backdrop for weddings and receptions. (Just ask Gretchen Merrick. She recently held her wedding reception at the family landmark.)

Dempster's words will forever remain the Gallery's foundation. "I think to paint a fine picture is one of the greatest achievements of man."

Horse nail, woodruff key, and cotter pin made at Standard Horse Nail (From Rosalind Candy Castle, right on 5th Avenue to see Standard Horse Nail.)

Standard Horse Nail Company

With Charles taking the lead, the three brothers Merrick — Frederick, Franklin, and Edward (Dempster) — established the Standard Horse Nail Company in 1872. Its headquarters are just a few blocks from the Merrick Gallery. Perfecting the hot-forged nail, the family business quickly made a name for itself.

When a fire swept through the original Standard Horse Nail building in 1884, the brothers salvaged what they could and quickly set up a new shop on nearby Fifth Avenue.

Now, more than a century later, the Merricks' Fifth Avenue enterprise continues to thrive — although horse nails are no longer its stock and trade. The advent of the automobile prompted Frank Woodruff, a friend of Silas Merrick (nephew of the company's founder), to design a "key" to hold gears on a shaft and keep them from stripping. Silas developed a means of gang-milling these keys for the automotive industry.

These days, Standard Horse Nail manufactures a variety of precision parts — including machine, woodruff, and gib keys and standard and threaded taper pins and cotter pins — for motors, engines, and pumps.

Currently under the leadership of Robert Merrick, Jr., Standard Horse Nail employs 35 at its New Brighton location and another 18 at its East Liverpool, Ohio, site.

Ohio-Beaver Route

BEAVER FALLS

ⓘ Antique Emporium
724–847–1919
818 7th Avenue, Beaver Falls
Mon, Tues, Wed, Th, Sat, 10AM–5PM; Fri, 10AM–8PM; Sun, NOON–5PM

This Victorian warehouse, with three floors of nooks and crannies to explore, features a variety of one-of-a-kind collector's items from the region.

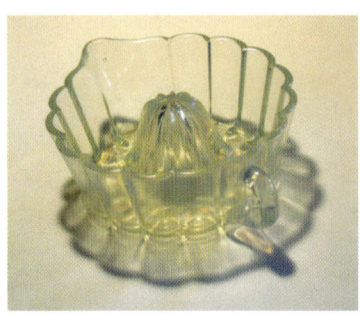

A vase made by Phoenix Glass, Monaca, and an opal juicer made by Fry Glass Company, Rochester

ⓘ Beaver Falls Historical Society / Museum
724–846–4340
1301 7th Avenue (in Carnegie Library), Beaver Falls
Museum in basement: Mon–Th, 9AM–2:30PM
Genealogy: Mon, 3PM–8PM; Tues–Th, 10AM–4PM; Sat, 10AM–3PM

The Beaver Falls Historical Society / Museum is housed in the first Carnegie Library built in Beaver County. Frederick J. Osterling, the architect who designed the library, also designed Clayton, the Frick mansion in Pittsburgh. Collections include vintage fire equipment, china, and locally produced cutlery.

Plates made by Mayer China, Beaver Falls

Northwest from Pittsburgh

Oram's Donuts
724–846–1504
1406 7th Avenue, Beaver Falls
www.orams.com
Mon–Sat, 5 AM–2 PM

What's that heavenly smell? Follow your nose to Oram's, a mom-and-pop institution in Beaver Falls since 1938. But don't oversleep — the early bird still gets the doughnut in this former factory town!

Carrie Graleski serves crullers at Oram's.

Locks and Dams

For the first decades of southwestern Pennsylvania's history, the Allegheny, Monongahela, and Ohio Rivers served as highways for trade, settlement, and industry. In the roadless wilderness, the rivers were the only way to efficiently transport raw materials, finished products, supplies, and people. But there was a big drawback to the rivers: they were unreliable.

The problems? Weather and terrain. Winter's ice made the rivers impassable for boats. Spring thaws turned the rivers into dangerous torrents that regularly flooded. In late summer and fall, drought often reduced the rivers to a trickle. Many sections were navigable for only a few months or weeks each year. The region's hilly terrain added to the difficulty. For example, the Monongahela River's elevation drops by 147 feet as it flows north to Pittsburgh.

The solution? Locks and dams. Dams create controllable pools at different elevations to help lessen flooding and to even out the water flow over the length of a river. Locks act like steps, allowing boats to "climb" up or down the river from one pool to the next.

The first lock-and-dam sets in the Pittsburgh area were built on the Monongahela River in 1844. After the Civil War, more locks were built on both the Mon and the Ohio. The Allegheny River, much shallower, had no locks until the 1930s.

The locks and dams helped spur the region's industrial growth. These marvels of design, now built and maintained by the U.S. Army Corps of Engineers, are still on the job, each year moving hundreds of barges carrying thousands of tons of material, as well as allowing recreational access to the rivers' full length.

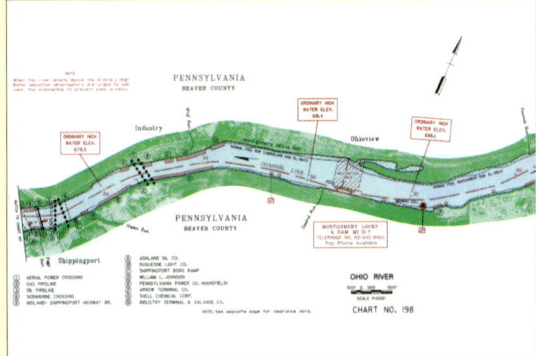

U.S. Army Corps of Engineers river pilot's map showing Montgomery Lock and Dam, downstream from Lock 6 Landing Restaurant on the Ohio River

Ohio-Beaver Route

MIDLAND AREA

From Pittsburgh: *Take PA 65 N to PA 68 W past Beaver.*

Half-Day Tour: Sites 22–24
Lock 6 Landing Restaurant: *Follow PA 68 W between Beaver and Midland. Lock 6 is on left.* **Rocca's Homestyle Pasta:** *Follow PA 68 W into Midland. Rocca's is on right.* ☎ **St. Nicholas Chapel:** *From Midland, take PA 68 E to PA 60 N to Brighton exit 14. At end of ramp, left at stop sign. Right at next stop sign on Tuscarawas Rd. Go 3 mi. Chapel is on right on Seven Oaks Country Club Grounds.* ***Return to Pittsburgh:*** *PA 68 E to PA 65 S to Pittsburgh.*

Go "barge spotting"! Along the rivers you will see tow boats propelling barges carrying loads of coal, stone, and steel, as they have for more than a century.

22

Lock 6 Landing Restaurant
724–728–6767
610 Beaver–Midland Rd. (PA 68 W)
Tues–Th, 5–9PM; Fri, Sat, 5–10PM; Sun, 5–9PM
Outside Marina: Fri, Sat, Sun, NOON–11PM

Overlooking river traffic since 1904, this historic lock house has been restored as a restaurant with a dock and a beautiful view of the Ohio River.

Historic photos at the restaurant tell Lock 6's 100-year story.

MIDLAND

Rocca's Homestyle Pasta
724–643–6333
323 Midland Avenue, Midland
Mon–Fri, 11AM–8PM; Sat, 4–8PM

One day in May 1982, Robert Rocca and three of his brothers, Teddy, Ike, and Anthony, went to work as usual at the Crucible mill. It was a routine Robert knew by heart. After all, from the day he graduated high school 19 years before, he had only one job — and it was at the mill.

But on this particular day, Robert learned that the mill was shutting down and that he, his brothers, and just about the entire town of Midland would soon be out of work. "I never saw it coming," Robert says. "It was ugly."

And it was scary. With a wife and four young kids at home, he wasn't sure where to turn. He never went to college, never earned a degree, never experienced the world beyond the mill. So Robert decided to turn to the one sure thing in his life — his family. "You go back to your roots," he says. "You do what you do best." What the Roccas do best is prepare food, specifically Italian desserts and pastas.

When Robert, his parents, and his three brothers left Italy for America in 1955 (two more brothers were later born in the United States), they brought with them some old family recipes.

Seeking self-sufficiency in his adopted homeland, Robert decided to use those recipes as the foundation for a new family-owned and -operated business. While two of his brothers went into the wholesale pasta business, Robert opened a takeout service. By 1992, he, his wife, and their four children and three grandchildren were running a restaurant.

With Dean Martin songs playing in the background, the Rocca family tree decorating one wall, and Midland memorabilia all around, the restaurant offers sustenance to both its patrons and proprietors. "We're luckier than some," Robert says. "Without the family, we never would have made it."

Patriotic pasta at Rocca's

Shutdown

Today, most of the Crucible Stainless and Alloy Division of Colt Industries is quiet. The finishing mill, the bar mill, the bloom mill. Silent. The strip mill, the molding yard. Silent. Blast Furnace No. 1 — 240 feet from tip to toe, mute against the open sky.

...Now, there is not even a mill. Today, Colt Industries, the parent firm for the last 14 years, closed Crucible. The mill is up for sale, but no one, it appears, wants to buy.

...The hope through much of Midland, the home of Crucible for the past 76 years, [is that] the mill will be resurrected. Today it may close, but tomorrow — maybe Monday — a buyer will appear.

It is wishful thinking tinged with savvy. Until today, a buyer would have been obligated to work under contractual agreements forged between the United Steelworkers union and Crucible. As of Saturday, a buyer is free to write his own ticket with the union.
—Beaver County Times, October 15, 1982.

Between Midland and Beaver you'll see the Shippingport Nuclear Power Station, opened in 1958 as part of the Atoms for Peace Program. This site was the first commercial central electric-generating station in the United States to use nuclear energy.

Ohio-Beaver Route

OHIOVILLE

24 ✠ ♪

GCU Saint Nicholas Chapel
800–722–4428
5400 Tuscarawas Road, Ohioville (Beaver)
👁 Phone ahead for tour.

The Birth and Baptism of Saint Nicholas

The spirit of the Carpathian Mountains of Europe and the sweat from the steel mills and coal mines of western Pennsylvania are at the heart of the Greek Catholic Union (GCU) Saint Nicholas Chapel. But perhaps its soul can be found in the incredible, and incredibly colorful, iconic scenes that line its walls. Each of the 10 paintings offers a glimpse into the life of Saint Nicholas of Myra. Born late in the 3rd century in Patara, a city in Lycia of Asia Minor, Saint Nicholas is celebrated as the patron saint of the GCU and the chapel's namesake.

The scenes depict Saint Nicholas' birth and acts of kindness and charity. The final painting portrays his funeral — and the sparing of the miners. On December 19, 1907, a number of GCU members living in Van Meter and Jacobs Creek, Pa., decided to attend church services for the Feast of Saint Nicholas rather than go to work in the Darr Mine. That same day there was an explosion in the mine, and some 200 men were killed. It's a true story.

Saint Nicholas Consecrated Archbishop of Myra

Dedicated in 1992 to commemorate the GCU's centennial, this New Brighton Township church also provides a glimpse into the lives of its founders. Leaving behind their homes in the northeastern portion of the former Austro-Hungarian Empire, these immigrants arrived in America in the late 19th century. In an effort to maintain their identity, customs, and culture, they established churches and lodges. By 1892, this loose affiliation became the foundation for the GCU. Today, the Union remains 40,000 members strong.

Seventy-five years later, the idea of recreating an old-world–style wooden chapel, like the ones that dominated their homeland, was first suggested. But it wasn't until 1988, when a site was chosen at the Seven Oaks Country Club (home to GCU's headquarters), that plans truly started to take shape.

Saint Nicholas Saves the Storm-tossed Sailors

Interior of GCU Saint Nicholas Chapel

A committee of Union members studied some 120 Slovakian and western Ukrainian churches. They categorized each church based on its components: the floor plan, the outside shape and roof, towers, domes, and structural framework.

The group soon learned that all these churches shared three aesthetic elements — the vestibule (entrance area), the nave (center section where the congregation gathers for worship), and the sanctuary (that is joined to the nave by an icon screen).

These characteristics were incorporated into the design of Saint Nicholas. The chapel's overlapping roofs stand at 45-degree angles and feature the traditional onion-shaped cupolas or spires. According to GCU's Frederick Petro, "Our church is a composite of existing structures in Saris County, Slovakia, the region native to most of our organization's ancestors."

Inside the 80-seat church, visitors need only look up to find an image of Christ Pantocrator looking down from the 40-foot-high ceiling. This traditional theme speaks to the belief that God comes down and touches us.

Also steeped in religious and ethnic tradition is the GCU Museum. Located in the lower level of the church, the museum houses an assortment of artifacts and memorabilia. Displays showcase prayer books and religious instructional manuals, as well as lodge sashes, pins, photographs, and other treasured relics of the past.

The church, now part of the Byzantine Catholic Archdiocese of Pittsburgh, holds services on Sundays and major feast days. Saint Nicholas Chapel was built to honor past generations of immigrants and to provide a place of worship for generations to come. "Our objective," Petro says, "was to create a prayerful and peaceful space."

The Real St. Nicholas

St. Nicholas, also called Nicholas of Bari, Nicholas of Myra, and Santa Claus, flourished in the 4th century in Asia Minor near the modern Turkish city of Finike. One of the most popular minor saints commemorated in the Eastern and Western churches, his feast day is December 6th. He is now traditionally associated with the festival of Christmas.

...Nicholas' reputation for generosity and kindness gave rise to legends of miracles he performed for the poor and unhappy. He was reputed to have given marriage dowries of gold to three girls whom poverty would otherwise have forced into lives of prostitution. In the Middle Ages, devotion to Nicholas extended to all parts of Europe. He became the patron saint of Russia and Greece; of charitable fraternities and guilds; of children, sailors, unmarried girls, merchants, and pawnbrokers; and of such cities as Fribourg, Switzerland, and Moscow. Thousands of European churches were dedicated to him, one as early as the 6th century, built by the Roman emperor Justinian I at Constantinople (now Istanbul).
— Louise Carus. *The Real St. Nicholas: Tales of Generosity and Hope from around the World*, October 2002

Ohio-Beaver Route

ENON VALLEY

From Pittsburgh: *Take PA 60 N.*

Half-Day Tour: Site 25

☎ **SNPJ Borough Recreation Center:** *PA 60 N (go through 2 toll booths: $1.50) to Mt. Jackson exit 43. At end of ramp, left on PA 108 W. Go 2 mi. to blinking light. Continue 2.5 mi. PA 108 W makes a right turn. Continue 2 mi. Left on Martin Rd. (SNPJ sign). Go 1.5 mi. to SNPJ Recreation Center.*
Return to Pittsburgh: *Take PA 60 S.*

SNPJ Borough Recreation Center
724–336–5180
270 Martin Road, Enon Valley
www.snpjrec.com
☎ Phone ahead.

Button-box polka bands from around the region will have your toes tapping every Sunday at this recreation center operated by the Slovenian National Benefit Society (SNPJ), a gathering place for people of all ages who love Slovenian culture. The public is welcome to visit the museum and gift shop (open during events).

Slovenian traditional crafts: *cipka* **lace (top) and embroidery (bottom)**

Slovenian Heritage

"Is there any other country in the world that has love in its very name?" Slovenians ask with pride. A small nation in southeastern Europe, Slovenia is the ancestral homeland of many people in southwestern Pennsylvania.

Most Slovenians came to the area in the late 19th century to work as coal miners, settling in small patch towns such as Yukon, Herminie, and Strabane. In 1904, they founded a fraternal club, Slovenska Narodna Podporna Jednota (SNPJ), the Slovene National Benefit Society, to "provide affordable life protection" and help immigrants preserve their culture in America.

With headquarters in Imperial, Pa., and lodges in Pennsylvania, Ohio, and Florida, the SNPJ still offers life insurance, but also sponsors sports events, scholarships, and cultural events open to the public, such as Slovenefest, National SNPJ Days, and Slovene Day at Kennywood Park. In 1977, the region's Slovenians established the Borough of SNPJ in Enon Valley as a year-round cultural center.

Slovenians take pride in their cultural heritage, especially crafts such as *cipka* bobbin lace; traditional dishes such as stuffed cabbages, *krofi* (lemon-flavored doughnuts), and *potica* (nut-roll pastry); and button-box accordion music, made nationally famous by Frankie Yankovich, the "Polka King."

The Joe Grkman Band plays for Slovenian dances and events.

Ⓔ EVENTS CALENDAR

For specific dates and times of events see:
www.riversofsteel.com

Events that occur in several months are abbreviated with an *. See Recurring Events for full contact information.

Recurring Events

*Farmers Market
Ambridge
Park Road and PA 65
May–December: Thursdays

*Farmers Market
Beaver County
Beaver County Courthouse, Beaver
May–December: Saturdays

*Farmers Market
Beaver Falls
8th Avenue and 12th Street
June–October: Mondays

Barbershop Chorus
Friendship Ridge
724–869–7574
932 3rd Street, Baden
Tuesday nights

Polka Bands
SNPJ Recreation Center
724–336–6518 or 800–843–7675
www.snpjrec.com/schedule.htm
270 Martin Road, Enon Valley
Sunday afternoons

*Pierogi Sales
St. John the Baptist Roman Catholic Church
724–869–2280
377 Linmore Avenue, Baden
Fridays except in summer
Eat in or take out

*Pysanky Egg Decorating
Saint John's Russian Orthodox Church
724–266–2879
5th Street and Elm Road, Ambridge
Fridays during Lent

*Ethnic Music and Dance
Brodhead Cultural Center
724–773–3600
J.P. Giusti Amphitheater, Brodhead Road, Monaca
June–August
Ethnic music and dance concerts

January
*Pierogi Sales

February
*Pierogi Sales

March
*Pierogi Sales
*Pysanky Egg Decorating (Lent)

April
*Pierogi Sales
*Pysanky Egg Decorating (Lent)

May
Nationality Days
Ambridge Area Chamber of Commerce
724–266–3040
Merchant Street, Ambridge
www.nationalitydays.org
3rd weekend

*Farmers Market, Ambridge
*Farmers Market, Beaver

June
Holy Family Parish Festival
Holy Family Catholic Church
724–847–3538
1851 3th Avenue, New Brighton
Early June

Greek Food Festival
Kimisis Tis Theotokou
Greek Orthodox Church
724–375–9058
2111 Davidson Street, Aliquippa
Ethnic foods, music, dance

*Farmers Market, Ambridge
*Farmers Market, Beaver
*Farmers Market, Beaver Falls
*Brodhead Ethnic Music and Dance

July
Old Economy Village Family Festival
Old Economy Village
724–266–4500
14th and Church Streets, Ambridge
www.oldeconomyvillage.org
Children's workshop

Slovenefest
SNPJ Recreation Center
724–336–6518 or 800–843–7675
www.snpjrec.com/festpg.htm
270 Martin Road, Enon Valley
Ethnic music, dance, food

*Farmers Market, Ambridge
*Farmers Market, Beaver
*Farmers Market, Beaver Falls
*Brodhead Ethnic Music and Dance

Ohio-Beaver Route

August

Rusyn Food Festival
Saint John's Russian Orthodox Church
724–266–2879
5th Street and Elm Road, Ambridge
Early August
Ethnic foods, music, dance, crafts

Greek Food Festival
Holy Trinity Greek Orthodox Church
724–266–5336
2930 Beaver Road, Ambridge
www.htgoc.org
Mid-August
Ethnic food, music, dance

San Rocco Festa
San Rocco Cultural Committee
724–378–6646
Lefty Cepull Field, Main Street, Aliquippa
www.sanrocco.org
Mid-August
Italian saint's day festival

Beaver County Riverfest
Rochester Borough
724–775–1200
Riverfront Park, Rochester
River activities, entertainment

Southside Historical Village Days
Southside Historical Village Association
724–643–9337
Hookstown Fairgrounds, Hookstown
History

Freedom Vicary Days
Vicary House
724–728–5744 or 724–775–1848
1235 3rd Avenue, Freedom
2nd weekend
Festival, historical tours

Ethnic Days
Good Samaritan Parish
724–266–6565
St. Veronica's Church, 8th Street, Ambridge
Late August–Early September
Ethnic foods, crafts, culture, music, dance

*Farmers Market, Ambridge
*Farmers Market, Beaver
*Farmers Market, Beaver Falls
*Brodhead Ethnic Music and Dance

September

Fall Festival
Saint Blaise Catholic Church
724–643–4050 or 724–643–8680
8th Street and Penn Avenue, Midland
Early September
Ethnic foods, live music

Erntefest Harvest Festival
Old Economy Village
724–266–4500 or 724–266–1803
14th and Church Streets, Ambridge
Late September
German festival

*Farmers Market, Ambridge
*Farmers Market, Beaver
*Farmers Market, Beaver Falls

October

Oktoberfest
Quad Mercantile
724–758–2292
598 Ellwood-Zelienople Road, PA 288, Ellwood City
Early October

Homewood Heritage Days
Homewood Borough Council
724–843–4076
wwww.homewoodjunction.com/heritage.htm
Buttermilk Falls, Homewood
1st weekend in October
Living history encampment area,
foods, music, crafts

Applebutter Fest
Vicary House
724–728–5744
1235 3rd Avenue, Freedom
Mid-October
Make and taste applebutter

American Indian Gathering
Community College of Beaver County
724–775–8561 ext.157
1 Campus Drive, Monaca
Mid-October
Ethnic activities

Greek Mini-Festival
Kimisis Tis Theotokou
Greek Orthodox Church
724–375–9058
2111 Davidson Street, Aliquippa
Traditional foods, entertainment

*Farmers Market, Ambridge
*Farmers Market, Beaver
*Farmers Market, Beaver Falls
*Pierogi Sales

November

Christmas with Belsnickel (Santa Claus)
Old Economy Village
724–266–4500 or 724–266–1803
14th and Church Streets, Ambridge
www.oldeconomyvillage.org
Late November

Northwest from Pittsburgh

Festival of Trees
Brady's Run Park
724–846–2411
PA 51, Beaver Falls
Late November–Early December
Traditional crafts

*Farmers Market, Ambridge
*Farmers Market, Beaver
*Pierogi Sales

December

Christmas at the Village
Old Economy Village
724–266–4500
14th and Church Streets, Ambridge
www.oldeconomyvillage.org
Early December
19th-century Christmas

Candlelight Tours
Vicary House
724–728–5744
1235 3rd Avenue, Freedom
Early December
18th-century traditional Christmas

Christmas Dinner Tour
Old Economy Village
724–266–4500
14th and Church Streets, Ambridge
www.oldeconomyvillage.org
Early December

*Farmers Market, Ambridge
*Farmers Market, Beaver
*Pierogi Sales

American Bridge Company caution sign

Songs

Solidarity Forever

*When the union's inspiration through the workers' blood shall run,
There can be no power greater anywhere beneath the sun;
Yet what force on earth is weaker than the feeble strength of one,
But the union makes us strong.*

*Chorus: Solidarity forever!
Solidarity forever!
Solidarity forever!
For the union makes us strong!*

*They have taken untold millions that they never toiled to earn,
But without our brain and muscle not a single wheel could turn;
We can break their haughty power, gain our freedom when we learn,
That the union makes us strong.*

*In our hands is placed a power greater than their hoarded gold,
Greater than the might of armies magnified a thousandfold;
We can bring to birth a new world from the ashes of the old,
For the union makes us strong.*

— Labor movement anthem, as shown on www.afscmelocal34.org/solidarity_forever.htm

Steel Mill Blues

*I went down to the steel mill,
I saw my paycheck there.
It was stretched out on the boss' table,
So thin, so small, so bare.*

*So I took that little old paycheck down to the grocery store.
I bought me a little can of baked beans
And I didn't have no paycheck no more.*

*Paycheck (paycheck) Paycheck (paycheck),
You just fly away.
Paycheck (paycheck) Paycheck (paycheck),
Tomorrow you're gone, though you were here today.*

*Now the moral of this story,
It's as simple as it could be.
If you want to fatten up that skinny paycheck,
Sign a card with the SWOC.*

— Adapted by Joe Glazer to fit the great organizing period of 1936–1942 when the Steel Workers Organizing Committee (SWOC) was active.

Alle-Kiski Route

Northeast from Pittsburgh

Mosaic of Industry

The Alle-Kiski Route leads up the Allegheny River valley and out along the Kiskiminetas River, focusing on riverfront communities in northern Allegheny, northern Westmoreland, and Armstrong Counties. Whereas some parts of the Rivers of Steel National Heritage Area were dominated by one industry, such as steel or coal, the Alle-Kiski Route had, and still has, a "mosaic of industries," all connected to or influenced by steel.

Aluminum grew to world prominence here. Plate glass was perfected here, and support industries for steel — refractory brickmaking, foundries, limestone quarries — flourished here.

Salt extraction methods developed here led to the first oil drilling. And, of course, there were steel mills and coal mines as well.

Many of the companies with large-scale plants in the area, such as Alcoa (Aluminum Company of America) and PPG (Pittsburgh Plate Glass), are household names throughout the United States. Some of their plants still are operating, such as those of Allegheny Ludlum Steel (ALC) and PPG's Creighton Works. Some now keep a quiet vigil as their communities consider how best to move beyond the industrial era. And still others, such as the Tour-Ed Mine and the Kiski Junction Railroad, afford visitors an up-close, rewarding glimpse into the world of industrial work.

The cultural heritage of the Alle-Kiski Route is no less varied. During the 18th century, early European fur trappers and explorers encountered Seneca and Delaware villages along the Allegheny River from Kittanning southward as Scots-Irish, German, and English settlers began to stake out farmsteads.

After the Revolutionary War, when treaties with the Native Americans assured peace in the region, the pace of European settlement quickened. Originally agricultural, the Alle-Kiski area soon began to attract workers for its burgeoning industries, especially after the opening of the Pennsylvania Canal and the rise of "Big Steel" in the region.

By the late 19th century, the Alle-Kiski area was home to many eastern Europeans, including Poles and Hungarians, as well as Italians and African-Americans. These immigrants brought new cultures and customs to the area. Today, the cooking traditions, sacred spaces, dances, and music of these groups, as well as their firsthand stories of life in the workplace, create a rich tapestry of cultural experiences for visitors who are willing to explore.

above: Retired miners lead tours at Tour-Ed Mine in Tarentum.

opposite page (clockwise from top left):
PPG, Creighton
Kiski Junction Railroad, Schenley
View of the Allegheny River, Creighton
Alcoa Research Lab, New Kensington
J. H. Shoop & Sons, Freeport
Alle-Kiski Historical Society, Tarentum
Rowley's Market, Vandergrift
Feast of Corpus Christi, Tarentum
Allegheny Ludlum, Brackenridge

left: This Automatic Guided Vehicle (AGV) picks up and delivers stainless steel coils to finishing operations throughout the ATI Allegheny Ludlum Vandergrift facility.

Courtesy ATI Allegheny Ludlum, Vandergrift

Alle-Kiski Route

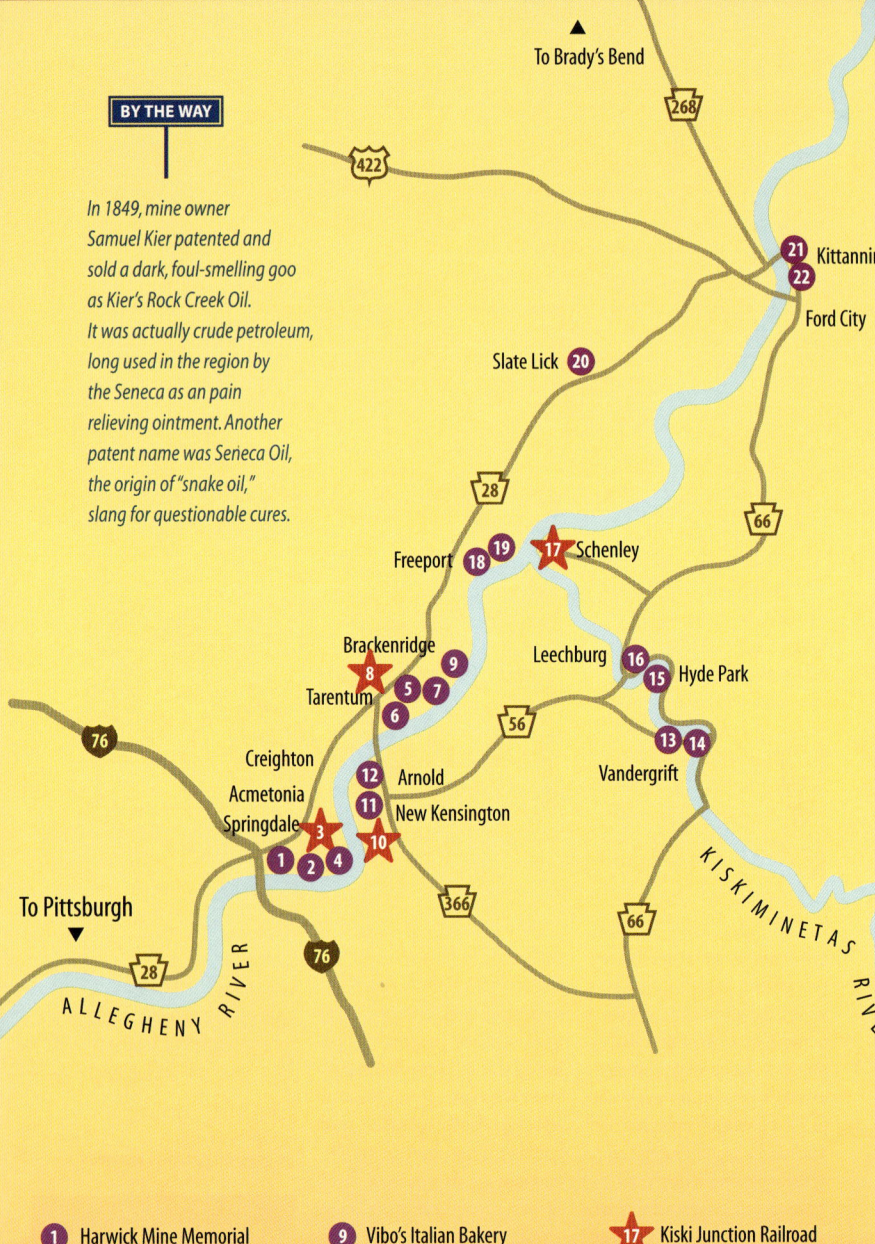

BY THE WAY

In 1849, mine owner Samuel Kier patented and sold a dark, foul-smelling goo as Kier's Rock Creek Oil. It was actually crude petroleum, long used in the region by the Seneca as an pain relieving ointment. Another patent name was Seneca Oil, the origin of "snake oil," slang for questionable cures.

1. Harwick Mine Memorial
2. Glen's Frozen Custard
3. Rachel Carson Homestead
4. Kleiner Deutschmann
5. A-K Valley Historical Society
6. Gatto Cycle Diner
7. Tarentum Station Restaurant
8. Tour-Ed Mine & Museum
9. Vibo's Italian Bakery
10. Mount Saint Peter Church
11. Mazziotti Bakery
12. Fazio's Italian Foods
13. Victorian Vandergrift Museum
14. Rowley's Market
15. Hyde Park Museum
16. Leechburg Area Museum
17. Kiski Junction Railroad
18. The Sheltering Tree
19. J. H. Shoop & Sons
20. Armstrong Co. League of Arts
21. Mulberry Street Creamery
22. Grace Presbyterian Church

Northeast from Pittsburgh

SPRINGDALE

From Pittsburgh: Take PA 28 N to Cheswick/Springdale exit 12.

Half-Day Tour: Sites 1–4

Harwick Mine Memorial: Left at exit ramp stop sign. Right on Pillow Ave. Left on Parkway Dr. Go 1 block. Memorial is on left. **Glen's Frozen Custard:** Follow Pillow Ave. down hill. Left at stoplight on Pittsburgh/Freeport Rd. Go 1.4 mi. Glen's is on right. **Rachel Carson Homestead:** Stay on Pittsburgh/Freeport Rd. Go .2 mi. Left on Colfax St. up hill 6 blocks. Right on Marion Ave. Homestead is on left. **Kleiner Deutschmann:** Stay on Pittsburgh/Freeport Rd. Restaurant is on left at the corner of Murtland St. **Return to Pittsburgh:** PA 28 S.

SYMBOLS	
★	Must-See Site
●	Point of Interest Site
🏭	Industry
✠	Folklife
🍃	Nature
ꕕ	Art & Architecture
☕	Food
🛍	Shopping
Ⓔ	Events Calendar
☎	Phone Ahead

❶ Harwick Mine Memorial

851 Parkway Drive, Springdale
Outdoors

Who will remember the men who worked — and died — in the Harwick Mine? A small group of former miners and other citizens have made sure no one forgets. In September 2000, after 10 years of planning, they unveiled a simple black granite monument inscribed with a photo taken January 25, 1904, the day of the explosion. Bricks bearing the names of coal miners, family members, or Harwick citizens form a base for the memorial, which is dedicated to everyone who shared in the life of the Harwick Mine.

❷ Glen's Frozen Custard
724–274–5516
400 Pittsburgh Street, Springdale
Spring: Mon–Th, 11AM–10PM; Fri, Sat, 11AM–11PM; Sun, NOON–10PM
Summer: Mon–Th, 11AM–11PM; Fri, Sat, 11AM–11:30PM; Sun, NOON–11PM

Glen's is a Springdale institution. Check out the stainless steel machines that keep churning out frozen custard.

Explosion Kills Many

With a concussion that shook the earth for miles around, a terrific explosion wrecked the mine of the Allegheny Coal Co., one mile from Cheswick [in Harwick], this morning entombing over 150 men…. So violent was the upheaval of the explosion that a mule was thrown from the bottom of the shaft to the mouth of the mine, a distance of 220 feet.
—*Pittsburgh Press*, Jan. 25, 1904.

Little Hope is Left

Pitiful, pleading, commanding with the sight of those crushed down by woe, this cry rises, then ends with a wail. None but women are left….

In the mine there are 182 men. Joe Puscley, the light tender, gave every man a light as he went down. He showed me the empty hooks where the safeties [lights] had hung….
—*Pittsburgh Press*, Jan. 26, 1904.

Alle-Kiski Route

My Favorite Recreation
by Rachel Carson (Age 14)

The call of the trail on that dewy May morning was too strong to withstand. The sun was barely an hour high when Pal and I set off for a day of our favorite sport with a lunch-box, a canteen, a note-book, and a camera. Your experienced woodsman will say that we were going birds' nesting — in the most approved fashion.

Soon our trail turned aside into deeper woodland. It wound up a gently sloping hill, carpeted with fragrant pine-needles. It was our own discovery, Pal's and mine, and the fact gave us a thrill of exultation. It was the sort of place that awes you by its majestic silence, interrupted only by the rustling breeze and the distant tinkle of water.

Late in the afternoon a penetrating "Teacher! Teacher! Teacher!" reached our ears. An oven-bird! A careful search revealed his nest, a little round ball of grass, securely hidden on the ground.

The cool of approaching night settled. The wood-thrushes trilled their golden melody. The setting sun transformed the sky into a sea of blue and gold. A vesper-sparrow sang his evening lullaby. We turned slowly homeward, gloriously tired, gloriously happy!
— Rachel Carson. *St. Nicholas League*, 1921.

Rachel Carson Homestead
724–274–5459
613 Marion Avenue, Springdale
www.rachelcarsonhomestead.org
Mar–Nov: Tues–Th, 10AM–2PM
Adults: $4; Seniors: $3; Children 5–12: $2.50;
Children 4 and under: Free

There is a tone of familiarity in Mary Beth Trout's voice as she tells the story of environmentalist Rachel Carson's childhood.

Leading a tour through the family's home in Springdale, Trout talks about Rachel, the little girl born in 1907 who could see the Allegheny River from her bedroom window; Rachel, the pre-teen whose article about her brother's experiences in World War I was published in a children's magazine; and Rachel, the young woman who set off for college to study English but instead discovered her true calling.

Although decades will forever separate Mary Beth and Rachel, Trout points out that they were both born and raised in the same neighborhood and both earned science degrees. She adds, "I will always remember reading that book." "That book" is *Silent Spring*, Carson's passionate and reasoned warning against the unbridled use of pesticides in general and DDT in particular. Published in 1962, it changed the way society thinks about the environment.

The world where Carson grew up was far less complicated, or so it may have seemed to a young girl coming of age in a time and place where heavy industry also was coming into its own. Rachel, often described as shy and reserved, had an inner strength of character that would define her life, and her life's work. Perhaps that's why her parents gladly struggled to pay the $1,000-a-year tuition at the Pennsylvania College for Women (now Chatham College) in Pittsburgh. Graduating in 1928 with a degree in zoology, Carson went on to earn a Master of Arts in marine zoology from Johns Hopkins University. By 1932, she found herself working as a junior aquatic biologist for the U.S. Bureau of Fisheries.

Hardly a glamorous job, it nonetheless gave Rachel Carson a voice. She began writing — first government documents and pamphlets, then articles for national magazines, and, ultimately, books. Her works include *Under the Sea-Wind* (1941), *The Sea Around Us* (1951), *The Edge of the Sea* (1955), *Silent Spring* (1962), and *The Sense of Wonder* (1965).

Sometimes labelled "a hysterical woman," Carson never lost sight of her commitment to celebrate and conserve the world we call home. In 1963, she became the first woman to receive the National Audubon Society's Audubon Medal. That same year, she was named the National Wildlife Federation's Conservationist of the Year.

On April 14, 1964, Carson died of breast cancer in her home in Silver Spring, Maryland. Nearly two decades later, her memory was honored when she was posthumously given the Presidential Medal of Freedom. The modest home at 613 Marion Ave. in Springdale — just downriver from the site of a former DDT manufacturing plant — stands as testament to her monumental achievements.

The fact that the house is still standing at all is a testament to the Rachel Carson Homestead Association. Founded in 1976, the organization fought to save the structure.

Restoration followed, and today the Association sponsors tours of the house and gardens, educational and outreach programs, and an annual Rachel Carson Day in late spring to commemorate her birthday.

"There is a quiet strength in this house," Trout affirms.

In the early 1900s, from her bedroom window, Rachel saw the Allegheny River, farmland, and woods, but little industry.

Kleiner Deutschmann
724–274–5022
643 Pittsburgh Street, Springdale
Dinner: Tues–Sat, 5–10PM

Decorated with heirlooms, this German family-owned restaurant specializes in spaetzle, sauerbraten, and many wursts — knockwurst, bratwurst, weisswurst, and bockwurst.

Silent Spring
by Rachel Carson (Age 55)

...With the advent of man the situation began to change, for man, alone of all forms of life, can create cancer-producing substances, which in medical terminology are called carcinogens. A few man-made carcinogens have been part of the environment for centuries. An example is soot, containing aromatic hydro-carbons. With the dawn of the industrial era the world became a place of continuous ever-accelerating change. Instead of the natural environment there was rapidly substituted an artificial one composed of new chemical and physical agents, many of them possessing powerful capacities for biologic change. Against these carcinogens, which his own activities had created, man had no protection, for even as his biological heritage has evolved slowly, so it adapts slowly to new conditions. As a result these powerful substances could easily penetrate the inadequate defenses of the body.
— Rachel Carson. *Silent Spring*, 1962.

BY THE WAY

PPG Creighton was the first PPG plant in 1883, and the first successful producer of thick, flat plate glass in the United States, ending reliance on Europe for plate glass.

Alle-Kiski Route

Twin Towns along the Allegheny: Tarentum and New Kensington

Parishioners at Holy Martyrs Catholic Church in Tarentum create traditional sawdust carpets in celebration of the feast of Corpus Christi.

Hugging the hillside along the Allegheny River near the mouth of Bull Creek, **Tarentum** began as a Native American village, then developed into a European trading settlement called "Chartier's Old Town" by 1734. Inhabited originally by German and Scots-Irish entrepreneurs and farmers, the village became an economic crossroads when the Pennsylvania Canal, via the Kiskiminetas River, came through town. In 1842, the town incorporated as Tarentum, named for Tarento, Italy. Wood, salt, coal, and glassmaking were the main industries.

In 1882, Captain John B. Ford, the same Scots-Irish immigrant who built the Pittsburgh Plate Glass plant in Ford City, decided to construct a plate glass works in Tarentum using the area's plentiful natural gas as fuel.

By the 1890s, there were iron and steel foundries as well, which attracted Polish and Slovak immigrants. Residents called West Tarentum "Little Europe," or "the Catholic part," while East Tarentum became known as "the Protestant side."

Today, folk place names such as "Hunky Alley" harken back to the early 20th century when Slovaks filled Tarentum's worker housing. Gardening and berry-picking are still serious passions for many in the community during the summer, and oldtimers still remember playing "mushball" (a form of softball).

Ethnic and religious traditions, such as the German sawdust carpet display for the feast of Corpus Christi at Holy Martyrs Parish, and events sponsored by the local Slovak Heritage Association, help keep Tarentum's cultural identity strong.

The Alle-Kiski Valley Historical Society and the Tour-Ed Mine, both in Tarentum, give visitors a good introduction to the cultural and industrial heritage of both the town and the entire Alle-Kiski area.

Across the Allegheny River from Tarentum lies **New Kensington**, long associated with aluminum, one of the major industries in the Rivers of Steel region. The Aluminum Company of America (Alcoa) began in Pittsburgh's Strip District as the Pittsburgh Reduction Works in 1888, and acquired its present name in 1891 when it moved up the Allegheny to what is now New Kensington.

Like the big steel companies, Alcoa drew thousands of immigrants from Italy and Poland, as well as Scots-Irish and German workers from the surrounding countryside, and African-Americans from the southern United States.

So important was the industry to the town that New Kensington was nicknamed "Aluminum City." There is even a section of town called "Aluminum City Terrace," a planned neighborhood built as a World War II Defense Housing project, in which the homes and community center, designed by Bauhaus architects Walter Gropius and Marcel Breuer, are partially constructed of aluminum.

The New Kensington Chamber of Commerce plans an Aluminum Heritage Museum in a former Alcoa building.

New Kensington's churches sponsor many ethnic festivals (Syrian, Polish, Italian) every summer at the nearby Lower Burrell VFW pavilion. And the African-American community holds an annual Juneteenth celebration in downtown New Kensington to commemorate the end of slavery in the United States.

More than 200 housing units make up New Kensington's Aluminum City Terrace. Strict rules regarding each unit's appearance were relaxed over the years, allowing for individual expression.

Northeast from Pittsburgh

TARENTUM AREA

From Pittsburgh: *Take PA 28 N to Tarentum exit 14.*

Half-Day Tour: Sites 5–9
Alle-Kiski Historical Society & Museum: *Right on PA 366/Bull Creek Rd. Left at second light on 7th Ave. Go 2 blocks to Lock St. Museum is on right. After Museum, walk down Lock St. to 6th Ave.* ***Gatto Cycle Diner:*** *Right 1 block on 6th Ave. to Wood Street. Gatto's is on corner.* ***Tarentum Station Restaurant:*** *Left 1 block on 6th Ave. Restaurant is on right.* ***Early Bird Special:*** *In the morning, visit* ***Vibo's Italian Bakery*** *in Brackenridge (p. 126) before visiting Tarentum sites.* ***Tour-Ed Mine:*** *Return via PA 366/Bull Creek Rd. to PA 28, passing under highway. Right on Ridge Rd. Left into Tour-Ed Mine parking.* ***Return to Pittsburgh:*** *PA 28 S.*

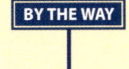

BY THE WAY

Lock Street in Tarentum is located on the site of one of the locks of the Pennsylvania Canal.

Alle-Kiski Valley Historical Society & Museum
724–224–7666
224 East 7th Avenue, Tarentum
Mon, Wed, Fri, 9AM–3PM
Adults: $3; Children: $2

Back in 1931, a group of Tarentum's War World I veterans joined forces to create a gathering place for friends and family. The result was an Art Deco American Legion Hall. Defined by a ballroom resplendent with panels of cobalt blue and gold mirrored glass made by PPG, Post 85 hosted its share of wedding receptions, bingo nights, and big-band dances.

But through the decades, veterans of other wars began to view the hall as a reminder of a time and place to which they no longer felt a connection. So, in 1967, the building was sold to the then-fledgling Alle-Kiski Valley Historical Society (AKVHS).

These days, the ballroom still dazzles, but now its primary function is to show off the displays accumulated by the AKVHS. The exhibits include glasswork from local companies — Challinor and Taylor, Richards & Hartley, and Tarentum Glass — and artifacts from a variety of wars dating back to the American Revolution.

"Most of the things have been given to us from families in the area," says AKVHS's Hartley Johnston. "Sometimes people just walk in with bags filled with stuff," and sometimes those items turn out to be priceless, such as the U.S. Navy uniform from World War I.

The AKVHS also boasts a standout collection of Kensington Ware from the nearby New Kensington Alcoa plant, and more than 500 glass plate negatives and prints of the region (circa 1906–1908) taken by local photographer George A. Burtner. A floor-to-ceiling mural portraying the region post–World War II greets visitors as they enter the building.

Downstairs, there's a saw shop, a vintage kitchen, a grocery store, Bain's Barber Shop, Dr. Bruno's dental office (with a foot-pedal drill), and the Eureka Hose & Fire Company. Johnston takes a hands-on approach to history at AKVHS. "Our goal is to preserve and celebrate the ethnic, cultural, and industrial heritage of the valley," he says. "It used to be just preservation, but that's not enough."

PPG made the cobalt blue and gold mirrored glass walls of the ballroom.

Aluminum and steel workers are depicted in a stairwell mural.

Alle-Kiski Route

6 ☕

Gatto Cycle Diner
724–224–0500
Corner of Wood Street and 7th Avenue, Tarentum
www.gattocycle.com/motorcycle/diner.html
Mon–Sat, 9AM–3PM

The Gatto Cycle Diner was made in 1949 by the O'Mahoney Company. The Gatto family restored the stainless steel structure to mint condition.

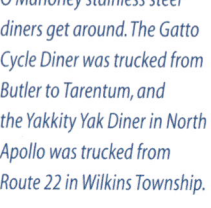

BY THE WAY

O'Mahoney stainless steel diners get around. The Gatto Cycle Diner was trucked from Butler to Tarentum, and the Yakkity Yak Diner in North Apollo was trucked from Route 22 in Wilkins Township.

7 ☕ 🏭

Tarentum Station Restaurant
724–226–3301
101 Station Drive, Tarentum
www.tarentumstation.com
Lunch: Mon–Fri, 11AM–3:30PM
Dinner: Mon–Th, 4–10PM; Fri, 4–11PM; Sat, 5–11PM; Sun, 4–8PM

Trains still rumble past this lively restaurant that occupies a restored railroad depot.

Northeast from Pittsburgh

Tour-Ed Mine & Museum
724-224-4720

748 Bull Creek Road, Tarentum
www.tour-edmine.com
Memorial Day–Labor Day: Wed–Mon, 1–4PM; Tues, closed
Sept & Oct: Fri, Sat & Sun, 1–4PM
Groups by appointment. Last tour each day: 3:30PM
Adults: $7; Children 12 and under: $4

If the walls and tunnels of the Tour-Ed Mine could talk, they would tell stories that date back more than 150 years. They would remember the miners who came armed with nothing more than candles on their helmets and picks in their hands. They would remember generation after generation of fathers and sons who labored inside the long horizontal shafts. They would remember so we wouldn't forget.

In a way, the walls and tunnels of this mine do talk. They speak through the voices of retired miners like Larry Kurtik. All we have to do is listen. At 50 years old, Kurtik still works the mines, but now his job involves taking the public on excursions inside the drift mine. As general manager, Kurtik oversees the 13.5 acres that make up the Tour-Ed Mine & Museum ("Tour-Ed" stands for tours and education).

Retired miner Pete Wahlen

Formerly known as the Avenue Mine, this tract in Tarentum served as a source of raw materials for Allegheny Ludlum Steel. In 1964, the Wood Coal Company took over operations, and for the next six years it supplied coal to local businesses like Tarentum Power and PPG.

Its purpose changed in 1970 when owner Ira Wood decided to use the mine to preserve the culture, the tools — the life — of the men who once worked there. Today, visitors come from nearby school districts or as far away as Japan to experience the mine from the inside out. Riding in trams for the two-hour tour, they can't help but notice that the ceiling, supported by wooden beams, is just 6 feet tall. Although electric lights illuminate the narrow paths, the darkness is ever present.

Along the way, Kurtik or one of his fellow miners-turned-docents explains the business of mining. They talk about state law, machinery, explosive "shots," the different kinds of mines and the different kinds of coal. As part of the Pennsylvania Mine Safety and Health Administration's Stay Out–Stay Alive program, they also make a point of telling kids about the dangers of abandoned mines and quarries. Then they invite their guests to check out the museum.

Coal Speak

afterdamp *an asphyxiating gas left in a mine after an explosion of firedamp.*

anthracite *hard coal that gives much heat and little smoke.*

banjo *a coal shovel.*

bituminous coal *soft coal mined in the western Pennsylvania/West Virginia region, used mainly for production of coke, the smelting agent in the iron production phase of steelmaking.*

black lung disease *a disease of the lungs caused by long-term inhalation of coal dust.*

cage *in a mine shaft, the device similar to an elevator car that is used for hoisting men and materials.*

coal *a solid, brittle, combustible carbonaceous rock formed by partial to complete decomposition of vegetation.*

creep *the forcing of pillars into a soft mine floor by the weight overhead.*

drift mine *an underground coal mine in which the entry or access is above water level and generally on the slope of a hill, driven horizontally into a coal seam. Tour-Ed is a drift mine.*

duly *an approved and permissible stick of explosive powder.*

firedamp *a gas, largely methane, formed in mines that is explosive when mixed with air.*

gob *that part of the mine from which coal has been removed.*

lignite *a brownish coal in which the texture of the original vegetable matter can still be seen. It is denser and contains more carbon than peat.*

man trip *a rail or rubber-tired carrier of mine personnel.*

methane *the most common explosive gas found in coal mines. It is tasteless, colorless, odorless, and nontoxic.*

Pennsylvania has 250–300 years worth of coal left to mine.

Alle-Kiski Route

peat *a dark-brown deposit resulting from the partial decomposition of vegetable matter in marshes and swamps. It is the first step in the formation of coal.*

permissible *approved by the U.S. Mine Safety and Health Administration, a federal agency of the Department of Labor, that governs the Federal Coal Mining Act of 1969. This act reformed the coal industry, which had claimed more than 100,000 lives since 1900.*

pot *a bad spot in the mine roof liable to fall without warning.*

seam *a thin layer or stratum of coal.*

shaft mine *an underground mine in which the main entry or access is by means of a vertical shaft.*

shot *a blast; also the amount of explosive used for a blast.*

slope mine *an underground mine with an opening that slopes upward or downward to the coal seam.*

trip *a train of mine cars.*

— Definitions provided by the Kentucky Mining Institute (©1996–2001) and from the U.S. Department of Labor Office of Administrative Law *Judges' Benchbook of the Black Lung Benefits Act*, January 1977.

When you're in Brackenridge take Brackenridge Avenue to Allegheny Ludlum, where stainless steel is produced.

Chock-full of stuff — figurines, photos, maps, laundry soap and starch, a 1908 Sears & Roebuck catalog, lanterns, lunch pails, blasting caps, a bicycle, a baby carriage — this cabin-like building houses the past. Period settings take center stage in the museum. With mannequins dressed in vintage clothing, these vignettes show a miner's kitchen (complete with a coal-burning stove, pump, sink, and icebox), a living room, a bedroom, and the neighborhood barber shop.

The Tour-Ed Mine is not out to impress. But if you look beyond the simplicity of the displays and collections, you'll get a glimpse into the life and times of the region's coal miners. The times may have changed, but Wood and Kurtik remain committed to the touring and educational components of the mine. These two men are not father and son, but clearly they share the kinship that is mining.

Miners' lunch buckets

BRACKENRIDGE

From Tarentum:
Vibo's Italian Bakery: *Take Lock St. toward river. Left on 1st Ave. through 3 stop signs. Left on Morgan St. Left 100 ft. on Brackenridge Ave. Bakery is in House on right.*

Vibo's Italian Bakery
724–224–0250
881 Brackenridge Avenue, Brackenridge
Mon, Wed, Th, Fri, 7AM–2PM; Sat, Sun, 7AM–1PM; Tues, closed

This small Italian bakery has provided bread for neighbors and neighboring businesses since the 1980s.

Giuseppe Lopreiato and his family make bread early each morning.

Northeast from Pittsburgh

Aluminum Industry

How important is aluminum in modern life? Think about the many uses of this versatile, lightweight metal: airplane frames, pots and pans, foil to cover a casserole. Now, how many people know that the center of aluminum production in America for more than 80 years was just upriver from Pittsburgh? With a name recognized in households around the world, Alcoa (originally the Aluminum Company of America) became famous for cooking utensils and, during World Wars I and II, for military hardware. From the 1950s on, Alcoa's aluminum began to find ever-wider peacetime use, for example, in the burgeoning automobile and construction industries.

Aluminum ware at the Alle-Kiski Valley Historical Society

Alcoa's corporate structure and the ethnic mix of its workforce reflected the influence of southwestern Pennsylvania's dominant industry, steel. Like many local steel companies, Alcoa was its town's primary employer and its primary corporate citizen, contributing funds for community projects such as the Italians' **Mount Saint Peter Church** (Alle-Kiski Route). While Alcoa's research and production facilities were based in New Kensington, the company's main offices in the **Alcoa Building** in downtown Pittsburgh were only a few blocks from the **U. S. Steel Tower.** (Three Rivers Route). The region's steel-related industries played a role equal to that of the steelmakers themselves in propelling America's post–World War II prosperity and in securing the nation's position of global economic leadership.

Brickmaking Industry

Wormy brick, shale brick, ladle brick, firebrick? Spiders, starters, piers, elbows? For most people, brick is just brick. But in southwestern Pennsylvania, from the early 19th century on, brickmaking became a highly specialized and diverse enterprise.

The story begins with this region's abundance and varieties of clay and sand. There are seams of clay, just as there are of coal. At first, only surface clay was extracted, but as demand grew, clay mining began.

Metal production requires brick for lining furnaces, ladles, and other equipment; however, ordinary house-brick cannot withstand the heat of molten metal (over 2,000°F). Industrial craftworkers in the region developed special bricks for the iron, steel, and, later, aluminum industries, by combining silica-rich clays with alumina from bauxite and other ores.

Stacked ladle bricks at the Freeport Brick Company

Mixed and fired together, silica and alumina produce yellow or white heat-resistant firebrick and refractory brick to line blast furnaces, open hearths, and ladles.

Metallurgical clay mines and industrial brickworks developed in several areas, but were concentrated along the Allegheny and Kiskiminetas Rivers. Early uses for brick were in home construction and road building, but brickmaking also propelled the growth of iron and steel. For over a hundred years, firms such as the Freeport Brick Company, Kittanning Brick Company, and Avonmore's Kier Brick Company have been mining clay and making ladle brick for the region's huge steel and aluminum plants.

During the height of industry, these steel-related firms employed hundreds of workers, as each plant needed thousands of bricks every year. Even today, firebrick and refractory brick are produced here to supply local steel and aluminum companies. The region's brickmaking industry also is part of the global economy; local brickworks import bauxite from China and precision equipment from Switzerland, while local craftworkers develop new bricks for applications as exotic as Venezuelan petrochemical processing.

Alle-Kiski Route

NEW KENSINGTON AREA

From Pittsburgh: Take PA 28 N to Tarentum exit 14. Bear right off ramp onto PA 366 toward New Kensington. Go straight through stoplights. Cross Tarentum–New Kensington Bridge.

Half-Day Tour: Sites 10–12
☎ **Mt. St. Peter Church:** Right at 3rd stoplight after bridge (Freeport Rd.). Go 2 mi. Church is on left. **Mazziotti Bakery:** Return on Freeport Rd. Go 1 mi. Left on Richmond St. Mazziotti's is on corner of Richmond St. and Constitution Blvd. **Fazios Italian Foods:** Right on Constitution Blvd. Right on Drey St. Fazio's is on corner of Drey and Leishman Sts. **Return to Pittsburgh:** PA 28 S.

Mt. St. Peter sits on a hilltop overlooking New Kensington.

NEW KENSINGTON

Mount Saint Peter Roman Catholic Church
724–335–9877
Freeport Road and 7th Street, New Kensington
www.mountsaintpeter.org
Year-round: Tues, Sat, Sun, open all day
School year: Weekdays, 6:30AM– 3:30PM
☎ Phone ahead for church tour.
Masses: Daily, 9AM; Sat, 9AM & 6PM; Sun, 8AM, 10AM, NOON
Closed during weddings and funerals. Please be respectful.

A mantlepiece from the Mellon Mansion, originally an altar from Pisa, Italy, became an altar once again in the new Mt. St. Peter Church.

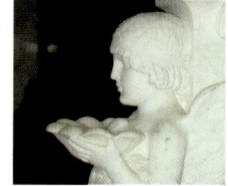

There is a presence in Mount Saint Peter Roman Catholic Church. That's not surprising — after all, churches are built on spiritual foundations that reach beyond the here and now. With a wide-open sanctuary that allows plenty of room for prayerful reflection, Mt. St. Peter is no exception to that rule. But there's another presence felt in this New Kensington church, one grounded in earthly trappings.

As fate — or perhaps divine intervention — would have it, the Richard Beatty Mellon Mansion in Pittsburgh was being demolished just as Mt. St. Peter was being constructed. The year was 1941 and John Stanish, a long-time Mellon employee and friend to the New Kensington Italian community, immediately saw the connection.

The lamp that crowns the canopy over the altar in Mount St. Peter once graced the billiard room in the Mellon Mansion.

Italian immigrant workmen constructed an airy sanctuary out of marble columns, a bronze banister, and a chandelier from the Mellon Mansion in Pittsburgh.

Northeast from Pittsburgh

Primarily through Stanish's efforts, the mansion's losses — marble columns and flooring, thick wooden banisters, stained-glass windows, alabaster fixtures, and cast-iron doors — became the church's gains. It wasn't until Monsignor Nicola Fusco brought the hearts, minds, and imaginations of his parishioners together that Mt. St. Peter truly began to take shape.

Many of the congregants had been stonemasons, carpenters, and metalsmiths in their native Italy. In their new homeland, where most found jobs in the nearby Alcoa plant, they set about using their old-country skills to make their dream a reality.

In their hands, the Mellon mansion's porch banister was transformed into the communion rail, a chandelier was reconfigured into the baptismal font, and doors that once enclosed the library now stand guard around the confessionals.

Antonio Muto spent more than six months on his knees, painstakingly cutting and placing pieces of marble to form the intricate pattern (pictured at right) that decorates the basement floor.

Four years later, in 1945, Mt. St. Peter came into full view on the hilltop where Freeport Road and 7th Street meet. "A church should be on a hill," Monsignor Fusco often said. "A church is something people should look up to."

A look inside this Romanesque structure, noted for its round arches and small windows, reveals an altar reminiscent of Saint Peter's in Rome. The ceiling, adorned with angels, stands 35 feet high and features casts of the gold and blue panels that once decorated the Mellon home.

In addition to the many Mellon artifacts, there is a red Verona marble pulpit commissioned by Andrew Carnegie but left crated for years in the basement of the Carnegie Library in Pittsburgh, and a 19th-century painting, *Behold the Lamb of God,* that first graced the Vatican and then the original Heinz Chapel on Pittsburgh's North Side.

Today, Mt. St. Peter is on the National Register of Historic Places. Eager to share its unique beginnings, the church offers tours to visitors while remaining the religious home to some 2,000 families — the sons and daughters, friends and neighbors of the people who so willingly contributed their hearts, minds, and imaginations.

Pittsburgh Mansion Meets the Wrecking Ball

The mansion in which the Mellons entertained royalty, celebrities, statesmen, and the best-known financiers of the world was the one built by Richard B. Mellon at 6500 Fifth Avenue, Pittsburgh, Pa. [now Mellon Park] *and now this magnificent building was being torn down...*

The Estate was a strip of terrestrial Paradise. ...The Mansion was built out of red Michigan sandstone. It was three stories high on the Beechwood Blvd. side, and four, on the opposite side. It numbered sixty-five rooms without counting halls or vestibules which were many. Both house and grounds required the skill of nearly one hundred servants. And now these were scarce. Hence the building had to be torn down before it would begin to fall of its own accord and embarrass the owner.

There were marbles from every corner of the world, even from India, China and Japan. There were bronze doors cast in England, wood-grilles carved in Bavaria, ceilings painted by Giovanni di San Pietro, magnificent mantlepieces, some of them adapted from ancient sculptured reredos, artistic bassorilievi, stately columns of rare brecciame, graceful arches of casotta, floors of tavanello and lignum vitae, steel beams especially built by the Carnegie Steel Company, some of the best masonry work in the State and one of the finest organs in the world.

— Nicola Fusco. *Mount Saint Peter,* 1944.

The Mellon Mansion in Pittsburgh's East End, as pictured on an early–20th-century postcard

As you drive on Freeport Road in New Kensington, you'll see the Alcoa Research Laboratory on the left. Note the distinctive architecture that once housed this specialty metals division.

Alle-Kiski Route

ARNOLD

11

Mazziotti Bakery
724–335–9376
1630 Constitution Boulevard, Arnold
Every day, 7AM–1:30PM

Get there early, before all the neighbors, for a loaf of Rina's beehive oven-baked Italian bread. Chances are you'll find it cooling in the backyard.

12

Fazio's Italian Foods
724–337–8521
1824 Leishman Avenue, Arnold
Mon–Sat, 9AM–7PM

Friendly clerks in this Italian market share great family recipes and sell imported cheeses, meats, and prepared foods such as lasagna, gnocchi, and stuffed shells.

BY THE WAY

Fannie Sellins, organizer for the United Mine Workers, was gunned down in Brackenridge on the eve of the Great Steel Strike in 1919. Look for her monument in the Union Cemetery along Freeport Road in Arnold.

Rivers of Steel Archives

Fannie Sellins

Spaghetti all'aglio e olio
(Spaghetti with Garlic & Oil)

1 lb. thin spaghetti or capellini
1/3 cup good olive oil
3 cloves garlic crushed
1 tsp. of hot pepper flakes
3-4 oz. Pecorino Romano cheese

Cook pasta according to directions. Meanwhile, make the sauce by heating oil in a small sauté pan, add the garlic and pepper, allow to simmer for 5 minutes. Drain pasta thoroughly. Turn into deep serving bowl. Add sauce and stir well to coat evenly. Serve at once with the cheese. (You may also add peas, artichokes, cooked bacon, cannellini beans, or anchovies.)
Enjoy!

—Fazio's Italian Foods

Italian Heritage

People of Italian background have been living and working in this region for more than 125 years. Large Italian communities can be found today in many industrial towns throughout the Rivers of Steel region, for example: New Kensington (Alle-Kiski Route), Jeannette (Youghiogheny Route), Ambridge and Aliquippa (Ohio-Beaver Route), the towns of Monongahela and Monessen (Monongahela Route), and the neighborhoods of Bloomfield and Panther Hollow in Pittsburgh (Three Rivers Route).

Like so many other southern and eastern European immigrants, Italians came to the region during the steel industry's boom years of 1880 to 1920. Young men far from home working long shifts as laborers saved money from their pay envelopes each week to bring wives from Italy. Uncles and brothers helped their newly arrived relatives find work.

While most Italian immigrants toiled at first in the mines and mills, many soon looked for other kinds of jobs. "Italians like to work daylight," said one older man, describing his family's early years. "They like to work outside."

Master mandolin player Joe Bucciero and his apprentice, Egidio Faiella

Today, throughout the Rivers of Steel region, you'll see Italian names in open-air businesses such as landscaping, gardening services, plant nurseries, stonemasonry, and construction. Skilled artisans in Italian immigrant communities often built their own, primarily Roman Catholic, churches. **Mount Saint Peter Church** in New Kensington (Alle-Kiski Route) is a beautiful example of this devotion. Christmas, Easter, and saints' days still provide occasions for music and pageantry in Italian neighborhoods. The San Rocco Festa in Aliquippa (Ohio-Beaver Route) is one such event.

In these milltowns and mine patches, immigrants from the same regions of Italy often settled near one another, recreating whole old-country villages, complete with local dialects, folk arts such as bobbin lace making and wind-band music, and, of course, food. Even today, homemade pasta dinners with Mama or Nonna on Sunday afternoons draw Italian families together across the generations. And food-related businesses help Italian communities continue their traditions and share their culture with visitors: bread from bakeries such as **Vibo's** or **Mazziotti's** (Alle-Kiski Route), sauces and sausages made from family recipes at places like **Rocca's Homestyle Pasta** in Midland and **Tony's Specialty Meats & Market** in Ambridge (Ohio-Beaver Route), and Italian groceries and restaurants throughout the region that feature specialties from old family recipes.

Antonella Dilanni carries on the tradition of bobbin lace making.

Alle-Kiski Route

VANDERGRIFT

From Pittsburgh: *Take PA 28 N to Tarentum exit 14. From exit ramp, bear right on PA 366, straight through stoplights. Cross Tarentum–New Kensington Bridge. Go through 3 stoplights, then take PA 56 E.*

Half-Day Tour: Sites 13 and 14
Victorian Vandergrift Museum: *Take PA 56 E through Vandergrift (one-way road). Angle right at Burger King. Follow Sherman Avenue .3 mi. to old elementary school on right. Museum is in school.*
Rowley's Market: *Back on Sherman Ave. to PA 56 E. Right to cross bridge. Rowley's is at end of bridge on right.* ***Return to Pittsburgh:*** *PA 28 S.*

Victorian Vandergrift Museum and Historical Society
724–568–1990
184 Sherman Avenue, Vandergrift
www.vvmhs.com
Mon–Sat, 10AM–3PM
Donations welcome

After serving as an elementary school and office building, the Sherman School was given a new lease on life in 2001. That's the year it officially became the home of the Victorian Vandergrift Museum and Historical Society. The former four-room schoolhouse now offers visitors lessons about the town's rich industrial heritage. Receiving a number of its objects from residents past and present, the Vandergrift Museum displays photographs and artifacts. A genealogy library is also on site.

Rowley's Market
724–567–6511
12 1st Street, Vandergrift
Wed–Sat, 10AM–5PM; Th, 10AM–8PM

Established in 1903, this general store is the one you've always imagined, where handcrafted pottery shares the same shelf as shiny new galvanized steel buckets. The Rowley family has operated the store for 100 years.

Early Steel Milltowns

There are no pavements, no fences, no space for gardens or flowers. Refuse and filth are allowed to collect in the alleys — there are no sewers, and no water piped into homes. The lack of proper water supply and sewage disposal was the cause of serious and deadly outbreaks of disease of all type.
— Ida Tarbell. *New Ideals in Business,* 1916.

One Man's Vision

We desire to have a town that in many features will be unique and in all respects more attractive than the average manufacturing town of the present day. In fact, we want something better than the best.
— George McMurtry. Letter to Frederick Law Olmsted, 1890.

BY THE WAY

The 3200 employees of the Kiskiminetas steel mills gave George McMurtry a Tiffany bowl when he retired. Look for it in the Senator John Heinz History Center in Pittsburgh.

BY THE WAY

Rowley's survived the flood of 1936. Look for the flood marker on the building.

Northeast from Pittsburgh

Vandergrift — "A Workingman's Paradise"

Travel through the gently winding streets of Vandergrift, just 30 miles northeast of Pittsburgh, and your car seems to transport you to a more gracious era. You can actually feel the town plan as you drive it. The grid is curved — even the houses are rounded.

Designed and laid out in 1895 by world-famous landscape architect Frederick Law Olmsted, Vandergrift embodies the vision of its founder, industrialist George G. McMurtry, president of Apollo Iron & Steel Company.

McMurtry's dream was to create a company town that would showcase good relations between management and labor, which would in turn result in high productivity and profits. The idea was to build the factory and the town at the same time, so that the site would be integrated.

Following the ideals of the late-Victorian era, the workers' homes were designed to be gracious as well as functional, using the most up-to-date building technology. The town plan included parks and other amenities for the workers' comfort.

The Casino Theatre is now a performing arts center.

From 1902 to 1988, the Vandergrift mill was associated with U. S. Steel. Still in operation and now owned by the Allegheny Ludlum Corporation, the mill sits on a flat bend along the Kiskiminetas River, its main gate opening off the Vandergrift town circle.

Around the upper part of the circle, visitors can get a good view overlooking the steel works from the town's newly restored Casino Theatre, a Greek Revival hall built in 1900 and located in the heart of the town's National Register Historic District. First a vaudeville theater and then a movie house, the Casino is now a performing arts center, the site of plays and concerts throughout the year.

A walking tour (map and audio cassette are available at the **Victorian Vandergrift Museum** and at the Casino Theatre) lets you enjoy the Historic District at your own pace, and imagine living in the "workingman's paradise."

Vandergrift's architecture reflects the gentle curves of Frederick Law Olmsted's town plan.

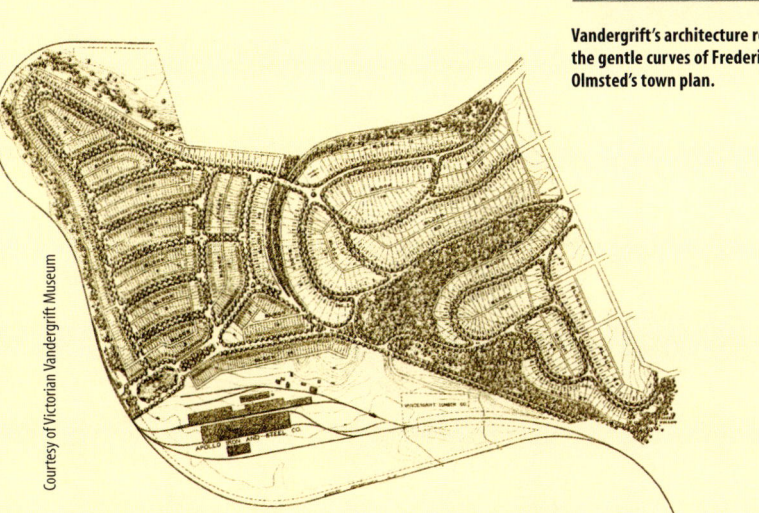

Courtesy of Victorian Vandergrift Museum

Alle-Kiski Route

Twin Towns on the Kiski: Leechburg and Hyde Park

Nestled cater-corner on opposite bends of the meandering Kiskiminetas River are two company towns worth a visit: Leechburg and Hyde Park. Each with its own character, the twin towns are connected not by road, but by a steel footbridge built in the 1950s.

Leechburg holds its annual community festival at its end of the bridge. On the Hyde Park side, visitors get a striking view of the bridge from the leafy path beside the railway along the river.

The larger of the towns, **Leechburg**, was founded by David Leech in 1827 as a stop on the Pennsylvania Canal. Visitors may stop in for a walking-tour map at the Leechburg Area Museum and Historical Society, which occupies a house, dating from the 1830s, that was owned by David Leech.

Once owned by David Leech, this building is now the Leechburg Area Museum and Historical Society.

In 1871, Leechburg entered the industrial age when an iron-works was built there. U. S. Steel later bought the plant, expanding with a cluster of mills to become the town's main employer from 1900 through the 1930s. Still operating, the plant is now owned by the Allegheny Ludlum Corporation.

During Leechburg's industrial heyday, immigrants from eastern and southern Europe and African-Americans from the southern states came to work in the mills. People couldn't choose their jobs — the company assigned jobs according to each worker's ethnic background.

Nowadays the mills assign work by skill and seniority, yet cultural identity remains important to Leechburg residents. With old-country traditions continuing to enrich community life at the Hungarian Club and the Marconi Club (Italian),

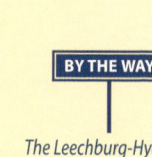

BY THE WAY

The Leechburg-Hyde Park footbridge connects not only two towns, but two counties.

The footbridge

Leechburg is a town that celebrates its cultural diversity and its shared industrial heritage.

Hyde Park is a small town, off the beaten path, but it's a can-do community. Visitors will be charmed by the town's open, neighborly spirit as they visit the Hyde Park Museum, housed in a historic Lutheran church, and enjoy a leisurely walk along the river.

Built on the "Great Bend," a peninsula jutting into the Kiskiminetas River, Hyde Park was laid out in 1893 by W. H. Hyde of the Hyde Land Company. The town was incorporated in 1898.

The Hyde Park Foundry & Machine Company was established in 1895 to produce machines for processing steel. An industrial company town right from the start, Hyde Park attracted immigrant workers from many parts of Europe.

Because of the town's isolation, residents had to learn to rely on their own ingenuity — and on each other — for support.

The grave of town founder David Leech overlooks Leechburg.

First Evangelical Lutheran Church

Northeast from Pittsburgh

LEECHBURG • HYDE PARK

From Pittsburgh: *Take PA 28 N to Tarentum exit 14. From exit ramp, bear right on PA 366, straight through stoplights. Cross Tarentum–New Kensington Bridge. Go through 3 stoplights. Take PA 56 E toward Leechburg.*

One-Day Tour: Sites 15–17

Hyde Park Museum: *Before reaching Leechburg, angle right at road sign "Hyde Park 1" on S. Glosser Hill Rd. Bear left at "Y." Right on Main St. Left on Center St. Museum is on left.* **Leechburg Area Museum and Historical Society:** *Return to PA 56 E to Leechburg. Cross bridge. At "Yield" sign, go straight. Right on Main St. Go 2 blocks to First St. Museum is on right.* **Kiski Junction Railroad:** *See Schenley, page 136.* **Return to Pittsburgh:** *PA 28 S.*

The Hyde Park Foundry, a pattern and machine shop, still operates in Hyde Park.

Hyde Park Museum
724–845–6525
Hyde Park Borough Building (the former Bethel Lutheran Church)
Corner of Main and Center Streets, Hyde Park
Wed, NOON–3PM, or by appointment

The Hyde Park Museum showcases artifacts from industries that have occupied Hyde Park throughout the years: a foundry and a brewery, and glove, brick, and glass factories.

Leechburg Area Museum and Historical Society
724–845–8914
118 1st Street, Leechburg
Wed and Sat, NOON–3PM

This memorabilia-filled museum is housed in an 1830s building and a 1900-era building. Visitors will find everything imaginable with the name "Leechburg" imprinted on it, as well as wasp-waisted Victorian wedding gowns and, on the second floor, an archive of old newspapers and books.

Tools, utensils, and building materials were both made and used locally.

Alle-Kiski Route

SCHENLEY

From PA 28 N exit 14: Take PA 56 E to PA 66 N to Schenley.

2-Hour Train Ride:
Kiski Junction Railroad: At top of hill, go left at blinking light on Schenley Rd. Go 4 mi. Kiski Junction Railroad is on Railroad St. next to Schenley Industrial Park (former Schenley Distillery).

Kiski Junction Railroad
724–295–5577
Railroad Street, Schenley
www.kiskijunction.com
May 25–Oct 31: Sat, Sun, Tues, 2PM
May 29–Aug 28: Wed, 7PM
Adults: $8; Seniors: $7; Children 12–17: $6; Children 4–11: $4; Children 3 and under: Free

Mary and Charlie Bowyer haul scrap metal and people from downtown Schenley to Bagdad, Pennsylvania.

The Kiski Junction Railroad track may be short in distance, but the ride is long on stories — especially when Mary Bowyer is doing the talking, which is pretty often.

Running parallel to the Kiskiminetas River, the railroad hauls freight and people — although not at the same time — from Schenley to Bagdad. Total round trip: just four miles.

Mary and her husband, Charlie (he doesn't really say much), have been working for Kiski Junction since the mid-1990s. Charlie is the engineer. Mary is his brakeman. They moved from Ohio and now make the nearby red caboose their home.

All year, every year, they ride the rails from downtown Schenley ("The population here is 70 plus two — we're the two," Mary says) to the Allegheny Ludlum specialty silicon steel plant in Bagdad. There they pick up gondola cars loaded with scrap metal and take them to the bridge overlooking the Kiski and Allegheny Rivers. Each car can hold a 99-ton payload, Mary says, and in 2001 they hauled about 600 cars.

At this interchange, Mary and Charlie leave the scrap metal behind for the Norfolk Southern Railway to take to Natrona–Brackenridge for "re-melt." Then Mary and Charlie make the short trip back to Schenley. That's the work part of their job.

The fun began in 1996. It started when a group from the local campground wanted to do something different, something special for the Fourth of July. At first Mary and Charlie just used an open flat car. Twelve passenger cars — and countless passengers from church outings, scout troops, and bus tours — later, the Kiski Junction Railroad has become a phenomenon.

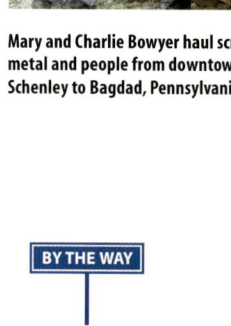

BY THE WAY

Here's why kids love this trip: "There are lots of sights and the trip is cool. It's a real diesel train. Kids get to go into the cab and pull the whistle. You even see a working steel mill!"
—Jeff & Jacob, ages 12 & 9

Northeast from Pittsburgh

That success can be attributed to the romance of the rails, and to the spirited commentary Mary is only too happy to share with her charges along the hour-and-a-half trip. "People always told me I should talk about this or that, so I started taking notes."

"This and that" now includes stories about former residents, such as Mary Schenley, for whom the town was named. Her family settled here, then moved to Pittsburgh and donated the land that became Schenley Park.

There are also stories about trillium that grows wild on the hillside, herds of deer, flocks of turkeys, bald eagles, horned owls, and one very outgoing bear. " 'Gilpin George' is a 300-pound-ish black bear that roams all over Gilpin Township and once stopped us dead in our tracks right down this straight stretch," Mary says.

There are tales about local employers, both past and present. Mary points out that the Schenley Whiskey Distillery, part of the local scene for many years, was originally 26 buildings on 42 acres. "It employed 1,200 people and closed in the 1980s. It's now a huge industrial park." The Allegheny Ludlum plant is still operating." In the 1960s, Ludlum bought the entire town of Bagdad, Pa., moved all 300 residents, tore down all the homes, and built the big mill up ahead."

And, of course, there is plenty of talk about the railroad, a four-mile branch line that was part of the Pennsylvania Main Line Canal. In the late 1800s, the canal was filled in and the railroad was built on top.

"You are riding on a railroad that has been in continuous operation for 144 years," Mary likes to point out.

Charlie's the engineer; Mary's the brakeman and tour guide.

The Pennsylvania Canal

The act of the Legislature authorizing the construction of the Pennsylvania Canal was passed in 1825 and the work of digging and blasting started in the following year. The length of the canal from Johnstown to the mouth of the Kiskiminetas River was sixty-four miles, in which space there were a number of locks. ...The distance covered by the canal within the bounds of Armstrong County was twenty-five miles, most of which was along the bank of the Kiskiminetas. At the mouth of that river the canal was carried across the Allegheny by means of a wooden aqueduct, resting on stone piers. Thence the course was through Freeport across Buffalo Creek on another aqueduct, and down the Allegheny to Pittsburgh.

The stone for the locks and bridge piers was obtained from the quarries near the rivers, and the work of construction was mostly done by Irish immigrants, who finally became settlers and landowners after their labors were ended. ...

After the completion of the Pennsylvania Railroad the trade of the canal languished, and in August 1857, the State sold the entire line of the canal, locks, etc. to the railroad for $7,500,000. That road having thus eliminated its only competitor, allowed the canal to relapse into ruin, using but a small portion of the route for a roadbed. For almost the entire length of the route through this county the canal is not used by the road, although upon that side of the river most of the towns are located.

—*Armstrong County, Pa.: Her People, Past and Present,* Volume One, J. H. Beers & Co., 1914.

Alle-Kiski Route

Old Freeport

Settled in the 1780s, Freeport provided a natural stopping-point on the Allegheny River. An eddy there slowed boats down, making it a good place to pull in and tie up. During those early years, the region had few roads, and transportation depended on the river. The settlement's importance increased in 1826 when Irish workers arrived to build the Pennsylvania Canal. By 1828, the town had 30 houses.

In 1829, the first passenger canal boat left Freeport for Pittsburgh — a five-hour trip!

By the 1850s, the community boasted a sawmill, a gristmill, a tannery, an iron foundry, a brickyard, a woolen mill, and even a distillery. One reason for the town's success was its status as a "free port" — no fees were charged to boats putting in there.

Cash money was scarce because there were no banks in the Allegheny–Kiskiminetas Valley for many years. Often trade relied on bartering. One of Freeport's earliest merchants recorded that he bartered a suit for 25 gallons of whiskey.

Mickey's Mill on Buffalo Creek dates from about 1871.

Through the 19th century, even after the canal's influence declined, Freeport boomed as fleets of barges carrying timber and (later) oil traveled through. People said that when the lumbermen and oilmen from upriver would come to town, the partying, fighting, and drinking in Freeport made the Wild West look tame! By the early 20th century, however, the boom had ended. Freeport became the quaint and quiet town that visitors see today — but a town that remembers its boisterous past.

Courtesy of AKValley.com © 1999 by Darren McPhilimy, all rights reserved.

Freeport, circa 1845

As you drive Route 28 north to Freeport, you'll see PPG Creighton on your right. This facility produces automobile windshields.

FREEPORT

From Pittsburgh: *Take PA 28 N to Freeport/Millerstown exit 16. Make a right at the bottom of ramp. At stop sign and light, make a left. Follow signs for PA 128 down hill into Freeport.*

Half-Day Tour: Sites 18 and 19
The Sheltering Tree: *Left onto High St. Store is immediately on right.*
Shoop & Sons: *Continue on High St. Right on 5th St. Shoop's is on corner of 5th and Market Sts.* **Return to Pittsburgh:** *Right on Market St. Right on 4th St. Left on High St. Right on 2nd St. to Buffalo St. At Gulf Station, left to PA 28 S.*

18

The Sheltering Tree
724–295–2730
210 High Street, Freeport
Tues–Sat, 10AM–5PM; Sun, NOON–5PM

This store is the primary retail outlet for Carson Statesmetal, located in nearby Slate Lick, a Pennsylvania maker of lead-free pewter ware. Look in the back room for an eclectic mix of sundials, dinnerware, wind chimes, and other metal items.

Northeast from Pittsburgh

J. H. Shoop & Sons
724–295–4126
201 5th Street, Freeport
Mon–Th, 9AM–5:30PM; Friday, 9AM–8PM; Sat, 9AM–4PM
(Memorial Day–Labor Day: Sat, store closes 1PM)
John Shoop is there: Mon, Tues, Fri, Sat

Long before credit came in the form of a card, when blue jeans were about function and not form, there was a Shoop's clothing store in Freeport.

When Jacob Shoop, a tailor by trade, opened the family business back in 1830, there wasn't even a paved road in town.

In fact, Freeport was just that — a port where boats could stop free of charge to refuel and restock provisions. The Allegheny River was the only passageway that mattered. But whether it was a pair of work boots or a Sunday suit for the local loggers and miners, the original Mr. Shoop understood that clothes mattered, too.

That bit of wisdom — along with the store itself — has been passed down through generations of Shoop sons. After Jacob, John Henry took over the register. Then there was William G., who was followed by Everett. Today, John E. Shoop is the proprietor of this local landmark. (It's been said that Shoop's holds the record as the nation's oldest men's clothing store continuously owned and operated by the same family.)

Stocked with artifacts like tailor's shears and business ledgers from Shoop's past, as well as with modern-day apparel for men of all professions, the store has stood at the same address for more than a century. It moved to its present location in 1890, the same year Freeport's main road was built. And, according to John Shoop, it really hasn't changed a whole lot since then.

DON'T READ THIS!
It will make your Headache.
LOOK A LITTLE OUT!
—FOR THE—
CHEAP CORNER
Clothing Store!
ON WATER STREET.

JACOB SHOOP
Has Just Received
The Largest Stock of Clothing
EVER BROUGHT TO THIS TOWN.
No more shivering and shaking when you can buy Clothing for a mere song. Look at what he offers:

Good Heavy Overcoats from $4 to $12.
Boy's Suits for $4.
Men's Suits from $5 to $16.
Boy's Vests at 60 cents. Good goods.

Underwear cheaper than you can steal it.
Drawers from 40 to 90 cents.
He has also a large and varied assortment of

Hats, Caps, and everything in Men and Boys wear that you can imagine.

But better than all else he has brought his prices down to the lowest notch, and is determined to sell for less money than any other man in town.

above: A vintage ad illustrates the attitude that's kept J. H. Shoop & Sons in business since 1830.

left: John E. Shoop represents the fifth generation to sell men's clothes in Freeport.

BY THE WAY

In 1852 John Shoop bartered tailoring services for 25 bushels of coal, which was worth $1.

Alle-Kiski Route

Frank Gatrell, caller

Square Dancing Calls
California Twirl
Coordinate
Dive Thru
Dixie Style
Do Paso
Do Sa Do
Ferris Wheel
Flutter Wheel
Grand Square
Kiss Your Wife
Ladies 'n Men Sashay
Load the Boat
Pass Thru
Ping Pong Circulate
Relay the Deucey
Roll Away
Scout Back
See Saw
Slip the Clutch
Spin Chain Thru
Spin the Top
Split the Ring
Star Thru
Swing
Tea Cup Chain
Track Z
U Turn Back
Wheel and Deal
Zoom

SLATE LICK

From Pittsburgh: Take PA 28 N to Slate Lick exit 18. Left at end of exit ramp. First right on Cadogan Rd. (PA 128 N). Go 2.5 mi. See sign for League of Arts on left.

20

Armstrong County League of Arts Center
724–763–7457
Cadogan Road (PA 128N), Slate Lick
☎ Phone ahead or visit during events.

Some buildings house artifacts that sit quietly in glass cases, far from the fingers of curious children. But other buildings shelter local customs — folklore and traditions kept alive by the warm embrace of friends and family.

For nearly 30 years, the Armstrong County League of Arts Center has been such a place, where western and hoedown square dances thrive. "For the people of this county," says League founder Marilyn Rea, "that was our American dance."

But this seemingly quintessential red-white-and-blue art form took many of its cues from the other side of the ocean. England's Morris and country dances and France's quadrille and cotillion all left their imprints. As generations of European settlers evolved into American pioneers, the dances came along for the ride.

Nowadays, different parts of the country have unique styles of dance. "We're stompers or flatfooters," Rea says of the western Pennsylvania contingent. "We shuffle our feet."

In addition, the advent of a caller who shouts out the steps and keeps the rhythm going with a steady round of chatter was an American contribution. A caller herself, as well as a musician and visual artist, Rea (with her husband, Red) keeps the League of Arts jumping. On various nights throughout most of the year, the unassuming log building shakes to the rafters with the sounds of bluegrass jams and country socials. "We fill the place," Rea says. "They come from all over — Maryland, West Virginia, New York." Dancers also come in all ages. "We taught our own two grandchildren to square dance," Rea says. "And I've taught at local schools."

Visitors will find the works of Rea and other local artists lining the walls. Rea's acrylic renderings depict rural landscapes and seafaring scenes.

And if you've come seeking the square dance, Rea asserts that, on any given day, somewhere in Armstrong and its surrounding counties, someone is bound to be calling your name.

Legend has it that country dance got its name from the word "contra," which refers to the opposing lines of dancers.

Northeast from Pittsburgh

Scots and Scots-Irish Heritage

Immigrants from Scotland began coming to southwestern Pennsylvania in the mid-18th century. While some Scots traveled here directly from Scotland, many more were "Scots-Irish," people who, after losing their lands in Scotland, first went to Northern Ireland before emigrating to North America. They were among the earliest permanent European settlers in southwestern Pennsylvania. Many served in the Revolutionary War and were among the ex-soldiers who received land as payment for service.

The Scots-Irish became the region's dominant social group. Their primary occupation was farming, at first, along with running small businesses. But they were entrepreneurs, taking advantage of the resources around them.

As the region's economy developed, they started many of the mills, mines, and factories and founded company towns. Several captains of the iron and steel industries were of Scots or Scots-Irish background: Andrew Carnegie, James Laughlin (of Jones & Laughlin Steel), and J. P. Morgan, for example. Most belonged to the Church of Scotland, a Protestant denomination known in America as Presbyterian. Throughout the Rivers of Steel region, you will find Presbyterian churches even now, large and small. **Grace Presbyterian Church** in Kittanning (Alle-Kiski Route) is a particularly beautiful example.

The long-term Scots-Irish presence is represented in county, town and street names — Armstrong, Braeburn, Leechburg, Arnold, Armagh — and in the region's strong work ethic. Quilting is one Scots/Scots-Irish folk tradition still practiced throughout the region by women's groups at local churches. Visitors can enjoy fiddle music and square dancing in Slate Lick at the **Armstrong County League of Arts Center** (Alle-Kiski Route), or at the monthly Old-Time Fiddlers' Jamboree in Connellsville (Youghiogheny Route).

Cassandra Sotos at the Armstrong County League of Arts

Rivers of Steel Archives

KITTANNING

From Pittsburgh: Take PA 28 N to US 422W/Butler exit. Then take West Kittanning exit. Follow Butler Rd. Go 2 mi. (past Franklin Village, bearing right through West Kittanning and down hill). Cross bridge.

Half-Day Tour: Sites 21 and 22
Mulberry Street Creamery: From bridge, right 2 blocks on Water St. Left on Mulberry St. Creamery is on right. ☎ **Grace Presbyterian Church:** Continue on Mulberry St. to "T." Left on Jefferson St. crossing Market St. Stay on Jefferson St. to Arch St. Church is on left.
Return to Pittsburgh: US 422 E to PA 28 S.

Mulberry Street Creamery
724–548–7328
103 Mulberry Street, Kittanning
www.mulberrystreetcreamery.com
1st week in Mar–Oct:
Weekdays, NOON–8PM; Weekends, NOON–9PM

Grandfather Mercurio came from Italy to work on the railroad. In 1998, his son opened the Mulberry Street Creamery.

Anthony Mercurio will tell you that he serves the best gelato this side of the Allegheny.

Alle-Kiski Route

㉒ ⚜

Grace Presbyterian Church
724–548–5609
150 North Jefferson Street, Kittanning
☎ Phone ahead for tour, or attend service:
Sun, 11ᴀᴍ (winter); Sun, 10ᴀᴍ (summer)

A stained-glass window depicting Jesus glows with the rising sun.

Faith is at the center of a trinity of windows.

From our 21st-century perspective, stained-glass windows do not generally reflect a political agenda. But in the 19th century, some windows — as well as furniture and architecture — came to symbolize the Arts and Crafts Movement.

Responding to the Industrial Revolution, specifically to the poor working conditions in the factories and the poor quality of goods they mass-produced, this crusade began in England.

By the late 1800s, it had spread across Europe and the Atlantic, where eventually Americans such as Louis Comfort Tiffany, Gustav Stickley, and Frank Lloyd Wright picked up the gauntlet. Adhering to the tenets of the Arts and Crafts Movement — hands-on attention to detail and pride in accomplishment — these gentlemen advanced the philosophy that a true craftsperson is nothing more, and nothing less, than an artist.

That philosophy shines through the stained-glass windows of Kittanning's Grace Presbyterian Church. Since 1911, when this Jefferson Street church first opened its doors, five original Tiffany works have graced the building. The most striking is the Jane Ross Reynolds memorial window, *Faith*.

Showing a woman holding the Scriptures in her arms and looking up to the "crown of glory," the window's "depth of color, general form and beautiful and wonderful iridescent effects are entirely dependent upon the Tiffany favrile and luster glass, in conjunction with the latest methods of 'plating,'" proclaimed the *Kittanning Daily Leader Times*.

This type of ecclesiastical art was a Tiffany trademark and a good source of revenue for the company. Often the windows were tributes to departed family members. And, thanks to the area's booming steel and coal industries of the early 1900s, Grace Presbyterian boasted its share of parishioners who could afford Tiffany's work.

But art glass was never simply about status. For the church, it was about love — love of community and love of God. And for Tiffany, perhaps it was about pride. After all, according to Grace Presbyterian's records, "Mr. Tiffany came here from New York to inspect the windows himself."

Northeast from Pittsburgh

Twin Towns on the Allegheny: Kittanning and Ford City

The histories of Ford City and Kittanning have been inextricably intertwined.

During the heyday of industry, Ford City was the manufacturing hub of Armstrong County, while Kittanning, the county seat, was home to managers and merchants. Like brothers, the two communities supported and competed with each other — in a friendly rivalry played out annually in the Kittanning–Ford City football game on Armistice Day.

For more than a hundred years, the Kittanning–Ford City Trolley line connected the towns — now they are joined by river and road.

Mansions line Kittanning's Water Street.

Kittanning invites you to slow down, breathe deeply, and enjoy the beauty of the Allegheny River. The tree-lined, landscaped walkway along the river's edge echoes the wooded hillside across the river. Beyond the bridge, gracious mansions and churches from another era line the town's riverfront road.

Although that time seems remote, Kittanning played an important role in the region's industrial history.

Settled by Scots-Irish and then German immigrants, Kittanning started in 1800, well

This Kittanning law office was once a library.

before the rise of steel. Even earlier, it had been a Native American settlement. In 1821, with only 321 inhabitants, it incorporated as a borough. By 1900, Kittanning was a thriving community. Pittsburghers regularly came by steamer to spend a few refreshing days in the country.

Kittanning's industries included an iron and steel works. Many local fortunes were built on coal mining. With abundant clay, Kittanning was known for producing refractory brick used to line furnaces in steel mills. A workers' neighborhood called Clay Hole was located near the present-day courthouse in the center of town.

But Kittanning was primarily a center of banking and commerce. Memberships in clubs, musical groups such as the firemen's band, and religious institutions marked social status and class. It is said that people here are joiners. At one time there were 32 churches, primarily English or Scots-Irish Protestant.

Today, many of the beautiful old homes have been renovated. Some of the most distinctive churches, such as **Grace Presbyterian**, are within walking distance in the town's historic district. "Originally, Grace Presbyterian was for the professionals, while Faith Presbyterian was for the merchants," remembers one resident, "but those distinctions have gone by the wayside now."

By contrast, **Ford City** began in the late 1880s as a riverfront company town and remains a working community to this day. The town was built by Captain John Ford to house the workers for his plant, the Ford City Plate Glass Company. In 1889, the firm merged with the Pittsburgh Plate Glass Company and became the largest plate glass manufacturer in the world. (Now known as PPG, the company still operates plants in the Rivers of Steel region.)

The promise of good jobs at PPG or at the Eljer china and porcelain works attracted workers from Germany, Italy, Poland, and other nations in Europe, as well as, after World War I, African-Americans from the southern states, and Mexicans. These people spoke many different languages, but the core of their lives was the same: religion and family. Each group had its own club. Companies donated land to any group that wanted to build a church.

Although the original PPG factory has closed, the town plans to renovate the building as a glass museum. Until then, visitors will want to attend the annual Ford City Heritage Days festival to sample food, music, and crafts representing the town's rich ethnic traditions, or enjoy a walk along Ford City's riverfront trail.

Ford City plans to open a glass museum in 2004.

Alle-Kiski Route

EVENTS CALENDAR

For specific dates and times of events see: **www.riversofsteel.com**

Events that occur in several months are abbreviated with an *. See Recurring Events for full contact information.

Recurring Events

Polka Dance
American Slovenian Citizens Association
724–274–9997
230 Heron Avenue, Acmetonia
Saturday and Sunday evenings

Traditional Musicians Jam
Armstrong County League of Arts
724–763–7457
Cadogan Road (PA 128 N), Slate Lick
Every 2nd and 4th Thursday
Banjo players, mandolinists, guitarists, monthly square dances, year-round classes in dances, crafts, and traditional music

*Bluegrass Day
Armstrong County League of Arts
724–763–7457
Cadogan Road (PA 128 N), Slate Lick
October–April: 2nd Sunday

*Country Day
Armstrong County League of Arts
724–763–7457
Cadogan Road (PA 128 N), Slate Lick
October–April: 4th Sunday

*Fleatique/Antiques Market
Alle-Kiski Historical Society
724–224–7666
Tour-Ed Mine and Museum
748 Bull Creek Road, Tarentum
May–October: 3rd Sundays

January

*Bluegrass Day
*Country Day

February

*Bluegrass Day
*Country Day

March

*Bluegrass Day
*Country Day

April

*Bluegrass Day
*Country Day

May

Alle-Kiski-Connie Canoe Sojourn
Strongland Chamber of Commerce
724–845–5426
One Parks Bend, Vandergrift
Mid-May

Syrian Food Festival
St. George Antiochian Orthodox Church
724–335–5223
1150 Leishman Street, New Kensington
Mid-May

Corpus Christi Celebration
Holy Martyrs Roman Catholic Church
724–224–0770
353 West 9th Avenue, Tarentum
Late May or late June
Traditional sawdust carpet display

Rachel Carson Day
Rachel Carson Homestead
724–274–5459
613 Marion Avenue, Springdale
Late May or early June

*Fleatique/Antiques Market

June

BlueGrass Festival
Mountain Top Campgrounds
888–224–1511
873 Sun Mine Road, Tarentum
1st full weekend

East Vandergrift Ethnic Days
724–567–7122
McKinley Avenue, East Vandergrift
Mid-June
Ethnic foods, hand-crafted items

Ford City Heritage Days
724–763–1763
Ford City Memorial Park, Ford City
Late June
Crafts, food, entertainment, parade, children's area

Juneteenth
New Kensington
724–339–6616
4th Avenue and 10th Street, New Kensington
Late June
African-American emancipation

*Fleatique/Antiques Market

August

Fort Armstrong Folk Festival
Riverfront Park
724–543–1045
Water Street, Kittanning
Early August
Crafts, foods, buggy rides, children's games

Italian Day
Mount Saint Peter Church
724–335–9877
100 Freeport Road, New Kensington
www.mountsaintpeter.org
Early August
Outdoor mass, Italian entertainment, food, children's area

(AVAC) Folk Festival
Allegheny Valley Association of Churches
724–266–0606
Bull Creek Presbyterian Church ballfield, Tarentum
Mid-August
Pig and corn roasts, entertainment

*Fleatique/Antiques Market

September

Syrian Picnic
St. George Antiochian Orthodox Church
724–335–5223
1150 Leishman Street, New Kensington
Mid-September

*Fleatique/Antiques Market

October

Harvest Festival
Burtner House
724–224–7999
Burtner Road, exit 15 off Route 28, Natrona Heights
Mid-October

Fall Hike
Roaring Run Trail Pavilion
724–478–3366
Deerwood Beers Community Park, Apollo
www.roaringrun.org
Mid- to late October
Includes a stream fording

*Fleatique/Antiques Market
*Bluegrass Day
*Country Day

November

*Bluegrass Day
*Country Day

December

Kolenda (Polish Christmas Caroling)
St. Francis of Paola Church
724–763–1196
736 5th Avenue, Ford City
Carols in Polish and English

Slovak Stedry Vecer
Holy Martyrs Roman Catholic Church
724–224–0770
353 West 9th Avenue, Tarentum
Traditional Christmas Eve Slovak dinner

*Bluegrass Day
*Country Day

Steel I-beam rolled in a structural mill

Song
March of the Rolling-Mill Men

*Rouse, ye noble sons of Labor,
And protect your country's honor,
Who with bone, and brain, and fibre,
Make the nation's wealth.
Lusty lads, with souls of fire,
Gallant sons of noble sire,
Lend your voice and raise your banner,
Battle for the right.
Heater, roller, rougher,
Catcher, puddler, helper,
All unite and join the fight,
And might for right encounter;
In the name of truth and justice,
Stem the tide of evil practice,
Mammon's sordid might and av'rice,
Our land from ruin save.*

*Ye who aid our locomotion,
Wield the "cord which binds the nation,"
Honest types of God's creation,
Honor to your names.
Hearts of oak and arms of metal,
Who by dint of skill and muscle,
Fashion bridge and iron vessel,
Ever true and brave.
Heater, roller, rougher,
Catcher, puddler, helper,
All unite and join the fight,
And might for right encounter;
Let's be firm, with soul unbending,
'Mid the flash and sparks ascending,
Vulcan's sons are now arising,
Comrades, all unite.*

— By Reese E. Lewis, in the *National Labor Tribune*, March 30, 1875

Youghiogheny Route

Southeast from Pittsburgh

Mountains of Fire

Coal barons and coke kings, coal workers and coke pullers, magnates and miners, patches and palaces were united in one industrial enterprise — making coal into coke, the fuel for steel. For most of a century, hundreds of beehive ovens burned day and night across the hills and valleys of Fayette and Westmoreland Counties, which are so quiet and green now. These "Mountains of Fire" produced millions of tons of the highest-quality coke to power steel mills throughout the Pittsburgh industrial district.

Spread through the Youghiogheny River area and centered along the Chestnut Ridge between Connellsville and Scottdale, the coal mining and coke production industry came to define and dominate this part of southwestern Pennsylvania. It reshaped and expanded older farming and market communities such as Uniontown. It created scores of company-built "patch" settlements such as Morewood, Leisenring, Bessemer, and Indian Head. It changed the human face of the region to a diverse mix of northern, eastern, and southern Europeans, and African-Americans as companies recruited immigrant workers by the thousands. It absorbed and built upon the technical know-how of the region's early iron-furnace industry. It spurred the growth of other industries, such as railroads and glassmaking, which in turn also prompted the development of new towns — Greensburg, Latrobe, Youngwood, and Mt. Pleasant.

Visitors to the Rivers of Steel's Youghiogheny Route today can travel back in time to the era when coke was king, as they tour Henry Clay Frick's birthplace in West Overton, gaze at the sumptuous Linden Hall mansion in Dawson, view the world-famous industrial scenes at the Westmoreland Museum of American Art in Greensburg, visit the exhibits at the Coal and Coke Heritage Center in Connellsville, and ride the rails at the Youngwood Railroad Museum. They can stop to see the Wharton Furnace or learn about the coke-making process at Mammoth Park's coke ovens. They can see how industrial and ethnic traditions have continued in the region as they watch glass blowers at the Youghiogheny Glass Company, see Benedictine monks grinding grain at the Saint Vincent Grist Mill, or view the Syrian Orthodox icons at Antiochian Village near Ligonier. Guests are always welcome at community events and church festivals such as the annual Mount Saint Macrina Byzantine Catholic pilgrimage in Uniontown or the Slovenian Grape Festival in Herminie.

top: **Henry Clay Frick**
bottom: **Coke oven worker**
opposite page: **Beehive coke ovens by night**

Youghiogheny Route

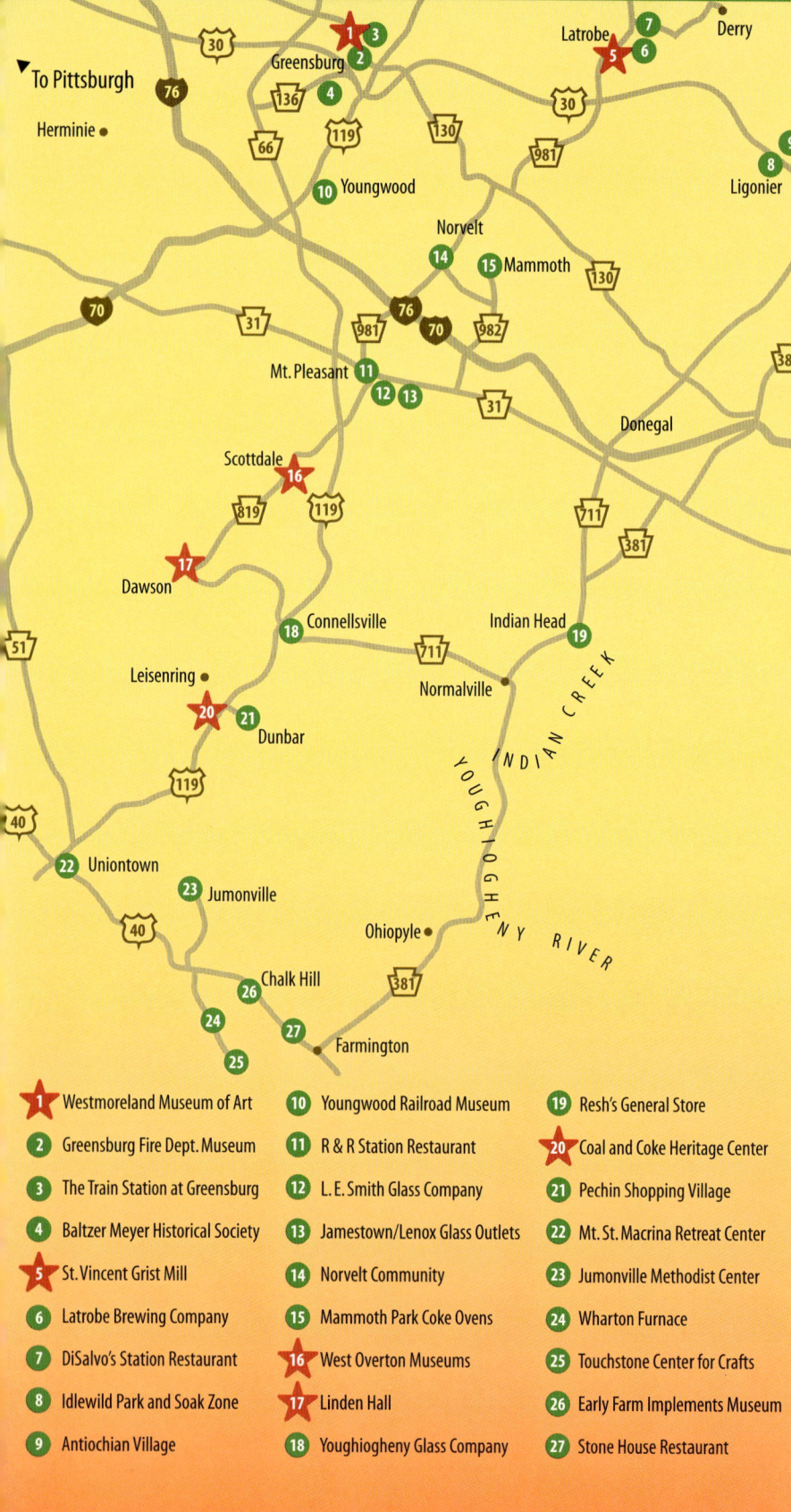

1. Westmoreland Museum of Art
2. Greensburg Fire Dept. Museum
3. The Train Station at Greensburg
4. Baltzer Meyer Historical Society
5. St. Vincent Grist Mill
6. Latrobe Brewing Company
7. DiSalvo's Station Restaurant
8. Idlewild Park and Soak Zone
9. Antiochian Village
10. Youngwood Railroad Museum
11. R & R Station Restaurant
12. L. E. Smith Glass Company
13. Jamestown/Lenox Glass Outlets
14. Norvelt Community
15. Mammoth Park Coke Ovens
16. West Overton Museums
17. Linden Hall
18. Youghiogheny Glass Company
19. Resh's General Store
20. Coal and Coke Heritage Center
21. Pechin Shopping Village
22. Mt. St. Macrina Retreat Center
23. Jumonville Methodist Center
24. Wharton Furnace
25. Touchstone Center for Crafts
26. Early Farm Implements Museum
27. Stone House Restaurant

Southeast from Pittsburgh

GREENSBURG

From Pittsburgh: Take I-76 E to Irwin exit 67. Follow US 30 E to Blairsville/ Connellsville exit. Left on US 119 N (becomes Main St.) into Greensburg.

Half-Day Tour: Sites 1–4
Westmoreland Museum of Art: US 119 N into Greensburg (becomes Main St.). Follow N. Main St. up hill to Museum on right. ☎ **Greensburg Fire Museum:** Left (south) 5 blocks on Main St. Just after City Hall, right into parking lot. Museum is in freight depot behind City Hall. **The Train Station at Greensburg:** Right (north) on Main St. to Westmoreland County Courthouse. Left on W. Otterman St. Right on Harrison Ave. into station parking lot. ☎ **Baltzer Meyer Historical Society:** Right on Ehalt St. Left 1 block on Vannear Ave. (PA 130 S). Right on W. Otterman St. Left on N. Spring Ave. Bear right on W. Newton St. (PA 136 W). Go 2 mi. Left on Baltzer Meyer Pike. The Historical Society is in Old Zion Lutheran Church on left. **Return to Pittsburgh:** PA 136 W to PA 66 S to I-76 W.

SYMBOLS	
	Must-See Site
	Point of Interest Site
	Industry
	Folklife
	Nature
	Art & Architecture
	Food
	Shopping
E	Events Calendar
☎	Phone Ahead

Westmoreland Museum of American Art
724–837–1500
221 North Main Street, Greensburg
www.wmuseumaa.org
Wed–Sun, 11AM–5PM; Th, 11AM–9PM; Closed most holidays
Adults: $3 donation; Children under 12, free

The Westmoreland Museum of American Art presides over Greensburg like a duchess — an elegant, columned building situated on a hill overlooking the city's main street. Opened in 1959, its focus from the beginning was to collect and exhibit American and southwestern Pennsylvania art. It quickly acquired works by world-renowned American artists such as Mary Cassatt, John Singer Sargent, and Winslow Homer. But it is two of the museum's regional collections that provide a high point to the visit: Southwestern Pennsylvania Landscapes and Valley of Work: Scenes of Industry. Together they portray the evolution of southwestern Pennsylvania's landscape from rural farmland to mighty industrial complex so vividly that they merit the annotation "Must-See Site."

Southwestern Pennsylvania Landscapes offers the works of George Hetzel, Charles Linford, Joseph Woodwell, and others who during the time of rapid industrialization captured the pastoral splendor of the region's mountains, woodlands, and streams.

Valley of Work records southwestern Pennsylvania's transformation into an industrial system through the eyes of artists such as Aaron Harry Gorson. A pioneer of industrial landscape painting, Gorson was an urban poet with a paintbrush, in love with the nighttime beauty of steelmaking Pittsburgh, the glow of the many lights and their effects on the multi-shaped clouds of smoke rising above the curving Monongahela and Allegheny Rivers.

These collections offer a stunning "before and after" view of our region and a chance to see top-notch works of art inspired by industry.

above: Pittsburgh Mills, **painting by Ernest Lawson (1873–1939), 1930.**

below: Pittsburgh, **painting by Otto Kuhler (1894–1976), n.d.**

Youghiogheny Route

②
Greensburg Fire Department Museum
724–832–7904
416 South Main Street, Greensburg
www.greensburgfire.org
☎ Phone ahead.

Tucked behind City Hall and dedicated to everyone's local heroes, the Greensburg Fire Museum opened in 1967 to preserve the region's 200-year history of firefighting.

The Museum's exhibits include antique firefighting equipment from Pittsburgh and Saint Vincent Archabbey in nearby Latrobe, as well as a display showing technical advancements in firefighting. For example, collaborating with the Jameson Coal & Coke Company, the Greensburg Fire Department adapted coal mine firefighting techniques, such as the use of foam, to extinguish intense fires in enclosed spaces of buildings.

Firefighting is not just a job — it's a way of life. Firefighters used to be organized in fraternal orders based upon ethnicity, religion, or social status. But, by the end of the 19th century in Greensburg, Poles, Germans, and Italians from all walks of life — bankers, shop clerks, and mill and railroad workers — served together to protect their community. The Parade Circle display shows the all-volunteer Fire Department as a vital social organization, complete with its own marching band. The whole family was involved and they have a right to be proud. The Greensburg Fire Department band has won more than twenty awards in local competitions!

This 1805 Pat Lyon pump wagon was acquired by the Greensburg Fire Department from the City of Pittsburgh shortly after the Civil War and restored in the 1990s by local Amish wagon makers.

③
The Train Station at Greensburg
724–850–7245 (Red Star Brewery)
101 Ehalt Street at Harrison Avenue, Greensburg
Mon–Th, 11:30am–10pm; Fri, 11:30am–11pm; Sat, noon–11pm

Designed by architect William Cookman for the Pennsylvania Railroad and opened to the public in 1911, the Train Station is still a working terminal. Within the restored station, the Red Star Brewery & Grille offers visitors a taste of German heritage.

Beer vats line the entry to the Red Star Brewery & Grille. The last time you could sip a locally brewed beer in Greensburg was before Prohibition.

Southeast from Pittsburgh

4
Baltzer Meyer Historical Society
724–836–6915
Baltzer Meyer Pike, Greensburg
April–Oct: Mon, Wed, 10AM–2PM; Nov–Mar: Wed, 10AM–2PM or
☎ Phone ahead.

People of German descent come from near and far to find their ancestors in the archives of the Baltzer Meyer Historical Society, named for one of Greensburg's earliest settlers.

Jackie Turney of Jeannette researches Turney ancestry in *Old and New Westmoreland*, a genealogy record book.

Greensburg and Latrobe

Strung like beads along the Pennsylvania Railroad mainline, Greensburg and Latrobe owe their development to the industrialization of the railroad era.

Once home to the Seneca and other Native Americans, Latrobe was explored by George Washington's surveyors around 1750 and later settled by Scots-Irish and German immigrant farmers. In 1851, Oliver W. Barnes, an agent for the Pennsylvania Railroad, bought 140 acres on which he established the

Westmoreland County Courthouse

railroad line, laying out streets for a new town that he named **Latrobe** after his college roommate. Irish immigrant David Williams, a contractor for the Pennsylvania railroad, helped organize the borough government in 1854 and donated land for a Catholic church and school. German Benedictine monks established Saint Vincent Archabbey in 1846.

The railroad encouraged firms such as Latrobe Electric Steel and McKenna Metals (now Kennametal), as well as brickmaking and ceramics operations, distilleries, and a woolen mill.

Greensburg was named for Revolutionary War General Nathaniel Greene. Incorporated in 1799 as Westmoreland's county seat, the town grew quickly in the late 19th century, spurred by the establishment of the Pennsylvania Railroad in the 1850s and the discovery of rich soft-coal deposits, which made Greensburg a commercial hub for the small mining communities in the area. Irish and German Catholic settlers

The Palace Theater

were later joined by Italian immigrants, who came to work in the area's glass and other industries. The Roman Catholic church established the Greensburg Diocese, and St. Joseph's Academy for women (now Seton Hill University) was founded in 1918. Greensburg now is a regional educational and cultural center, with a University of Pittsburgh branch campus and the **Westmoreland Museum of American Art,** which features works by local and national artists.

Youghiogheny Route

LATROBE • LIGONIER

From Pittsburgh: *Take I-76 E to Irwin exit 67. Take US 30 E to stoplight at St. Vincent Dr.*

One-Day Tour: Sites: 5–9
St. Vincent Grist Mill: *Left on St. Vincent Dr. past church and monastery. Left at "T" in road. Grist Mill is first building on right.* ***Latrobe Brewing Company:*** *Continue on US 30 E. Left on PA 981 N. Cross small bridge into Latrobe. Bear left at "Y." Left on Ligonier St. Follow signs to Brewery.* ***DiSalvo's Restaurant:*** *From Brewery driveway, right on Ligonier St. Left on Washington St. Right on Alexandria St. under trestle to stoplight. Right on Depot St. Restaurant is on right.* ***Idlewild Park and Soak Zone:*** *Go 5 mi. on US 30 E toward Ligonier. Park is on right.* ☎ ***Antiochian Village:*** *Follow US 30 E into Ligonier. Left on PA 711 N. Go 4 mi. Left at "Y" (Sheetz Gas Station). Stay on PA 711 N. Go 4 mi. Antiochian Village is on right.* ***Return to Pittsburgh:*** *US 30 W to I-76 W.*

Famous as the hometown of Fred Rogers and Arnold Palmer, Latrobe also claims the first banana split sundae and the first professional football team.

LATROBE

Saint Vincent Grist Mill and General Store
724–537–0304
300 Fraser Purchase Road, Latrobe
www.stvincent.edu
Mon–Sat, 9 AM–4 PM; Sun, NOON–4 PM

St. Vincent Gristmill

The Miller's Knot

Around the turn of the 6th century, a young student of law and philosophy went in search of God. When Benedict of Nursia finally emerged from his solitude, prayer, and penance, he established a monastery near Cassino, Italy. As word of Saint Benedict's exploits began to grow, so did his following.

Centuries later, one follower was Boniface Wimmer. A monk from the Benedictine Abbey of Metten, Bavaria, Father Wimmer left his homeland for America. His mission was to educate the sons of German immigrants and to establish a new monastery in the new world. By 1846, Father Wimmer had accomplished his goal — and much more. Settling in the foothills of the Chestnut Ridge (near Latrobe), he assumed responsibility for the existing Saint Vincent parish, and then founded the Saint Vincent Archabbey, Seminary, and College.

Today, the Saint Vincent Archabbey — the first Benedictine order in the United States — has 185 monks living, working, and studying in the community or serving in other parishes. It remains true to Father

Wimmer's vision of self-sufficiency: the community boasts its own power plant, fire department, machine shop, printing press, and gristmill.

Still turning wheat into flour, the gristmill operates much as it did in the beginning. Built in 1854, the three-story mill was originally powered by steam generated by a coal furnace, which was stoked by the monks who mined their own coal. Employing an elaborate series of elevators and chutes and two burrstones (each weighing one ton), the milling process can transform a single bushel of wheat into 36 pounds of unbleached flour.

Throughout the decades, the gristmill has undergone expansions, renovations, and a conversion to electricity in 1952. Today, the mill and general store stand as the cornerstones to Saint Vincent's museum and visitor's center.

The public is invited to watch the gristmill in action and purchase bags of Saint Vincent's own whole wheat flour, unbleached flour, corn meal, and bran — all hand-tied with the traditional miller's knot. Although the monks no longer bake their own bread for sale, nearby Friendship Farms (established in 1795) has filled the void, following the Saint Vincent recipes. Loaves of Monastery Bread are available at the mill's general store.

Visitors are also welcome in the museum's Environmental Education Center. Here Saint Vincent students, with Department of Environmental Protection, Pennsylvania Mountain Service Corps, and AmeriCorps volunteers, monitor the watershed restoration efforts known as the Monastery Run Improvement Project.

Part of the region's legacy can be found in what the mining industry left behind. For more than 75 years, the Westmoreland and Fayette Coal Company, Mount Pleasant Coke Company, Latrobe Coal Company, Mount Pleasant By-Product Coal Company, and the Benedictine Society worked the local mines. But as the plants shut down and the mines stood idle, contaminants — like alkaline and iron — began to seep into the groundwater. The Monastery Run Project was created in the early 1990s to find an effective way to deal with the ongoing challenge of abandoned mine drainage. The project consists of 20 acres of wetlands treatment facilities.

Saint Vincent College helps to prepare its 1,200-plus students to deal with the challenges of life after college. The school offers a four-year, co-ed, liberal arts education, while the Saint Vincent Basilica provides spiritual guidance. Construction of the Romanesque church was started in 1892 and completed 13 years later. The Benedictine monks gather there twice a day to pray.

St. Vincent Archabbey

Wheat Becomes Bread

 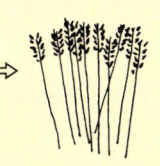 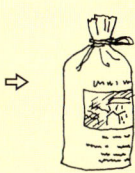 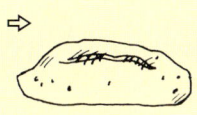

St. Vincent's leases land to a farmer in New Alexandria who grows grain to make flour.

St. Vincent's buys the grain from the farmer, grinds the flour at their grist mill, and sells it to Friendship Farms in Lycippus.

Friendship Farms Bakery bakes "Monastery Bread" using St. Vincent's grains and recipe, and sells it back to St. Vincent's.

St. Vincent's sells the bread at the Gristmill General Store.

Youghiogheny Route

Latrobe Brewing Company
724–537–5545 or 724–532–5540
119 Jefferson Street, Latrobe
Gift shop and video tour: Mon–Fri, 9AM–5PM; Sat, 9AM–3PM

Latrobe Brewing Company opened its doors in 1893 when the town was a growing center of industry and trade, and the area offered natural resources and easy railroad access. In 1899, the company was sold to Pittsburgh Brewing Company and became one of that company's 16 western Pennsylvania breweries. The company closed its doors during Prohibition, but in 1933, after Prohibition ended, the Tito brothers bought the brewery. They developed Rolling Rock, an extra-pale lager, in 1939. Over the next decades, Rolling Rock grew into a well-known regional brand.

Some people believe the number "33" on the back of the Rolling Rock bottle stands for 1933, the year Prohibition was repealed.

Courtesy of Latrobe Brewing Company

DiSalvo's Station Restaurant
724–539–0500
325 McKinley Avenue, Latrobe
www.disalvosrestaurant.com
Tues–Fri, 11AM–10PM; Sat, 4–11PM; Sun, 10AM–9PM

Uniting the tastes, sounds, and sights of the region's ethnic and industrial heritage, DiSalvo's offers the chance to savor local Italian cuisine in a restored passenger station as trains rumble overhead.

DiSalvo's features a real dining car... a restaurant within a restaurant!

LIGONIER

Idlewild Park and Soak Zone
724–238–3666
US 30 E, Ligonier
www.idlewild.com
Park gates open at 10AM.
Attraction times vary; see Idlewild's web site for information.

When William Darlington decided to sell a tract of land in Ligonier, he stipulated that the property be used for "picnic purposes or pleasure grounds." On paper, those words were nothing more than a simple clause in a contract. In reality, however, they have served as the foundation of fun that has become Idlewild Park.

On May 1, 1878, Judge Thomas Mellon agreed to Darlington's terms and soon began developing the land, which happened to be a railroad right-of-way. He built campgrounds, a man-made lake, picnic areas, and a large hall on both sides of the tracks.

As the owner of the Ligonier Valley Railroad, he recognized the opportunity to not only create a destination, but also provide the primary means of getting there.

Up until that time, the sole function of the Ligonier Valley Railroad was to move coal from the Fort Palmer mines (located five miles north of Ligonier) to Latrobe. With the addition of a stop at the newly created Idlewild Park, some of the trains were pressed into passenger service. As a result, city dwellers could travel from nearby Pittsburgh to Ligonier for a fun-filled day in the country.

Through the years, a bandstand, pavilions, and rides were introduced. The three-row Philadelphia Toboggan Company Carousel, the Whip, Skooters (bumper cars), and the Rollo Coaster still run today.

Eventually, people started to find their own way to Idlewild via the automobile. So when the Ligonier Railroad made its final run in 1951, the park, under the new ownership of the Macdonald family, hardly missed a beat. Kennywood Park Corporation took over operations in 1983, and Idlewild kicked into high gear.

Nowadays, Idlewild is home to Jumpin' Jungle (a hands-on play area), Story Book Forest, Mister Rogers' Neighborhood of Make-Believe, a nine-acre kiddie-land called Raccoon Lagoon, Hootin' Holler (built to look like a mining town), Olde Idlewild, and the Soak Zone, which features 14 wet rides.

Visitors used to come by train to the park. Today you can ride a mini-train to re-create that experience.

Photos courtesy of Idlewild Park

Hootin' Holler replicates a turn-of-the-century mining town.

Youghiogheny Route

Philip Zimmerman, Iconographer

It is of this world, yet otherworldly. It is of this moment, yet timeless. Iconography — the highly stylized depiction of religious figures or events — is an art form characteristic of Eastern Orthodox religions.

Often featuring gold-leaf backgrounds and strong geometric patterns, icon paintings are about expressing spirituality, not human sentimentality. As a result, the seemingly expressionless faces of Christ, the Virgin, and the saints are designed to serve as visual reminders of the divine.

This ancient art has found new life in the hands of modern-day practitioners like Philip Zimmerman. After completing a seven-year apprenticeship with Bishop Job at St. John the Baptist Orthodox Church in Black Lick, Pa., Zimmerman opened his own studio in 1988.

Now a teacher himself, Zimmerman also paints for churches throughout the country and for private clients. Locally, his icons can be seen at SS. Peter and Paul Chapel in Antiochian Village near Ligonier, the Holy Ghost Orthodox Church in Ambridge, and St. Mary's Carpatho-Russian Orthodox Church in Jenners.

But don't expect to find Zimmerman's signature on any of his works. "Icons are always derived or copied from something before," he says. "Painting icons is being creative within a boundary. It's remaining faithful."

9 Antiochian Village
724–238–3677
PA 711 N, Ligonier
www.antiochianvillage.org
Bookstore: Mon–Fri, 9AM–5PM
☎ Phone ahead for museum tour.

It is a place where beauty is appreciated, spirituality is affirmed and business is conducted. For nearly 25 years, the Antiochian Village Heritage and Learning Center has been offering people of the Christian faith a temporary respite from the real world.

Purchased in 1978 by the Antiochian Orthodox Christian Archdiocese of North America, the 300 acres that make up the village were home to one of the earliest Presbyterian worship centers and schools in western Pennsylvania. When Metropolitan Philip, the archbishop of the Antiochian Orthodox community, was told that this parcel of land was for sale, he traveled to the site. He found the perfect setting for a refuge where youth could learn a Christian way of life, and where all ages could learn about their faith.

The Antiochian Orthodox Christian faith has its roots in Syria, and can be traced back to the first followers of Christ. Today, Antiochian Village is headquarters for its archdioceses and home to campgrounds, recreational facilities, meditation trails, an ecumenical chapel, a theological library with some 21,000 books, lodging facilities, a dining room, meeting rooms, and a museum.

Throughout the year, Orthodox, Christian, and nonprofit groups hold conventions and retreats on the grounds. The museum, however, is currently open to the public by appointment only, but that's about to change. Continuing to fulfill Metropolitan Philip's vision, the village has announced an expansion project. Plans call for the construction of a new wing to house the museum's collection of icons (some dating back centuries) and artifacts, including a Damascene tea service, drums and zithers, and articles of clothing, such as a *jallabiyah* (caftan) and an *aba'ah* (cloak).

top: **Icon:** *The Virgin Hodegetria,* **12th or 13th century, Middle East**

center: **Enameled brass teapot and pitcher, 19th century, Damascus, Syria**

bottom: **Terracotta oil lamps, 5th or 6th century, Tunisia**

Southeast from Pittsburgh

MT. PLEASANT AREA

From Pittsburgh: *Take I-76 E to New Stanton exit 75.*

One-Day Tour: Sites 10–15

☎ ***Youngwood Railroad Museum:*** *Take US 119 N to Youngwood. Right on Depot St. Railroad Museum is on the right before tracks.*
R & R Station Restaurant: *Take US 119 S to PA 31 E (becomes Main St.) into Mt. Pleasant. Restaurant is on the right before tracks.*
L. E. Smith Glass Company: *Stay on PA 31 E. Right on Factory St. Outlet is on corner of Factory and Liberty Sts.* ***Jamestown Crystal Outlet & Lenox Outlets:*** *Continue .25 mi. on PA 31 E. Outlets are on right.* ***Norvelt Community:*** *Stay on PA 31 W. Go 1.5 mi. to traffic circle. Take PA 819 N. Go 1.5 mi. Take PA 981 N into Norvelt.* ***Mammoth Park Coke Ovens:*** *Stay on PA 981 N. Right at brown Mammoth Park sign (SR 2012 E) to PA 982 N into Mammoth. Left at main Park sign. Follow signs to coke ovens.* ***Return to Pittsburgh:*** *PA 982 S to PA 31 W to US 119 N to I-76W.*

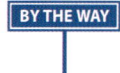

Youngwood was the first "hump" railroad sorting yard in the United States. A hump yard has a central mound from which rail cars are released to coast to the correct track.

YOUNGWOOD

Youngwood Historical & Railroad Museum
724–925–7355
1 Depot Street, Youngwood
www.yrrm.org
☎ Phone ahead.

Bill Marietta helps keep Youngwood's railroad heritage rolling.

Viewed in strictly practical terms, trains are about transporting things — people, steel, scrap iron, coal — from one place to another. But when seen from a more romantic vantage point, trains are about the journey, the wanderlust, the adventure. The Youngwood Historical & Railroad Museum seeks to pay tribute to both sides of the track.

The museum arrived on the scene in 1982, the year Youngwood's depot building was set to be demolished. Working up a full head of steam, concerned citizens and railroad enthusiasts joined forces to save the building and preserve the town's locomotive legacy.

That legacy got its start during the 1870s when the original train crossing was established at the junction of John Young's and James Woods' properties. By 1902, the newly chartered borough of Youngwood boasted a 15-bay roundhouse, a switch tower, machine shops, a sand house, tool and rail-line sheds, miles of mainline and spur tracks — and the depot building, home to the Pennsylvania Railroad's baggage and passenger station.

Courtesy of Youngwood Historical & Railroad Museum

Youghiogheny Route

Twenty years later, one-seventh of the nation's supply of coal and coke passed through the Youngwood yard. And those train cars — sometimes as many as 700 a day — ran during the Great Depression and World Wars I and II. It wasn't until the region's industrial stronghold began to weaken that the trains began to slow down.

In the 1980s — with the fate of Youngwood's depot building hanging in the balance — the idea of creating a museum picked up speed. Nowadays, this modest structure is home to an assortment of locomotive paraphernalia, including photographs, paintings, maps, miniature train collections, uniforms, a telegraph machine, lanterns, time books, and the original crew board.

And with the help of the Westmoreland Scenic Railroad, events such as Civil War Train Raids, Western Train Robberies, Bob Day, the Polar Express, and other excursions are scheduled from late April (Arbor Day) through late December.

Wooden trainset designed and built by Mr. Gettamy of Greensburg

The Bobs

In July 1999, a letter arrived at the Youngwood Historical & Railroad Museum. "Dear Friends," it read. "Here's a contribution of $500.00 if you will set up a binder display at the museum listing all the friends and neighbors named 'Bob' who are interested in railroading. I will send an additional $500.00. I will remain anonymous and will follow your progress."

This Youngwood native went on to say that he was a fireman on the Pennsylvania Railroad, "and you never forget the great experiences."

Well, one Bob led to another. The first to join the brave new world of Bobs was Robert "Bob" Geiger. He was quickly followed by the father–son Bobs, Robert "Bob" Stephen Reintgen and Robert "Bob" Joseph Reintgen.

Soon, Bobs from near (Greensburg) and far (Kailua, Hawaii) were lending their names to the cause. At last count, there were some 250 Bobs and even a few "Wannabes" on board.

To thank all the wonderful Bobs, August is now officially Bob Month in Youngwood. And, as if that weren't enough, the museum hosts a party on the last Saturday of the month inviting every Tom, Sue, and Mary to become a "Bob for the Day."

True to his word, Bob Anonymous sent that additional $500.

MT. PLEASANT

11

R & R Station Restaurant and Inn
724–547–7545
19 West Main Street, Mt. Pleasant
www.mtpleasantpa.com/randr
Sun–Th, 7AM–9PM; Fri & Sat, 7AM–MIDNIGHT

Since 1883, this local landmark's proximity to the railroad tracks has made it instrumental in the town's transportation history. The family-owned hotel's 17 rooms are all appointed in train décor. Guests can enjoy homestyle cooking in the dining room or in the Caboose Lounge.

Railroad memorabilia surround Stanley Lingelbach, Dick Hartman, and Joe Hlinka as they enjoy lunch at the R & R.

Mount Pleasant

Probably named for Mount Pleasant Presbyterian Church, built by settlers in 1774, the town of Mt. Pleasant was laid out by Andrew McCready in 1797 and incorporated in 1828. In addition to Scots and Scots-Irish, early community residents included Germans, particularly Mennonites. In the late 19th century, coal and coke began drawing workers from Poland, Hungary, and Italy. Mt. Pleasant played a significant role in the 1891 "Morewood Massacre," the struggle between management and the immigrant miners at H. C. Frick's Morewood Mine. From the 1850s on, the labor force and abundance of coal fuel attracted the glass industry, later including such firms as L. E. Smith Glass Company and Lenox China.

Each September, the Mt. Pleasant Glass and Ethnic Festival highlights the town's industrial and cultural heritage with bagpipers and polka bands, ethnic foods, and glass-blowing demonstrations.

The New Haven Hose Company Bagpipe Band on parade at the Mt. Pleasant Glass and Ethnic Festival

L. E. Smith Glass Company
724–547–3544
1900 Liberty Street, Mt. Pleasant
www.lesmithglass.com
Factory Tours: Mon–Fri, 9AM–2PM
Factory Store: Mon–Sat, 9AM–5PM; Sun, NOON–5PM
Closed on weekends Jan–Mar and on national holidays

The beginnings of the American glass industry can be traced back to the Jamestown Colony, circa 1608. According to the L. E. Smith Glass Company, not much has changed in 400 years. Workers at the plant still use many of the same tools and techniques their forebears did.

That's something visitors can see for themselves during daily factory tours. Past the double doors that separate the gift shop from the plant, tanks of molten glass reach temperatures as high as 2,500° F. Silica sand, ash, potash, limestone, and cullet (broken or crushed glass) melt to a red-hot, honey-like liquid.

Dipping into the tank, the gatherer takes a gob of molten glass onto the end of a punty (a solid iron rod with a clay head). Working with the presser, he drops the gob into a mold. The newly formed and still-hot candy dish, dinner plate, or bunny rabbit figurine is then carried on a simple wooden paddle to the lehr (a long annealing oven) to cool. From there, each piece is inspected for chips, cracks, and bubbles.

Following the tour, visitors are ushered back to the factory outlet. Using many of its original molds, some forged nearly a century ago, the company makes colored and crystal glass items, such as punch bowls, vases, and pitchers.

The company got its start in 1907, producing mustard containers and inkwells. By the early 1920s, L. E. Smith added automobile headlight lenses to its list of products, and for the next two decades made more than half of all Ford lenses. Recognizing the value of handmade glass, L. E. Smith carries on the traditions of this time-honored industry.

Pressed glassware at the L. E. Smith showroom

Youghiogheny Route

Handmade glass pieces by regional artists

Jamestown Crystal Outlet
724–547–7630
Route 31 E, Mount Pleasant
Mon–Fri, 10AM–5:30PM; Sat, 10AM–6PM; Sun, 11AM–5PM

Lenox Outlet
724–547–9555
Route 31 E, Mount Pleasant
www.lenox.com
Mon–Sat, 10AM–6PM; Sun, NOON–5PM

The Lenox China Company was founded in 1889 in the United States by artisan Walter Scott Lenox. In 1918, Lenox China became the first American company to create an official table service for the White House. The company's Mount Pleasant plant operated from 1970 to 2002. Today, sharing a building that housed the Lenox factory retail store, the Jamestown Crystal Outlet and the Lenox Outlet showcase the region's handcrafted glass and chinaware. At the Jamestown Outlet, visitors can choose pieces by glass artists working throughout southwestern Pennsylvania. The Lenox Outlet offers items in many well-known patterns made by Lenox, still America's major producer of fine china.

Glass and China Industries

Southwestern Pennsylvania's abundance of silica-rich sand prompted the early establishment of china and glass industries in the region. Was there a connection to iron and steel? Yes — it was the presence of a workforce skilled in glass and china production that helped make possible the rapid rise of steel in the region, because the skills of the one industry transferred readily to the other.

In the first decades of the 19th century, English and German craft-workers established china and glass factories in Allegheny County, using local coal as their fuel. Along the south shore of the Monongahela River in Pittsburgh, for example, Bakewell & Pears produced flint china, including some specially commissioned for the White House in Washington, DC.

After the Civil War, the discovery of natural gas deposits in outlying areas prompted several Pittsburgh china and glass companies to relocate to Westmoreland, Armstrong, Beaver, and Washington Counties. From its original site in downtown Pittsburgh, Pittsburgh Plate Glass (now PPG) expanded to Creighton and Ford City. Duncan and Miller Glass relocated to "little" Washington. New firms built plants as well. The region became known for companies such as Mayer China in Beaver Falls and Lenox China in Mt. Pleasant. Blown glass and pressed glass for tableware, and plate glass for the construction and later the automobile industries, were produced in the region. Skilled Italian immigrants found work at the "glass houses" in Jeannette and Latrobe.

China is no longer made in southwestern Pennsylvania, but glass continues to flourish. PPG operates a plant near Creighton and a museum of plate glass is planned for Ford City (Alle-Kiski Route). Visitors can watch art glass being made at **Youghiogheny Glass**

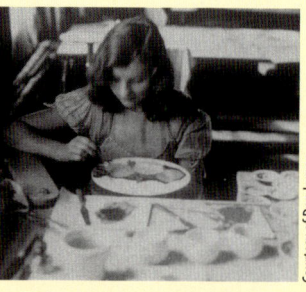

In Beaver Falls, steelworkers' wives and sisters earned money at Mayer China by hand-painting floral designs on dinnerware.

Courtesy of Don Inman

in Connellsville and see tableware production at **L. E. Smith Glass Company** in Mount Pleasant (Youghiogheny Route). They can enjoy gallery displays of locally made art glass at the **Jamestown Crystal Outlet** in Mount Pleasant (Youghiogheny Route) and the **Duncan and Miller Glass Museum** in Washington (Monongahela Route). Those with time to spend can learn glassmaking at **Touchstone Center for Crafts** (Youghiogheny Route) and at **Pittsburgh Glass Center** (Three Rivers Route).

Southeast from Pittsburgh

NORVELT

Norvelt Community
PA 981 N and SR 2021, Norvelt

Built by the U.S. government during the 1930s to promote self-sufficiency among unemployed coal miners, Norvelt was named for First Lady Eleanor Roosevelt, who championed both this "subsistence homestead" and its privately developed counterpart, Penn-Craft (Monongahela Route).

Courtesy of Library of Congress

MAMMOTH

Mammoth Park Coke Ovens
724–830–3950
Poker Road and PA 982 N, Mt. Pleasant
www.fay-west.com/westmoreland/mammoth_park/guide
Outdoors: Open year-round

Near a lake in Mammoth Park, visitors can explore a row of preserved beehive ovens and two narrow-gauge "larry" cars. Interpretive signs explain the cokemaking process.

During the Depression, the government hired artists and photographers to document Works Progress Administration (WPA) and Farmers Home Administration projects.

Courtesy of Library of Congress

One of artist Ben Shahn's photos of Norvelt life in the 1930s

Westmoreland Homesteads

The Norvelt Community, originally known as the Westmoreland Homesteads, sought to address the needs of unemployed bituminous coal miners and their families. It was designed by the Division of Subsistence Homesteads for "stranded industrial" workers to "help them build new lives."

Work began on the site in 1933 and, by 1937, 254 homes had been constructed. Government administrators and homesteaders worked together to develop Norvelt's community life.

A cooperative farm, store, and garment factory were developed. In addition, 23 social and community groups were organized in Norvelt. Today, a number of original houses remain, and Norvelt has been integrated into the surrounding community.

— www.lib.iup.edu/depts/ speccol/exhibits/norvelt.html (Indiana University of Pennsylvania web site).

Youghiogheny Route

Along PA 119 north of Scottdale, the 650-acre Sony Technology Center manufactures televisions and refurbishes computer monitors.

SCOTTDALE AREA

From Pittsburgh: Take I-76 E to New Stanton exit 75.

Half-Day Tour: Sites 16–17
West Overton Museums: Go 5 mi. on US 119 S. Take PA 31 E to Mt. Pleasant. Go 3 mi. on PA 819 S to West Overton Museums. **Linden Hall:** Stay on PA 819 S. Go 7.5 mi. Right on Dawson-Banning Rd. (SR 1002). Go 3 mi. Left on Linden Hall Rd. **Return to Pittsburgh:** Take US 119 N to I-76 W.

SCOTTDALE

West Overton Museums
724–887–7910
West Overton Village, Scottdale
www.westovertonmuseum.org
May 15–Oct 15: Tues–Sat, 10AM–4PM; Sun, 1–5PM
Adults: $6; Seniors: $4; Youth 7–17: $4; Youth 6 and under: free

above: The old distillery is now a main exhibit hall.
below: Whiskey bottle label

Sometimes it's difficult to imagine an icon of industry as a child. That's because history often brushes over those early years as it rushes to paint a portrait of power.

But everyone starts his or her journey in diapers — even Henry Clay Frick. By the time this coal and coke baron died in 1919, he had amassed a fortune and had earned a reputation as a ruthless businessman. But his story started nearly 70 years earlier.

Born in the rural town of West Overton, young Henry's greatest influence was his grandfather, Abraham Overholt. (Abraham's daughter, Elizabeth, married John W. Frick, and the couple had six children, including Henry Clay.) The Overholts were part of a community of German Mennonites who had immigrated to Bucks County, Pennsylvania. Led by Abraham's father, Henry Overholt, the group crossed the Alleghenies in the early 1800s and made a new home in Westmoreland County.

Today, West Overton encompasses 43 acres and is the only pre–Civil War village still standing in Pennsylvania. And the West Overton Museums — consisting of the Overholt Homestead, summer kitchen, wash house, springhouse, big red barn, carriage house, distillery, and other buildings yet to be restored — stand as a tribute to the town and its people, most notably Henry Clay Frick.

The Overholt Homestead

Southeast from Pittsburgh

That was the mandate set forth by Henry's daughter, Helen Clay Frick, when she founded the Westmoreland–Fayette Historical Society in 1928 to oversee the site. Nearly 60 years later, West Overton Village was named to the National Register of Historic Districts as an outstanding example of a 19th-century rural industrial village.

While touring the buildings, visitors will discover Clay (as he was called during his time at West Overton), the boy who was often ill, who worked the fields and fired the ovens and was a champion fiddle player. As Clay grew older, his grandfather paid him to keep the books in the family-owned and -operated distillery. Despite the fact that the Overholts were strict Mennonites, they recognized the value in producing rye whiskey from their grain.

The hay barn and the summer kitchen

Apparently, recognizing opportunities ran in the family. Seeing that the region was rich in bituminous coal deposits, Frick formed his own company and began buying land, building beehive coke ovens, and making a lot of money. By his early 30s, he was a millionaire living in Pittsburgh with his new bride, Adelaide Howard Childs.

Although he never again called West Overton home, his presence continues to be felt. Two floors of the distillery now house a number of Frick artifacts, including the chair he was sitting in when an attempt was made on his life during the Homestead Strike of 1892, as well as Overholt heirlooms like the family's hand-made coverlet collection and original whiskey bottles. There are also mining, glass (from L. E. Smith, Bryce, and Lenox), and pottery exhibits. Tours are available May 1 through October 31.

The coke king Henry Clay Frick

Throughout the year, West Overton hosts Civil War encampments, juried quilt shows, storytelling festivals, barn dances, and other seasonal activities. The 150-seat auditorium (located in the basement of the distillery) is a venue for lectures, musical presentations, and banquets. The former general store (once owned by Christian Overholt) is now The Quilt Patch, a retail shop.

Scottdale's "Coke King"

The H. C. Frick Coke Company was the largest coke producer in the world, operating nearly 40,000 acres of coal and 12,000 coke ovens, with a daily capacity of 25,000 tons. Frick prospered at a time when heavy industries and private fortunes were growing to unprecedented sizes. By the late 1870s, Frick bought out his partners. The company had nearly 1,000 employees, and Frick was a millionaire by the time he was 30.

— James Howard Bridge. *The Inside History of the Carnegie Steel Company; a Romance of Millions*, 1903.

Youghiogheny Route

DAWSON

Linden Hall
724–529–7543
432 Linden Hall Road, Dawson
www.lindenhallpa.com
Mansion: April 15–Oct: Mon–Fri, 11AM–3PM; Sun, by appointment only
Adults: $8; Seniors (62 yrs): $7; Groups (25 or more): $7 per person; Youth (12 and under): $4

On September 25, 1879, Sarah Moore married Philip Cochran. Her life was forever changed, although perhaps not in the ways she anticipated.

above: Linden Hall's formal gardens and spacious grounds invite a stroll.

below: Light floods Linden Hall's beautiful circular solarium.

Sarah Moore was the farmer's daughter from Lower Tyrone Township; Philip Cochran was the oldest son of Irish immigrants who made their family fortune mining coal and manufacturing coke in the Dawson–Vanderbilt area.

A year after the wedding day, the couple's only child, James, was born. But the happily-ever-after picture Sarah may have envisioned was not to be. As the turn of the century approached, tragedy followed. In 1899, Sarah's husband died, and then, in 1901, so did her son. While in mourning for Philip, Sarah built a Methodist Church in his honor. It stands today in the town of Dawson. But the loss of her son was more difficult to overcome.

Mrs. Cochran spent the next several years traveling abroad. During one visit to London's St. James's Palace, she conceived the notion of building an English Tudor mansion near her hometown, but it wasn't until 1911 that construction began. To that end, 60 stonecutters from Italy were commissioned to quarry stone on the property and then hand-cut it for the house. European artisans were called upon to cross the Atlantic to work alongside local craftsmen in carving the ornate woodwork and fashioning the marble, crystal, gold leaf, and sterling silver fittings.

Southeast from Pittsburgh

left top: **The formal dining room**
left center: **Signed Tiffany windows**
below: **Sarah Cochran**

Named for the linden trees Mrs. Cochran imported from Germany and planted throughout the 785-acre estate, Linden Hall was dedicated on December 25, 1913. The four-story mansion boasts 35 rooms, 27 fireplaces, 13 bath and powder rooms, and a tiled basement complete with billiard tables and bowling alleys.

Pipes from the hand-carved Aeolian organ (one of only three in the world) in the first floor's Great Hall, as well as on the third floor, create a stereo effect, and the signed Tiffany windows

gracing the main entranceway depict the property's formal gardens and fountain.

The final price tag exceeded the $2 million mark. Part of those expenses can be attributed to Mrs. Cochran's insistence on such modern conveniences as electricity (the rest of the town didn't turn on the lights until the 1930s), an elevator, and bathroom showers.

In its heyday, Linden Hall employed eight maids, two manservants, and 20 day workers. In her prime, Mrs. Cochran entertained every day, inviting Sunday school classes to visit and symphony orchestras to perform.

In 1936, Sarah Cochran died and her mansion became a seminary for a Ukrainian Byzantine order, a gambling casino, and, with the additions of a golf course, a swimming pool, tennis courts, and picnic grounds, a country club.

However, it wasn't until the United Steelworkers of America purchased the estate in 1976 that the grandeur of Linden Hall — a mansion built with coal and coke money — was restored.

Maintaining the country club amenities, the Steelworkers added a conference center, restaurant, and 74-room lodge to the grounds. Listed on the National Register of Historic Places, the mansion is now open for tours, holiday festivities, wedding receptions, and private parties.

Turn-of-the-century shower bath

Sarah Cochran

As a poor farmer's daughter, Sarah Moore married into a wealthy family. As the widow of a coal baron, she took control of her husband's business. As a woman, she redefined the roles of her society.

After the deaths of her husband, Philip Cochran, and her only child, James, Sarah found herself taking charge of Cochran Coal & Coke, personally supervising the building of Linden Hall, and making significant contributions to charities, schools, and other organizations throughout the region.

Her legacy, in the form of the Philip Cochran United Methodist Church in Dawson and the East Connellsville United Methodist Church, still stands today.

Youghiogheny Route

Glass Speak

cane *a strand or rod of glass.*

cold shop *a glassworking facility without a furnace or a glory hole.*

cut glass *glass ornamented or shaped by cutting or grinding with abrasive wheels.*

direct carving *shaping a block of glass by cutting portions of it away.*

enameled glass *glass decorated by fusing opaque glass powders to its surface.*

engraving *ornamenting glass by marking its surface with a diamond point or abrasive wheel.*

etching *marking or texturing glass by applying an acid solution.*

glass blowing *shaping glass by blowing air through an iron tube into a mass of molten glass.*

glory hole *an auxiliary furnace for reheating glass that has cooled while being worked on.*

gob *a lump of molten glass.*

hot shop *a glassworking facility with a furnace and a glory hole.*

lamp work *shaping glass rods or tubes softened by the flame of a blow torch.*

millefiori *decorative glass made by fusing multicolored glass canes together and melting and manipulating the resulting mass.*

punty *an iron rod used for handling molten glass.*

right: **Steve Fenstermacher shapes molten glass.**

below: **Youghiogheny Glass's glory hole**

CONNELLSVILLE AREA

From Pittsburgh: *Take I-76 E to New Stanton exit 75.*

One-Day Tour: Sites 18–21
Youghiogheny Glass Company: US 119 S to Connellsville. Left on PA 711 N (Crawford Ave.) past church. Youghiogheny Glass is on left. **Side trip to Resh's General Store:** Left on PA 711 N (Crawford Ave.) Go 13.5 mi. through Connellsville past Normalville. Right on Indian Head Rd. Resh's is on right. **Coal and Coke Heritage Center:** From Youghiogheny Glass, right on Crawford Ave. Left at stoplight on US 119 S. Go 6 mi. Right into Penn State/Fayette Campus. Heritage Center is in lower level of library. **Pechin's:** Return 1.5 mi. on US 119 N. Right on Pechin Rd. Go 1.7 mi. Pechin's is on right. **Return to Pittsburgh:** US 119 N to I-76 W.

CONNELLSVILLE

18 Youghiogheny Glass Company
724–628–0332
900 West Crawford Avenue, Connellsville
www.stainedglassbiz.com/youghiogheny
Mon, Tues, Wed, Fri, Sat, 10AM–5PM; Th, 10AM–7PM; Sun, NOON–4PM

Steve Fenstermacher sits patiently on a bench. He's not waiting for a train or a bus, but rather for his apprentice, Dave Bloom, to deliver the next gob of glass held high on the end of a punty rod.

With the iron rod braced across the arms of the bench, Fenstermacher begins the slow process of transforming the molten gob into a one-of-a-kind work of art. As his left hand spins the rod, his right hand uses a folded newspaper doused with water to gently tame the gob. (A folded newspaper is a time-honored tool of the trade.)

On cue, Bloom retrieves the punty and plunges the gob back into the "glory hole" or oven. Without missing a beat, he returns the rod to Fenstermacher's bench. Hardly glancing up, Fenstermacher takes a pair of calipers and starts to coax the glass into the shape of a giraffe.

For the next half-hour—the average time required to craft a single giraffe—Fenstermacher and Bloom continue their give and take. This pas-de-glass is performed within the confines of a building adjacent to the Youghiogheny Station Glass Gallery.

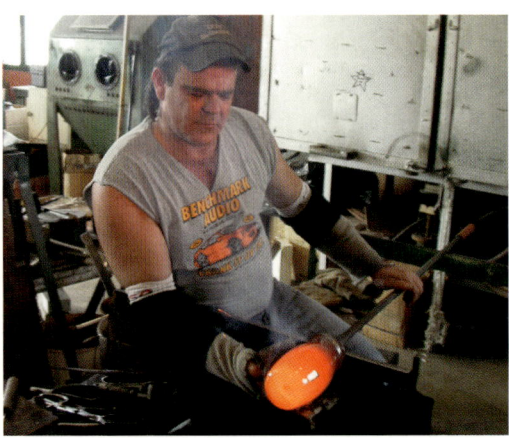

Southeast from Pittsburgh

Fenstermacher began his glass career as a bit gatherer, one of many jobs performed in a glass studio, when he was just 12 years old. After enrolling in an apprenticeship program at Steuben Crystal in Corning, New York, he emerged as the youngest person in the company's history to achieve "gaffer" or master glassworker status. He was just 24.

In 1989, he took on the role of research and development glassworker for Lenox Crystal in Mount Pleasant and then six years later moved his bench to Youghiogheny Station Glass. With Fenstermacher's skills and talents in place, Youghiogheny Station Glass has been able to add offhand (handblown) art glass to its line of sheet and stained-glass products.

Fenstermacher's work — including the giraffes — is on display and for sale in the gallery building at Youghiogheny Station. Housed in the old P&LE Railroad passenger station, the gallery highlights the work of regional and national glass artisans. Youghiogheny Glass also offers classes in stained-glass making for both beginners and advanced students.

Preserving many of its original features — like the ticket office, departure board, lighting fixtures, and wood and marble — the station is a registered site with the National Register of Historic Places.

top: Blown glass
bottom: Sheet glass

Connellsville — Coke Capital of the World

Connellsville, one of the oldest towns in southwestern Pennsylvania, has a rich industrial and ethnic history. Named for Zachariah Connell, an early settler, the town was founded along the Youghiogheny River in 1793, at a place navigable for rafting, near a stone quarry, a coal bank, and stands of timber. Flatboat building for westward pioneers became an important industry during the town's first 50 years. Iron-smelting furnaces were built to produce nails and tools, using charcoal made from the nearby forests, and, by 1830, brickyards operated as well.

From the 1860s on, boat building gave way to the railroads, whose tracks provided a more economical method of shipping cargo. At the height of the region's industrial period, almost every major rail line went through Connellsville.

Connellsville became most famous, however, for producing coke fuel for the steel industry, utilizing the area's rich deposits of low-sulphur, metallurgical bituminous coal. The first successful beehive coke oven had been built only a short distance from the site of Zachariah Connell's original stone house. In 1865, a local brickyard began making firebrick for the coke ovens. By the late 19th century, the town had become the center of the Connellsville Coke District, a huge coke-producing area that stretched over 20 miles along the Chestnut Ridge.

The town's boom years came to an end early in the 20th century when the invention of by-product coking made the beehive coke oven process obsolete. In place of coke, new industries, especially glass, were started. In Connellsville today, the skies are clear. Visitors can take a walking tour to learn about the town's coal-dominated industrial past, and watch glass being made in its industrial present. On a pleasant day, they can stroll or ride along the Youghiogheny Trail, one of the region's finest hiking and biking trails, converted from the riverfront railroad beds.

1900s postcard showing Connellsville coke ovens by night

Rivers of Steel Archives

Youghiogheny Route

Coal and Coke Industries

Steelmaking starts with smelting iron ore to produce usable iron. The best fuel is coke, which burns hot, long, and evenly. Coke is made by baking coal for many hours. The finest metallurgical coke is made from the kind of low-sulphur, bituminous coal found in much of southwestern Pennsylvania.

Through the 19th century, coke was made in beehive-shaped, stone-and-firebrick ovens built near the coal mines, filling the air with smoke by day and a fiery glow by night. Railcars and barges carried the coke downriver to fuel the huge steel mills. At the height of the Steel Era, the Chestnut Ridge in Fayette and Westmoreland Counties and the hillsides of Greene and Washington Counties were lined with hundreds of beehive ovens operated by industrialists such as Henry Clay Frick and J. V. Thompson. Thousands of immigrant workers from southern and eastern Europe streamed into the company-built "patch towns," laboring round the clock.

But change was imminent. By 1920 beehive ovens were obsolete. Huge, centralized by-product coking plants were built near steel mills along the Monongahela River. They not only produced coke more efficiently, but also captured valuable gases, tar, and other by-products from the coke-baking process.

Today, coal is still mined in the region, generating electricity and fueling the remaining steel mills. Built in 1918, U. S. Steel's Clairton plant, the largest coke plant in the United States, produces 4.8 million tons of coke annu- ally — 20 percent of America's output — and 55 million gallons of by-products used for plastics and other goods.

Visitors can gaze in awe at the vast **RAG Cumberland Mine** coal tipple (Monongahela Route), follow former miners into the earth at the **Tour-Ed Mine** (Alle-Kiski Route), inspect beehive ovens at **Mammoth Park Coke Ovens** (Youghiogheny Route) and Marianna (Monongahela Route), and get a panoramic view of the by-product plant, **U. S. Steel Clairton Coke Works** (Three Rivers Route).

"Larry" cars deliver coal to charge the coke ovens.

Making Coke

Beehive ovens were built into a hillside in banks of ovens, called a **battery**. A wood fire was started in an oven and gradually increased in intensity. A small **charge** of coal was dumped through the **trunnel head**, and the front door was partially bricked up, leaving a gap for draft. By the fourth or fifth day, the oven was sufficiently hot.

Coal was delivered to the oven by a **larry**, a small coal car. An average charge for a 12-1/2´ diameter oven was 5 to 5-1/2 tons of coal. About 1-1/2 tons of coal would yield 1 ton of coke.

A **leveler** leveled the charge with a tool resembling a large toothless rake, and the door was bricked up by a **mason** to within 1-1/2˝ of the top. Burning time varied from 44 to 72 hours. A **puller** then opened the door and inserted a pipe to spray water to quench the coke. He then used a bar to break up the coke and draw it out through the door onto the wharf. Workers loaded the coke into wagons and then loaded it into railroad cars.
— www.lehigh.edu/~kaf3/cokedata/coking.html

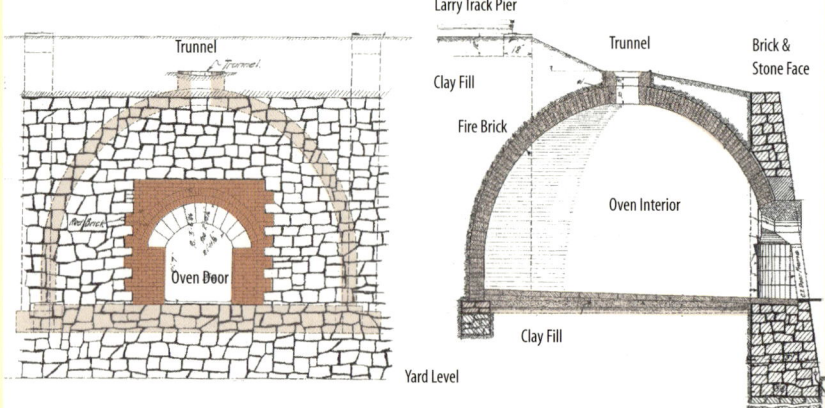

Front and side view drawings of H. C. Frick Coke Company beehive coke ovens, Scottdale, Pa., 1909

INDIAN HEAD

Resh's General Store
724-455-3416
2018 Indian Head Road, Indian Head
Mon–Sat, 8:30am–8pm; Sun, 9am–8pm

The Indian Head Trail starts near Resh's General Store. This hike/bike trail used to be a railway and is part of the regional "Rails to Trails" program.

"Hi, Gladys, how you doing?" asks Pete Resh as he walks through the aisles of his general store. "Hi there, Robbie," he says to another customer in another aisle.

It's not surprising that Pete, a.k.a. Clarence Wesley Resh, knows just about everyone in the place. After all, he grew up helping his dad (Charles William Resh) run the store, and now he's helping his son (Chris William Resh) carry on the family business.

But back when Indian Head was a bustling coal town, a family by the name of Mellon laid claim to the shop. From 1929 to 1940, the Mellons owned and operated the mine, and, in keeping with the practices of the time, they owned and operated the company store as well.

Employed by the Mellons, Charles Resh managed what was then called Sparks Supply Store, selling food and other essential items for scrip, or "jinky tin," as the locals called the company-issued currency.

In 1940, the Mellons decided to shut down the mine and sell their holdings. Charles Resh saw an opportunity to transform the company store into a general, community-oriented shop. Pete Resh was 10 years old when his father became the new owner.

"My father wanted me to go to college," Pete recalls, "but I told him I like the store. I like the people." So father and son worked together until Pete bought out his father in 1960. Today, it's Pete's son, Chris, who's in charge. "I think my dad would be real proud," Pete says.

Artifacts courtesy of Clarence Resh

Pete and Gladys Resh remember when workers shopped with "jinky tin."

Youghiogheny Route

Coal and Coke Heritage Center
724–430–4158
Penn State University Fayette Campus, Uniontown
www.coalandcoke.org
Mon–Fri, 10AM–3PM

top: **Coal miner**
bottom: **Coke oven mason**

Evelyn Hovanec hears voices, but there's no need to worry. As one of the directors of the Coal and Coke Heritage Center, Dr. Hovanec has spent the past 25 years listening to local miners, their wives, and their children talk about life, love, and work in the Connellsville Coke Region.

Encompassing 137 square miles along the base of the Laurel and Chestnut mountain ridges, the coal patches of the area stretched from Latrobe to Smithfield. And the stories of the men and boys who worked in the mines, as well as of the women and girls who worked at home, span nearly a century.

Those stories have become the Patch/Work Voices Project. With more than 700 hours of taped interviews, and a collection of music, videos, and slides, the project speaks to the heart of the Coal and Coke Heritage Center.

"When we started," Dr. Hovanec recalls, "a lot of people didn't think it was very important. But it's a project of the little people, not the corporate giants. That's where the history truly is — with the people."

Located on Penn State University's Fayette campus, the Heritage Center tells the history through artifacts, photographs, maps, blueprints, documents, scrapbooks, journals, newspapers, and an array of artwork featuring regional painters. "We have thousands of artifacts," Hovanec says, "and every one of them is my favorite."

But perhaps the soul of the center can be found in those items that have been created or donated by members of the community. For example, there's a replica of the Davidson Mine tipple that Ted, a retired draftsman for U. S. Steel, was building to scale in his basement. When his wife suggested he find another hobby, Ted called the Heritage Center.

By 1905, the Connellsville Coke District alone produced an amount of coke that "would have made a train so long the engine in front would have gone from Connellsville to San Francisco and back before the caboose had moved from the starting point!"

Working model of a coal tipple

Southeast from Pittsburgh

Then there are the displays — one of a miner in full regalia, the other of a coke oven — that were the result of Eagle Scout projects. And there's the ethnic dress and shawl that were passed down from mother to daughter to granddaughter. The colorful garb originally belonged to Josephina Rudinska Kubachka, who came to this region from Czechoslovakia in 1929.

It's these personal connections, Hovanec says, that prompt people from all parts of the country — in fact, from all parts of the world — to visit the center. Not surprisingly, it was Hovanec's own connections that initially fueled her interest in establishing the Coal and Coke Heritage Center.

"This region is my home. This is where I went to school. I thought everyone's father was a miner," she says. "As a small child, I can remember seeing the glow from the ovens, the sky was still bright at night, and hearing the sound of the 'larry' going up and down." But as the mining industry fell into sharp decline, families — including Hovanec's own — began searching for work beyond the patches.

Although many people left the mining communities, Hovanec says, they never lost contact. "I have three cousins who recently visited the center and brought their daughters with them."

For Hovanec, that's what the center is all about — future generations recognizing the meaning, value, and worth of the Patch/Work Voices Project.

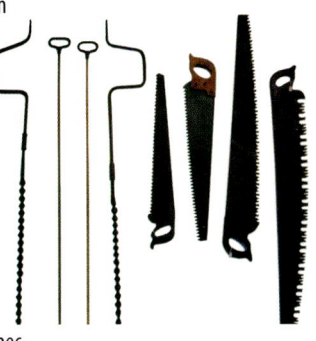

Coke worker's tools

Photos courtesy of Coal and Coke Heritage Center, Penn State Fayette Campus, Uniontown

Coke Patch Scrapbook

Life in patch towns was hard under the coal companies' round-the-clock control. The pay was low and the workers, most of whom were immigrants, were often paid with company-issued "scrip," so cash was scarce. Many families grew their own vegetables to supplement the staples such as flour and sugar they had to buy at the company store. Fathers and sons came home each day covered with soot and grit after long hours bent over in the mines or sweating at the fiery coke ovens. Mothers and daughters cooked and baked, sewed and cleaned, and washed endless loads of work clothes. But patch life also had its rewards. Families reached out to help each other in times of need. And children formed lifelong friendships as they played together, overcoming barriers of language and custom.

Youghiogheny Route

Pechin Shopping Village was featured on the front page of the Wall Street Journal *on March 5, 1984.*

DUNBAR

Pechin Shopping Village
724–277–4251
449 Pechin Road, Dunbar
www.pechin.com
Open every day. Cafeteria/Bakery: Mon–Sat, 7AM–9PM; Sun, 9:30AM–5PM. Check website for hours of other stores.

Dubbed the "Appalachian Mall of America," Pechin's claims to have "the lowest prices on everything" — in 2004, a cup of coffee was a nickel and a hamburger just 19 cents in the cafeteria! Started in 1947, this rambling jumble now includes hunting and fishing outfitters; a supermarket; discount stores selling beer, herbs, carpet remnants, and auto supplies; and a bakery (try their Slovak *kolachi*).

Local shopper Bobbie Kay Brown loads up on discounted items at Pechin's.

The National Road, now US 40, was the first highway built entirely with federal funds. Started in 1818, it stretched from Cumberland, Maryland, to Vidalia, Illinois, opening the Midwest to settlement and commerce. Look for roadside markers.

UNIONTOWN • FARMINGTON

From Pittsburgh: Take I-76 E to New Stanton exit 75. Take US 119 S to Uniontown exit US 40 W (Main St.).

One-Day Tour: Sites 22–27
Sites along US 40 from Uniontown to Farmington
☎ **Mt. St. Macrina:** Right on US 40 W (Main St.). Right at first stoplight. Look for red-brick mansion on right. **Jumonville Methodist Training Center:** Take US 40 E-Bus. through Uniontown. Go 10 mi. to Summit Inn. Left on Jumonville Rd. Go 3 mi. At welcome sign, go straight to entrance of Jumonville Center on right. **Wharton Furnace:** Return by Jumonville Rd. Left on US 40 E. Go .5 mi. Right on Wharton Furnace Rd. Go 2 miles. Wharton Furnace is on right just before Shepard Rd. ☎ **Touchstone Center for Crafts:** Follow Wharton Furnace Rd. another 2.5 mi. to Touchstone. **Early American Farm Implements Museum:** Return to US 40 by Wharton Furnace Rd. Go 1.3 mi. on US 40 E to Chalk Hill. Outdoor Museum is on left. ☎ **Stone House:** Continue 1 mi. on US 40 E. Stone House is on left. ***Return to Pittsburgh:*** US 119 N to I-76 W.

Southeast from Pittsburgh

Slovak and Rusyn Heritage

Slovak Easter egg made by Sister Rita Keshok

Slovakia is a small country in eastern Europe, yet it played a large role in the steel history of southwestern Pennsylvania. In the late 19th century, hundreds of immigrant workers from eastern Slovakia poured into the region's mill and coke patches. All spoke the Slovak language, but some were ethnic Slovaks and others were Rusyn, a related cultural group sometimes also called Carpatho-Rusyn or Ruthenian or, mistakenly, "Russian."

Most of the Slovaks were either Roman Catholic or Protestant. Like other immigrants, the Catholic Slovaks founded "ethnic" parishes, several honoring the patron saint of Slovakia, Saint Michael. The Rusyn were primarily Eastern Orthodox. Early in the 20th century, some Orthodox Rusyn in the United States formed a new denomination, Byzantine Catholicism, which acknowledged the leadership of the Roman Catholic Pope, but retained Orthodox symbols, such as onion-shaped domes and the triple cross; other Rusyn remained fully allied with the Orthodox Church.

Slovak and Rusyn parishes today are centers of ethnic identity. In Homestead and Braddock (Three Rivers Route) are two Catholic churches originally dedicated to Saint Michael, with Slovak inscriptions and murals of "old country" life. The interior of **Holy Ghost Byzantine Catholic Church** in Charleroi (Monongahela Route) is a feast of floral murals created local artists. **Mount Saint Macrina** in Uniontown (Youghiogheny Route), a Byzantine Catholic convent run by the Sisters of Saint Basil, is the site of an annual pilgrimage. Many Slovak and Rusyn churches around the region hold weekly "Lenten kitchens" on Fridays before Easter, serving fish sandwiches, *haluski* (cabbage and noodles), *pyrohi* (dumplings filled with potato, cheese, prunes, or kraut), nut rolls, and other delicacies.

Other Slovak and Rusyn cultural arts continue in the region as well. Ensembles such as Slavjane and PAS (Pittsburgh Area Slovaks) perform dances and music at local festivals. Visitors can learn more about Slovak-Rusyn heritage at the **Czechoslovak Nationality Room** at the University of Pittsburgh, or by tuning into WEDO radio (810 AM) on Sundays at noon for the Slovak Hour. University of Pittsburgh's Slovak Association holds an annual Slovak Festival in the fall.

UNIONTOWN

Mount Saint Macrina Retreat Center
724–438–7149
500 West Main Street, Uniontown
www.byzcath.org/ssb
☎ Phone ahead for tour.

Once upon a time, Oak Hill led a life of disquieting opulence. Everything about the 43-room, two-story manor — the silk tapestries, Tiffany lamps, ornate woodwork, imported marble — spoke to the virtues of wealth and power.

But times change. Now known as Mount Saint Macrina, the house leads a quiet, simple life of devotion as a retreat center. The Sisters of Saint Basil, an order of the Byzantine Catholic Church, acquired the mansion and nearly 200 acres of property in 1933 for the miraculous sum of $50,000.

Originally constructed in 1909, Oak Hill cost its benefactor, Josiah Van Kirk Thompson, $3 million. As president of Uniontown's First National Bank, J.V. Thompson made his fortune buying coal-rich land and then leasing the mining rights. He also made a family with his first wife, Mary. But Mary died after a brief illness, leaving him with two sons.

A view of the columned entry from the back lawn

Youghiogheny Route

above: **Interior chapel**
right: **The garden grotto invites meditation.**

Enter Hunney Hawes, an aspiring actress. Thompson and Hawes met, fell in love, and married in 1903 at New York's Waldorf-Astoria. They returned from their honeymoon to Oak Hill. Built to last, the mansion was fitted with a steel frame, and the concrete floors were 13 inches thick. The estate was self-sufficient, generating its own electricity, gas, and water. Unfortunately, the foundation of the marriage was not as strong. In 1913, Hawes received a $1 million divorce settlement and moved to New York.

A year later, the bottom fell out of Thompson's business ventures, leaving the financier broke, but not homeless. Although Oak Hill was purchased by the Piedmont Oil Company, Thompson was allowed to stay in the mansion until the day he died. Upon his death, Thompson's possessions and furnishings were sold at auction (netting considerably less than market value), and, shortly afterward, the Sisters of Saint Basil moved to their new home.

The casino is now a chapel. The grounds that once housed stables, tennis courts, and a swimming pool are now dedicated to meditation. The estate also includes the motherhouse, a nursing home, a personal care home, and pilgrim houses. Each September, Mount Saint Macrina hosts one of the largest pilgrimages in the United States. As many as 7,000 travel to the Mount.

Uniontown

Founded July 4, 1776, Uniontown, the Fayette County seat, had two periods of prominence. From 1818 to the 1850s, the town was a market center along the National Road. During the Coal and Coke Era, from 1880 to 1950, it was the financial hub of the Connellsville Coke District. Several places relate directly to millionaire J.V. Thompson, one of the region's many wealthy "coal barons." The round-cornered Fayette Bank Building was built around 1900 by Thompson. Dating from 1894, Trinity United Presbyterian Church at Fayette and Morgantown streets, with its Romanesque round stone arches, its stone carvings, and seven Tiffany windows, was the church that Thompson and other magnates attended. And, the estate now called Mount Saint Macrina was originally the opulent home that Thompson built as a gift to his wife.

The Fayette County Courthouse, State Theatre Center for the Arts, and the Fayette Bank Building

JUMONVILLE

Jumonville Methodist Training Center
1-800-463-7688
887 Jumonville Road, Hopwood
www.gospelcom.net/jumonville
The cross is open to the public until dusk.

What a difference a few centuries make. In 1754, the stretch of land now known as Jumonville Glen was the site of a battle between the Virginia Militia (led by then-Lieutenant Colonel George Washington) and French troops. Just 15 minutes after the first shot was fired, 10 Frenchmen, including Ambassador Jumonville, were dead and the French and Indian War was under way.

Nearly 200 years later, a 60-foot-high steel cross was erected at nearby Dunbar's Knob. According to the dedication plaque, the Cross of Christ "towers high on this mountain top as an enduring symbol that life triumphs over death."

The cross is the focal point of Jumonville, a United Methodist Church camp, and conference and retreat center. Dating back to the 1940s, Jumonville has occupied 280 acres in this scenic and historic part of western Pennsylvania.

The story of the cross dates back to the Great Depression. That's when Methodist churches throughout the country first started collecting money to build the massive structure. Counted among the many pledges were the pennies and dimes donated by Sunday school children. However, plans to construct the cross were put on hold as World War II began to rage and steel became a vital war commodity. Once peace was declared, the project was resurrected.

First, a 183-ton concrete foundation was poured on which the 47,000-pound shaft of the cross would rest. The arms, each spanning 12 feet, were brought in separately and welded to the main frame at the site. The cross was fabricated by Moore Metal Works of Greensburg using structural steel made at local U. S. Steel Corporation mills. (By the way, the names of all the children who donated their coins were sealed in the cross's foundation.)

Jumonville chapel

Visitors to Dunbar's Knob, which rises nearly 2,500 feet above sea level, can look out over seven counties and three states.

The Great Cross on Dunbar's Knob can withstand winds of 100 miles an hour, and on a clear day can be seen from miles away.

Youghiogheny Route

FARMINGTON AREA

24 Wharton Furnace
724–238–1200
Wharton Furnace Road (SR 2003)
www.geocities.com/SoHo/Square/6835
Outdoors: Open year-round

Made from local fieldstone, Wharton Furnace is a well-preserved example of the iron-smelting furnaces that dotted the early-19th-century landscape in southwestern Pennsylvania.

Iron furnaces were fueled with charcoal from the nearby forests.

Early Iron Furnaces

...The furnace was charged with iron ore, charcoal and limestone, through a cupola in the stack. The charcoal acted as the fuel, and the limestone combined with the impurities in the ore to form slag, leaving relatively pure molten iron as the desired end product.

The raw materials were kept at a point roughly level with the charging point and were run across a trestle in ore carts to the charging point. After the charge was ignited, the fire was supplied with a continuous blast of cold air provided by a large bellows, which was operated with water power.

The air was piped from the bellows through the blower pipe, or bustle pipe, through the tuyere and into the furnace itself. When the molten iron collected to the point where it was about level with the cinder hole, or cinder notch, the clay plug was removed from the cinder hole and the molten slag, which floated on top of the ore, ran off into the waste area.

Then the clay plug was taken out of the tap hole, or iron notch, and the iron would run out into sand molds in the casting area. At that point, the tap hole and cinder hole were replugged and the operation continued.
— *Foxfire 5*, Garden City, N.Y.: Anchor Books, 1979.

Cross section of iron furnace in operation

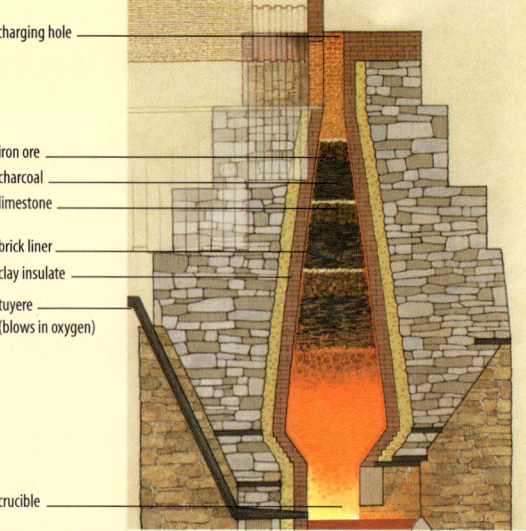

Touchstone Center for Crafts

800–721–0177
1049 Wharton Furnace Road, Farmington
www.touchstonecrafts.com
Mon–Fri, 9AM–4PM
☎ Phone ahead Nov–Mar.

Just like the mountains themselves, the traditional crafts that have grown up in the shadow of the Appalachians are both beautiful and rugged. Preserving the heritage and fostering the artistry of such age-old trades as blacksmithing, weaving, quilting, and woodworking is the mission of Touchstone Center for Crafts.

Founded in 1972 as the Pioneer Crafts Council in Mill Run, Pa., the Center now occupies 150 acres at the site of the former Camp Dunneback in Farmington. Featuring eight state-of-the-art studios, a gallery/gift shop, a library, 20 rustic cabins, camping sites, two recently built dorm units, a dining hall, and nature trails, Touchstone is the only residential arts and crafts facility in the state.

Touchstone's mission is to bring aspiring as well as accomplished artists and master craftspeople together amid the inspirational surroundings of Pennsylvania's Laurel Highlands. Each year, starting in May and ending in September, weeklong and weekend courses in blacksmithing, metalsmithing, jewelry making, textiles, ceramics, sculpture, papermaking, basketry, oil and watercolor painting, printmaking, drawing, photography, and glassmaking are taught by many of North America's most renowned artisans.

With class sizes often restricted to just 12 students, the opportunity for hands-on learning is limited only by time and imagination. Traveling from virtually every state in the United States, students arrive ready and willing to learn.

Part of the learning process includes nightly lectures and/or slide shows presented by the instructors. Instructors and students are encouraged to donate some of their work to the Touchstone Art Auction, held every Thursday evening from June through August and open to the public. Touchstone also offers summer programs for pre-schoolers, kids 6 to 12 years old, and teens. College internships and student work–study programs are offered, as well as field trips for nearby public schools.

above: **Blacksmithing classes**
center: **Hand-wrought iron door handle to Touchstone's blacksmith studio**
below: **Touchstone offices, gallery, and giftshop**

Youghiogheny Route

Early American Farm Implements Museum
724–438–5180
8 miles east of Uniontown on US 40
Outdoors: Open year-round
Free.

Jim and Jeanette Silbaugh have gathered over 1,000 items of antique farm machinery and display this amazing collection on the front lawn of their motel. This place is worth a stop for an up-close glimpse of a coalmine car, blacksmith tools, or a steam-engine tractor.

Fallingwater and Kentuck Knob, two homes built by Frank Lloyd Wright, are located within four miles of each other not far from Farmington.

Stone House Restaurant
1–800–274–7138
US 40, Farmington
www.stonehouseinn.com
April & May: Sun, NOON–6PM; Fri & Sat, 4–9PM
June–Oct: Sun, NOON–6PM; Wed–Sat, 4–9PM
☏ Phone ahead or check web site Sept–Mar.

Opened in 1822 as the Fayette Springs Hotel, the Stone House has provided fine dining and rest to weary travelers for more than 175 years. Entertainment during the 19th century featured minstrel shows and local fiddlers. Today, in addition to award-winning cuisine, visitors can enjoy a variety of special events and activities in this restored historic site.

Southeast from Pittsburgh

ⓔ EVENTS CALENDAR

For specific dates and times of events see:
www.riversofsteel.com

Events that occur in several months are abbreviated with an *. Full contact information can be found under Recurring Events.

Recurring Events

Architectural Tours
Fallingwater
724–329–8501
PA 381, Farmington
www.wpconline.org/fallingwaterhome.htm
April–Nov: Tuesday–Sunday;
Dec: Weekends only;
Jan & Feb: Closed; March: First two weekends
Reservations recommended
Tours through Frank Lloyd Wright's masterpiece

Architectural Tours
Kentuck Knob
724–329–1901
Kentuck Road off US 40, Chalk Hill
www.kentuckknob.com
Tuesday–Sunday
Reservations recommended
Tours of the region's "other" Frank Lloyd Wright landmark house and its sculpture gardens

*Old Time Fiddlers' Jamboree**
Fayette County Fairgrounds
724–438–0502
US 119 between Connellsville and Uniontown
March–December: 3rd Sundays

*Nature Tours**
**Powdermill Nature Reserve/
Nimick Nature Center, Cook Twp.**
724–593–6105
Southeast of Ligonier on SR 0381
www.powdermill.org
June–August: Wednesday–Sunday;
April–May & September–October: weekends only
Tours, displays of regional flora and fauna

Regional Art
Westmoreland Museum of American Art
724–837–1500
221 North Main Street, Greensburg
www.wmuseumaa.org
Changing exhibits and events involving southwestern Pennsylvania art

*Art Auction**
Touchstone Center for Crafts
800–721–0177
1049 Wharton Furnace Road, Farmington
www.touchstonecrafts.com
June–August: Every Thursday evening

February

Robert Burns Banquets
Various Locations
724–379–6600
Call for times and locations.
Events honoring the Scottish poet

March

Sacred Art Series
Antiochian Village
724–238–3677
PA 711 N, Ligonier
www.antiochianvillage.org
4 days
Byzantine chanting, Pysanky egg painting

*Old Time Fiddlers' Jamboree

April

*Old Time Fiddlers' Jamboree
*Nature Tours

May

Blacksmith "Hammer-In"
Touchstone Center for Crafts
800–721–0177
1049 Wharton Furnace Road, Farmington
www.touchstonecrafts.com
Mid-May

National Road Festival
Route 40
724–437–9877
www.nationalroadpa.org
Events held at various places along Route 40
3rd weekend

*Old Time Fiddlers' Jamboree
*Nature Tours

June

Quilt Show
West Overton Museums
724–887–7910
PA 819 between Mount Pleasant and Scottdale
www.westovertonmuseum.org

Founder's Day
West Overton Museums
724–887–7910
PA 819 between Mount Pleasant and Scottdale
www.westovertonmuseum.org

Slovenian Polka Dance
Slovenian National Benefit Society
800–THE–SNPJ
Evanstown SNPJ Picnic Grounds, Herminie

*Old Time Fiddlers' Jamboree
*Nature Tours
*Art Auction

Youghiogheny Route

July

Westmoreland Arts and Heritage Festival
Twin Lakes Park
724–834–7474
US 30 to Donohoe Road, Greensburg
www.artsandheritage.com
Early July

Salute to the Classics
Linden Hall
724–529–7543
432 Linden Hall Road, Dawson
www.lindenhallpa.com
Early July
Oldies bands, vintage cars, food

Parish Festival
Saint Rita Church
724–628–4015
120 Second Street, Connellsville
Mid-July
Italian food specialities

Ice Cream Festival
Fort Allen Antique Farm Equipment Assoc.
724–668–7897
PA 819 between Mt. Pleasant and Scottdale next to West Overton Museums
Mid-July
Music, hayrides, crafts

Festival of St. Vincent Basilica Parish
Saint Vincent Grove
724–539–8629
300 Fraser Purchase Road, Latobe
Late July
Features ethnic food, flea market

Fayette County Fair
Fayette County Fairgrounds
724–438–0502
US 119 between Connellsville and Uniontown
www.fayettefair.com
July–early August
Entertainment, farming exhibits

Slovenian Polka Dance
Evanstown SNPJ
800–THE–SNPJ
Evanstown SNPJ Picnic Grounds, Herminie

Sacred Music Institute
Antiochian Village
724–238–3677
PA 711 N, Ligonier
www.antiochianvillage.org
5 days in late July
Sacred music for liturgy and feast days, Byzantine chanting, and children's music

*Old Time Fiddlers' Jamboree
*Nature Tours
*Art Auction

August

Arts and Heritage Day Festival
Lynch Field
724–838–9146
PA 119 North, Greensburg
Early August
Ethnic food, music, entertainment

Bob Day
Youngwood Historical & Railroad Museum
724–925–7355
1 Depot Street, Youngwood
www.yrrm.org
Last Saturday

Italian Day Festa
Westmoreland Columbus 500
724–238–3666
Idlewild Park
US 30 E, Ligonier
www.idlewild.com
Mid-August

*Old Time Fiddlers' Jamboree
*Nature Tours
*Art Auction

September

Pilgrimage Honoring Our Lady of Perpetual Help
Mount Saint Macrina
724–439–4940
500 West Main Street, Uniontown
www.byzcath.org/ssb
1st weekend
Liturgies, candlelight procession, Slovak-Rusyn ethnic foods including *medveniki*, special travelers' cookies made by the Sisters of St. Basil

Derry Station Railroad Days
Derry
724–694–2538
PA 217
Late September
Crafts, gift shop, demonstrations, and dance

Scottdale Fall Festival
Scottdale Chamber of Commerce
Gazebo area, Scottdale
www.scottdale.com
Mid- September
Family-oriented event featuring the town's history in industry, railroading, coke and coal, quilt shows, food, and crafts

Ligonier Highland Games
Ligonier Highland Games Association
412–851–9900
Idlewild Park
US 30 E, Ligonier
Early September
Scottish pipe bands, dancing competitions, athletics, and sheepdog trials

Southeast from Pittsburgh

Heritage Musical
West Overton Museums
724-887-7910
PA 819 between Mt. Pleasant and Scottdale
www.westovertonmuseum.org/

Glass and Ethnic Festival
724–547–7521
Mt. Pleasant
Last full weekend
Ethnic foods, crafts, glass blowing and cutting demonstrations, and musical entertainment

Grape Festival
Evanstown SNPJ
800–THE–SNPJ
Evanstown SNPJ Picnic Grounds, Herminie
Early September
Food, games, and Slovenian music and dance

SS. Thekla and Raphael Pilgrimage
Antiochian Village
724–238–3677
PA 711 N, Ligonier
3 days
Spiritual pilgrimage includes worship sessions and activities

*Old Time Fiddlers' Jamboree
*Nature Tours

October

*Old Time Fiddlers' Jamboree
*Nature Tours

November

Greater Pittsburgh Arts and Crafts Festival
Expo Center at Greengate Mall
724–863–4577
US 30, Greensburg

*Old Time Fiddlers' Jamboree

December

*Old Time Fiddlers' Jamboree

Miner's hat and lamp, 1920s

Songs

Which Side Are You On?

Come all you good workers,
Good news to you I'll tell
Of how the good old union
Has come in here to dwell.

> Chorus:
> Which side are you on?
> Which side are you on?
> Which side are you on?
> Which side are you on?

My daddy was a miner,
And I'm a miner's son,
And I'll stick with the union
'Til every battle's won.

Oh workers can you stand it?
Oh tell me how you can?
Will you be a lousy scab
Or will you be a man?

Don't scab for the bosses,
Don't listen to their lies.
Us poor folks haven't got a chance
Unless we organize.

— By Florence Reece, 1931, as reprinted in *Songs for Political Action* liner notes, 1996

Two-Cent Coal

Oh, the bosses' tricks of 'seventy-six
They met with some success,
Until the hand of God came down
And made them do with less.
They robbed the honest miner lad
And drunk his flowin' bowl,
Through poverty we were compelled
To dig them two-cent coal.

But the river it bein' frozen—
Of course, the poor might starve;
What did those tyrant bosses say?
"It's just what they deserve."
But God who always aids the just,
All things He does control,
He broke the ice and He sent it down
And sunk their two-cent coal.

Their tipples, too, fled from our view,
And down the river went.
They seemed to cry as they passed by:
"You tyrants, now repent!
For while you rob the miner lad,
Remember, you've a soul,
For your soul is sinkin' deeper
Than the ice sunk your two-cent coal."

It's to conclude and finish,
Let us help our fellow man,
And if our brother's in distress
Assist him if you can,
To keep the wolf off from his door,
And shelter him from cold,
That he never again shall commit the crime
Of diggin' two-cent coal.

— Folk ballad sung by David Morrison in Finleyville, Pa., Recorded in 1940 by folklorist George Korson

Monongahela Route

Southwest from Pittsburgh

Fueling a Revolution

One of the hardest-working rivers in the United States, the Monongahela, runs through the Pittsburgh region. For more than a century "the Mon" has carried millions of tons of high-quality bituminous coal to power southwestern Pennsylvania's steel mills and electrical generation plants — the fuel for America's Industrial Revolution.

Meandering northward from its origins in West Virginia, the Monongahela offers breathtaking views and enjoyable pastimes such as fishing and boating. Yet the fleets of barges that ply its waters today speak to the river's long history as the Steel Era's most vital industrial artery.

Early in the 20th century, as by-product coke production replaced the older beehive method, the Monongahela became indispensable for transporting raw coal from the mines to the processing plants. The efficiency of newer longwall coal mining techniques only increased the river's importance as industry's water highway. The river's system of locks and dams was built to facilitate the transportation of coal. The coal companies' riverside barge loading facilities, as well as river-related industries such as barge building and repair, provided employment for many.

The Monongahela has both united and divided those who live along its shores. During the height of industrial activity, smoke from the mills and coking plants prevented residents on either side of the river from seeing each other. Their lives, however, were intertwined through the experiences they shared in industrial centers.

Bridges such as those at Masontown, Brownsville, Charleroi, and Elizabeth became valuable all-weather connectors, but still are few and far between. Historically, ferries at Fredericktown and many other locations linked towns where bridges could not, and generations of local residents served as ferrymen. Even towns and cities distant from the river, such as Waynesburg and Washington, were tied to the river as the steel makers, coal companies, and glass manufacturers extended their reach.

The people of this complex area come from diverse cultural backgrounds. In the milltowns along the river and in the inland mine patches and factory towns such as Cokeburg and Washington, eastern and southern European traditions mix with African-American, Middle Eastern, and others. The more rural communities show the region's connection to Appalachia, as Scots-Irish, German, and Native American heritages define the cultural landscape. Visitors can see Byzantine and Eastern Orthodox churches tucked in out-of-the-way spots, enjoy hiking along riverfront trails, watch artisans make pottery from the area's rich clay deposits, and learn more about the network of huge coal plants, barge fleets, and other industrial facilities, above and below ground, that still shape daily life in this part of the Rivers of Steel region.

below: The Coal Pickers by Frank L. Melega, 1952

opposite page: Coal Barges on the Monongahela by John Shryock, 1980s

Courtesy of Frank L. Melega Museum

Monongahela Route

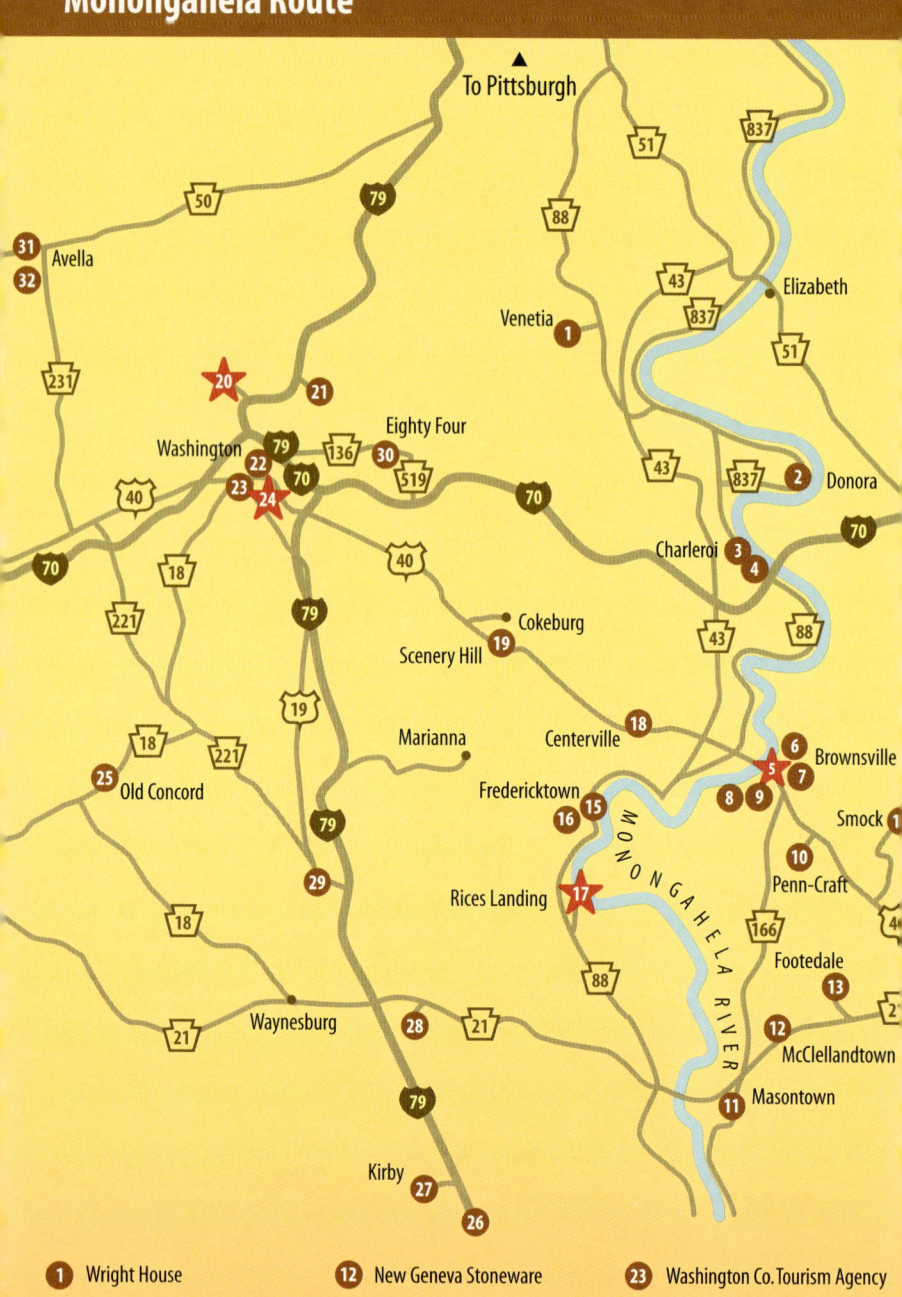

1. Wright House
2. Cement City
3. Holy Ghost Byzantine Church
4. Speers Street Shops and Dining
5. Flatiron Heritage Center
6. St. Peter's Church
7. Nemacolin Castle
8. Thompson House Restaurant
9. Elmo's
10. Penn-Craft Historical District
11. Fort Mason Historical Society
12. New Geneva Stoneware
13. St. Maximilian Kolbe Shrine
14. Smock Historical Society
15. Fredericktown Ferry
16. Coal Miner Memorial
17. Rices Landing Riverfront
18. McCutcheon Monument
19. Westerwald Pottery
20. Pennsylvania Trolley Museum
21. Quail Acres
22. Artists' Co-op
23. Washington Co. Tourism Agency
24. Duncan and Miller Glass Museum
25. Old Concord Presbyterian Church
26. Welcome Center
27. RAG Cumberland Mine
28. Greene County Historical Society
29. Ruff Creek General Store
30. Spring House
31. Meadowcroft Museum of Rural Life
32. Tudor Ironworks

Southwest from Pittsburgh

VENETIA · DONORA · CHARLEROI

From Pittsburgh: Take PA 51 S to PA 88 S.

Half-Day Tour: Sites 1–4

☎ **Wright House:** Take PA 88 S to "Y" at Amoco in Finleyville. Bear right on Washington Ave. (becomes Venetia Rd.). Go 1.3 mi. Wright House is on right. **Cement City:** From Finleyville, take PA 88 S to PA 837 S. In Donora, left on McKean. Right on the third (!!!) Walnut St. up hill 4 blocks to Modisette St. ☎ **Holy Ghost Byzantine Catholic Church:** From Donora, take PA 837 S to PA 88 S into Charleroi. Bear right at "Y" onto Lincoln Ave. Go 4–5 blocks. Right on 8th St. (no sign). Right on Meadow Ave. Church is on right. **Speers Street Shops:** Continue 3 mi. on PA 88 S. Left at Lower Speers sign (State St.). Go down hill. Right on Speers St. to shops. *Return to Pittsburgh:* PA 88 N to PA 51 N.

SYMBOLS
- ★ Must-See Site
- ● Point of Interest Site
- Industry
- Folklife
- Nature
- Art & Architecture
- Food
- Shopping
- E Events Calendar
- ☎ Phone Ahead

VENETIA

Wright House
724–941–5024
815 Venetia Road, Venetia
☎ Phone ahead.

A less-famous pair of Wright Brothers — James and Joshua — arrived in western Pennsylvania in 1764. In 1815, Joshua's son, Enoch, and Enoch's son, Joseph, decided to build a house for their families to share.

That house now is home to the Peters Creek Historical Society. Founded in 1967, the Society is dedicated to preserving local history for future generations to enjoy. Members have taken an interest in genealogy, coal mining, architecture, and historical sites and activities.

The Society has amassed a collection of memorabilia and artifacts that is displayed in the Wright House. The late–English Georgian vernacular house features two kitchens (one of which has been restored to an early–19th-century décor), two parlors, a dining room, a quilting room, two bedrooms (one with original Wright family furnishings), and a room dedicated to coal mining.

Much of the mining collection, including models, dioramas, lamps, and helmets, was donated by retired miners. But one item, a plaque commemorating the 96 miners and one rescue worker who were killed in the 1913 Cincinnati Mine explosion, was a roadside discard discovered and donated to the collection.

Thanks to the Peters Creek Historical Society, the Wright House remains a work in progress. Renovations continue inside, while outside the Giant Oaks Garden Club is busy cultivating herb and vegetable patches.

Fred Braun of the Peters Creek Historical Society shows the coal heritage room at the Wright House.

Monongahela Route

DONORA

Cement City
Walnut, Modisette, Ida, Bertha, and Helen Streets, Donora

They say people in glass houses shouldn't throw stones, but what about folks living in "cement houses"? Do the same rules apply? It seems doubtful that the builders of Cement City pondered such questions when they set out to create a community of cement homes in 1916. Their concerns were more immediate and practical.

Construction of Cement City in 1916–17

Years earlier, the Cleveland-based Union Steel Company sent William Donner to southwestern Pennsylvania. Charged with brokering a deal that would net the corporation 300 acres of land along the Monongahela River's horseshoe bend, he worked with Thomas Mellon to secure financing. The plan became a reality in Donora, the town that developed in the steel mill's wake, and is forever linked to the two men.

Once the mill was up and running, housing — or rather the lack of housing — was a problem. Cement City was the solution.

A typical Cement City parlor

Photos courtesy of Donora Historical Society

The notion of building a house out of cement was the brainchild, albeit one of the least successful offspring, of Thomas Edison. The inventor proclaimed that, in addition to being fireproof and termite proof, cement homes would provide affordable housing to the poor. (In reality, they proved to be more expensive to build than traditional wood frames, and presented more than their share of challenges for occupants trying to repair or update wires and pipes encased in cement walls.)

But Union Steel embraced the concept and began constructing Prairie-style cement houses specifically for the Donora mill's middle managers and foremen. By 1917, a total of 80 homes — 60 single-family dwellings and 20 duplexes — were completed on a hill overlooking the mill. The demand was immediate, but because the supply was limited, a waiting list quickly developed. Rent ranging from $22.50 to $40, depending on square footage, was paid directly to Union Steel in real money, not scrip. In return, the company handled all home maintenance.

Cement City today

Southwest from Pittsburgh

According to self-professed historian and current Cement City resident Brian Charlton, it took about 10,000 yards of cement to build the homes. The process involved putting the steel forms in place (which took a crew of 10 men an entire day to accomplish) and then pouring each floor of each house separately.

Far from looking like bunkers, the houses are warm and charming. Nowhere is that more evident than at the Charltons'. Brian and Nancy Charlton bought their duplex in 1984. (Union Steel sold its Donora Works and Cement City in the 1940s.) After purchasing the adjoining side four years ago, the Charltons broke through the wall, creating one big, happy house.

Despite that renovation, Brian, Nancy, and their 17-year-old daughter Kate are committed to preserving their home's vibrant past. Visitors will find a plaque affirming Cement City's status as a site on the Register of National Historic Places on the Charltons' front porch.

Along the Donora riverfront, you'll see the former facilities of the U. S. Steel Donora Zinc Works and the American Steel & Wire Plant.

Donora

Donora was built as a steel town in 1900 by William Donner, an industrialist from nearby Monessen, with financing from Andrew Mellon and other Pittsburgh investors. Mellon created the town's name by contracting Donner's last name and adding the first name of Donner's wife, Nora. Quickly becoming a boom town with a large wire mill, zinc mill, tin mill, and blast furnaces, **Donora** attracted Scottish iron workers, Spanish zinc workers, and workers from many other cultures including Slovaks, Rusyns, Croatians, Hungarians, Italians, and African-Americans.

The mill was on a flat tract of land in a sharp bend of the Monongahela River. Unfortunately, this area was often subject to fog. In October 1948, weather conditions combined to produce a climatic inversion. The zinc mill's chemical fumes became so dense that driving became almost impossible and many residents could not breathe. About 200 people checked into local hospitals; and 20 of them later died. The famous "Donora Smog" brought widespread media attention and eventually caused the demise of the mill, the loss of 8,000 jobs, and a drastic population decline. The severity of the disaster, however, also acted

A case worker interviews a smog victim in Donora in 1948.

as an alarm to the Pittsburgh region and the entire nation. The tragedy helped to spur the enactment of laws limiting industrial pollution and ushered in a new era of environmental awareness. Donora itself became an example of how a community can rebound from calamity. The old mill was torn down and later a new industrial park brought 2,000 jobs back to town.

Today, visitors can see the curve of the river where the mill stood and drive through **Cement City**, a neighborhood of poured-cement homes built for the mill's middle-management families. Churches representing the Slovak and Rusyn ethnic communities are still standing, as is as a building that once housed the Spanish Club. The Donora Historical Society is creating a community heritage center in the Slovak Sokol, a fraternal hall built around 1900.

In October of 1948, a temperature inversion created smog that killed 20 and sickened 6,000.

187

Monongahela Route

CHARLEROI

3

Holy Ghost Byzantine Catholic Church
724–483–8622 or 724–489–0500
828 Meadow Avenue, Charleroi
☎ Phone ahead or attend Mass: Sat, 5 PM; Sun, 9:30 AM

Icons grace the interior of Holy Ghost Byzantine Catholic Church.

It has been said that entering Holy Ghost Church is like walking into an icon. Every surface — the walls, the ceiling, the arches, the icon screen, the altar — is covered with bright, colorful images. The premise, based on St. John Chrysostom's assertion, is simple: the house of God must be the happiest place under the heavens, and whatever meets the eye should call the viewer to the contemplation of God.

However, the process of funding and then developing, designing, and painting 250 icons was decidedly more complicated. At the time, the late 1980s, the region was in the midst of a serious economic decline. The once-thriving glass, coal, and steel industries were not only cutting their payrolls, but in many cases were shutting down.

As young people began moving out of the Mon Valley in search of jobs, they left behind aging, struggling communities. Originally built in 1899 with the financial and spiritual support of eastern European immigrants, the Holy Ghost parish also was struggling. But instead of giving in to hopelessness, the congregation found strength and purpose in a renovation project that took more than two years.

Iconographer Mila Mina was called upon to bring visions of the Pantocrator (a traditional portrayal of Christ), the Icon of the Sign, and a host of saints and Biblical scenes to life. The job proved to be bigger than any one person could handle, so a staff of volunteers moved the pews, built the scaffolding, hoisted the buckets of supplies, and helped with painting and mounting the icons. One of those volunteers was Judy Lauderbaugh. Now an iconographer in her own right and still a member of the Holy Ghost Church, Lauderbaugh has contributed angels and curtain borders to the massive canvas.

It is a joyful sight to behold.

BY THE WAY

River workers don't go home at 5 pm. On the Mon, they work 6 days on and 6 days off.

4

Speers Street Shops and Dining
Shops 724–483–2290, Restaurants 724–483–1911
Speers Street, Lower Speers
Shops: Tues–Sat, 11 AM–9 PM; Sun, NOON–6 PM
Restaurants: Tues–Th, 11 AM–9 PM; Fri–Sun, 11 AM–10 PM

The eclectic mix along Speers Street includes the Heritage Wine Cellars (featuring Pennsylvania wines), the Riverside Village Shops (including The Baggy Cat craft shop), the Back Porch Restaurant and the Speers Street Grill.

Crafts from the Riverside Village Shops reflect life along the Monongahela.

Southwest from Pittsburgh

Barges

Most of the tugs I worked on were non-union and we ran two eight-hour shifts. You basically worked 16 hours in every 24. This allowed for four deck hands, two pilots, and two engineers. We cooked for ourselves, cleaned the boat and dishes, did our own laundry, and looked after the boat.

Most of the deck work was building a tow and dropping a tow. A **tow** is the barges you hook up to the tug. This can be anything from 1 to 12 on the Mon or up to 50 on the Mississippi. **Jumbo** barges can hold 1,600 tons, **stumbo** barges about 1,200 tons, and **standard** barges 800 to 900 tons.

This meant being good on your feet and strong enough to lift heavy cables, crowbars, and sledgehammers. When you built a tow, you went into a fleet of barges with a list of barge numbers and picked out the ones assigned to you. It was a test of skill to build your own tow in the least amount of moves possible. You tie up alongside and find your barges, then you move the ones in the way and tie yours together. Then hook up the tug and away you go.

Coming into a lock chamber, one of us called out the position of the lead barge in relation to the chamber. Once inside, we'd secure the tow to the chamber wall and wait for the river to rise or fall.

Both engines were never turned off. If the engineer changed oil, he shut down one engine and we ran on the other. The oil was changed once every two weeks. This meant we had waste oil to get rid of. We would pick up the food and drop off the waste oil and refuel all at the same time. The tug only made money pushing barges.

Pushing coal is a dirty job. When it rains, everything is wet and coal dust sticks to everything. When you go inside, everything gets dirty from your boots and clothes. When it is dry, the coal dust blows over everything.

When you meet another tug, you talk by radio on channel 13. Most of the talk was about work and who was doing what. They don't use the whistles as much any more—too noisy. Yet we still ask the other boat if he wants to pass on one whistle (port to port) or two whistles (starboard to starboard). Anyway, traffic coming downstream has the right of way. You have less control going with the current than against it.
—Jim Corr, barge hand

Barge Speak

Many barge terms relate to parts of the body:

breast wire a hard lashing run between two barges.

deadhead to run a tow boat without barges.

deadman a heavy anchor used to secure a mooring line.

eyeballs spotlights and field glasses or radar.

hand wire a small line usually some 30 feet long, which crewmen carry and throw.

head the bow of a boat or barge.

heel the temporary sideways tilt of a vessel.

jewelry rachets, chains, and wires for barge rigging.

knees plates mounted on the tow boat's bow, used to push barges.

on the hip towed alongside the boat.

rubbing elbows conversing at a meal.

walking making a boat move sideways by running one engine ahead and the other astern.

A towboat crew's living quarters are on the main deck, just above the waterline. Topside are the pilot house and engineer's cabin.

From the High Point Restaurant on PA 88 south of Charleroi, view the Monongahela River as it wraps around Coal Center at the Greenfield Bend.

Courtesy of California Area Historical Society

Monongahela Route

BROWNSVILLE AREA

From Pittsburgh: Take PA 51 S to PA 88 S to PA 43 S (Toll $.50) to US 40 E to Brownsville.

One-Day Tour: Sites 5–10
Flatiron Heritage Center: Take US 40 S across Lane-Bane Bridge. First right down exit ramp. Left .1 mi. on Brown St. Flatiron Center is on right. Parking lot is on left. ☎ **St. Peter's:** From Flatiron parking lot, right on Market St. under bridge overpass. At stop sign, straight 2 blocks. Left on 5th Ave. Right on Church St. **Nemacolin Castle:** Down Church St. Left on Fifth Ave. Cross Market St. (US 40). Right on Brashear St. to Castle. **Thompson House:** From Flatiron Building, right on Market St. Bear right on Water St. Thompson House is on left. **Elmo's:** From Thompson House, right on Water St. Right on Angle St. Left on 2nd St. Elmo's is on the left. **Penn-Craft Historical District:** From Brownsville take US 40 E. Right on Stone Church Rd. (SR 4020). Go 7 mi. Left at Penn-Craft sign. Go .5 mi. Left into Penn-Craft. **Return to Pittsburgh:** US 40 W to PA 43 N to PA 88 N to PA 51 N.

On the Brownsville waterfront, HBC Barge, LLC operates a barge repair facility.

BROWNSVILLE

Flatiron Heritage Center
724–785–9331
69 Market Street, Brownsville
www.flatironcenter.com
Mon–Sat, 11AM–8PM; Sun, 12 NOON–8PM

Lou Orslene

above: **The Flatiron Heritage Center**
below: **River and rail transportation are themes at the Flatiron Building.**

When Lou Orslene visits Brownsville's Flatiron Heritage Center, it's as if he's coming home. And in a way, he is. Lou, along with his three sisters and brother, grew up not too far from here in the coal-patch town of Filbert. In fact, his mom still lives in the same house. "We'll drive by later," he says. "You've got to see her garden. It's beautiful."

After living and working in various parts of the country and in England, Lou returned home — not as the prodigal son, but rather as an adult hoping to make a difference in the life of a struggling community. As the executive director of the Brownsville Area Revitalization Corporation (BARC) from 2000 to 2004, Lou became the resident visionary. Looking beyond the boarded-up buildings that so starkly define present-day Brownsville, he could see both a vibrant past and a purposeful future.

"Come on in," he says, holding open the door to the Flatiron Building. "This is an important part of our community." Dating back to the 1830s, the building housed ethnic banks, taxi services, a trolley stop, and a number of different tailors, as well as the original Brownsville library and post office. Lou remembers a Mr. Moskovitz setting up his vacuum-cleaner repair shop. "His business was right where we're standing on the checkered floor."

Named for its shape, the Flatiron currently houses BARC's offices, a first-floor museum, and an upstairs art gallery. In the museum, visitors learn about Brownsville's Colonial past. The town took root at the western point of Nemacolin's Trail, now known

Southwest from Pittsburgh

as U.S. Route 40 or the National Road. Brownsville's role in river travel and commerce includes the production and launch of the nation's first steamboat, the *Enterprise,* in 1814. And as for Brownsville's industrial legacy, the coal and coke mined in Fayette County passed through Brownsville on its way to feed the steel mills in Pittsburgh. These stories are told through artifacts, a topographical map, photographs, scale models, and paintings.

The paintings and sculptures in the second-floor gallery tell the story of local artist Frank L. Melega (1905–1997). Melega got his start creating signs for Brownsville businesses. Intrigued by everyday life in and around the region's coal patches, he began to paint images, including *Sunday Morning* in a patch town, *Rescue* from a mining accident, and *Mine Explosion*. Many of those images are now on permanent display in the Flatiron Building, thanks to donations by the artist and his son.

Mine Explosion, by Frank L. Melega, circa 1937

Lou pauses at the painting titled *Mine Explosion* and talks about his personal connection to its subject matter. "When I was five, my dad was blinded in an accident at the Maple Creek Mine. I imagine this scene playing out on that day. While it's a very dim scene," Lou says, "Mr. Melega uses light to depict hope and optimism."

That hope and optimism became a guiding force for Lou's father as well. Although he never regained his sight, he went back to college and eventually became an organizer and director for the United Mine Workers of America. He died in 1993.

"My Dad was amazing," Lou marvels.

Brownsville

Overlooking the Monongahela River in Fayette County, on a site that had been home to Native Americans, and later a fort, the town of Brownsville was mapped out in the mid-18th century. Named for founder Thomas Brown, the town rose to prominence just after 1800 as a trade stop along the National Road. Brownsville became one of the country's earliest inland boat-building centers, at first producing keelboats for pioneers heading West, then steamboats carrying passengers and freight, then coal barges.

Brownsville was the regional economy's rising star until the mid-19th century, when the Pennsylvania Railroad mainline connected Pittsburgh to Philadelphia. As the industrialization of southwestern Pennsylvania increased through the late 19th century and into the 20th, the town's early Scots-Irish and German settlers were joined by eastern and southern Europeans. Through the heyday of steel, Brownsville served as a commercial and industrial center, shipping coal and coke to the mills by river and rail.

top: The *Enterprise,* the first steamboat to travel to New Orleans and return, was built and launched from the Brownsville wharf in 1814.

bottom: The nation's first cast-iron bridge was built in 1839, and still spans the Monongahela River.

Monongahela Route

6

St. Peter's Roman Catholic Church
724–785–7781
18 Church Street, Brownsville
☏ Phone ahead for tour.

Not surprisingly, Church Street is home to several houses of worship, among them St. Peter's Church. Now on the National Register of Historic Places and the Pennsylvania Landmark Register, the church was built by Irish masons using locally quarried stone. Dedicated in 1845, it is the oldest continuously operating church in western Pennsylvania and the first Catholic parish in Fayette County.

The early congregants believed that Brownsville would be the headquarters for the soon-to-be-established Western Pennsylvania Diocese and that St. Peter's would become a cathedral. Thus, the church was equipped with a burial crypt (the final resting place for higher-ranking members of the clergy) and configured with a pulpit and sedile, or bishop's seat, on the right side of the altar. However, both Brownsville and the church were passed over.

The church at one time boasted the only heated cemetery in the world. It seems heating ducts used to run under the church graveyard — a distinction that landed it in *Ripley's Believe It or Not*. From its vantage point atop Church Street, St. Peter's Church offers an impressive view of the bend in the Monongahela River. And inside, its stained-glass windows offer a view of local history.

7

Nemacolin Castle
724–785–6882
100 Front Street, Brownsville
www.nemacolincastle.org
Mid Mar– mid-Oct: Sat & Sun, 11AM–5PM;
June 1–Aug 31: Tues–Th, 11AM–5PM
Adults: $6, Children: $3

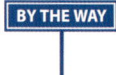

BY THE WAY

Look for a panoramic view of the Monongahela River from St. Peter's Church and Nemacolin Castle.

Presenting the grand appearance of a castle — complete with turret, 22 rooms, and a hallway that stretches 70 feet, this building is listed on the National Register of Historic Places. It is open to the public for regular and holiday tours, as well as "ghost tours" that tell of supposed ghostly activity within the castle's walls.

This manor was home to three generations of the Bowman family, through wars, economic twists and turns, and the rise and fall of industry.

Courtesy of Flatiron Heritage Center

Southwest from Pittsburgh

8
Thompson House Restaurant & Tavern
724-785-4744
815 Water Street, Brownsville
www.thompson-house-rest.com
Tues–Sat, 11:30AM– MIDNIGHT

Fine dining and flawless restoration double your enjoyment of this historic site that features a tavern as well as a bookstore and reading room. The Thompson House received an award in 1994 for outstanding achievement in historic preservation.

9
Elmo's
724–785–2232
210 2nd Street, Brownsville
Tues–Sat, NOON–MIDNIGHT; Sun, 4PM–MIDNIGHT

From the sacred to the secular, Brownsville's former synagogue has been transformed into a restaurant and cyber-café.

A visit to Elmo's is a family affair for Arthur and Brad Paluso of Charleroi.

Drowned or Crowned

"That South Brownsville team was almost unbeatable," recalled Howard Duff of Dawson. Howard witnessed some epic water battles between local fire departments. He was seven years old in 1936, living near the Park and Tilford Distillery in South Brownsville.

"The battles I remember best occurred down by the wharf in Brownsville. On different occasions, there would be teams from California, Fredericktown, and other communities, as well as from Brownsville area fire companies. The spectators would line the inter-county bridge and the river bank to watch the water battles.

"Nowadays each team stands on the ground and aims its fire hose at a barrel that is suspended on an overhead wire, but in those days, firemen stood on barges in the river and no barrel was used.

"Each team of firemen aimed its fire hose at the other team and blasted away with a powerful stream of water. The battle ended when all members of one team had been swept off their barge into the river.

"Since the stream of water that comes from a fire hose is very forceful, even the members of the winning team emerged from the battle black and blue and bruised all over.

"After the last losing fireman had been blasted into the waters of the Mon and the winning team had been crowned, one last spectacle capped the day's events.

"As a grand finale," Howard said, "the firemen would aim their hoses up into the air toward the inter-county bridge and pump water clear over the bridge! On a sunny day, it would make a beautiful rainbow."

—Glenn Tunney writes about Brownsville for the *Uniontown Herald-Standard*, April 13, 2003.

Monongahela Route

PENN-CRAFT

Penn-Craft Historical District/Redstone Knitting Mill
Bounded by PA 4020, Twp. Road 326, and Twp. Road 549, Penn-Craft

From scenes of everyday life to panoramic landscapes, the photos lining the walls of the Redstone Knitting Mill tell the history of Penn-Craft, from 1937 to the 1940s. Located near Brownsville, Penn-Craft was the site of a social and economic experiment that evolved into the nation's first privately funded subsistence community.

At a time when the Great Depression was claiming a 30 percent unemployment rate in coal towns throughout Fayette County, the American Friends Service Committee (AFSC) saw an opportunity for its "back to the land" philosophy to take root.

In 1937, the Quaker-based AFSC purchased 200 acres from Isaiah Craft and selected 50 families of different ethnic, racial, and religious backgrounds to live and work together. The participants were required to help build each other's homes and to contribute time and labor to the cooperative farms, store, and Redstone Knitting Mill.

For Lou Orslene, former director of the Brownsville Area Revitalization Corporation (BARC), those pictures tell the history of his grandparents, Joseph and Elizabeth Shaw. "My grandfather worked on the railroad," Lou says. "They had nine children and had been living in Brownsville."

As Penn-Craft pioneers, the Shaws were there that day in 1937 when First Lady Eleanor Roosevelt came to visit. A strong proponent of self-help, Mrs. Roosevelt said: "The value of the Penn-Craft project would be only partly realized if we view it as just an adventure in community development. We must see that its basic motivation of respect for the human spirit and faith in human resourcefulness have deep meaning for every area of economic and social life, not only in America, but in all lands." Penn-Craft served as a model for some 80 other subsistence communities established in the United States and around the world.

Today Penn-Craft is listed on the National Register of Historic Places. Its homes are privately owned, and the Redstone Mill has been given new life as a public meeting space.

Courtesy of Penn-Craft

above: The newly renovated Redstone Mill is used for special events and quilting classes.

below: In the 1930s, Penn-Craft women found employment at the knitting mill.

An Italian master mason named Billiani built this house for his family, and taught other families how to build their own houses.

Southwest from Pittsburgh

MASONTOWN AREA

From Pittsburgh: Take PA 51 S to PA 88 S to PA 43 S (Toll $.50) to US 40 E.

Half-Day Tour: Sites 11–14
Fort Mason Historical Society: From Brownsville, US 40 E to PA 166 S to Masontown. Right on Main St. Historical Society is on left. ***New Geneva Pottery:*** Return on PA 166 N to PA 21. Go 3 mi. on PA 21 E to McClellandtown. Left at firehouse (Puritan Rd.). Left on Main St. Go halfway down hill. Pottery is on left. ***St. Max. Kolbe Shrine:*** Stay on PA 21 E. Go 3.2 mi. (to DiCenzo sign). Left on SR 3023. Go 2 mi. to Footedale. Shrine is at St. Thomas Church on right. ***Smock Historical Society:*** Stay on PA 21 E to US 119 N to Pittsburgh St. exit (PA 51 N). Go 6.7 mi. on PA 51 N. Left at Smock sign on SR 4016. Go 1.6 mi. Historical Society is on right. ***Return to Pittsburgh:*** SR 4016 to PA 51 N.

On the river near Masontown, you'll see Duke Energy, a huge 630-megawatt, natural gas–fired electricity generation plant.

During the industrial boom of the early 20th century, Masontown was the center of the "Klondike" coke district, a nickname alluding to the money-making opportunities in the Alaskan frontier during the gold rush days.

MASONTOWN

11

Fort Mason Historical Society
724–583–8849
548 North Main Street, Masontown
Sat & Sun, 10AM–4PM

Although the doctor is no longer in, the home of a well-known local physician now houses the Fort Mason Historical Society.

Historical Society members Clara Pento (left) and Kay Rendina work to preserve the life and times of this coal-mining region.

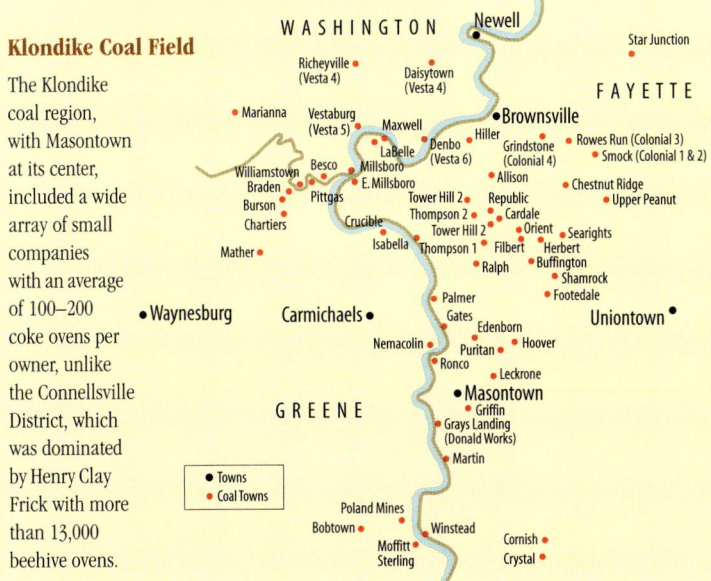

Klondike Coal Field

The Klondike coal region, with Masontown at its center, included a wide array of small companies with an average of 100–200 coke ovens per owner, unlike the Connellsville District, which was dominated by Henry Clay Frick with more than 13,000 beehive ovens.

195

Monongahela Route

McCLELLANDTOWN

New Geneva Stoneware
724–737–1370
840 Main Street, McClellandtown
www.newgeneva.com
Mon–Sat, 9AM–5PM

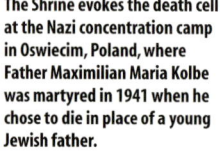

right: New Geneva Stoneware owner Lynn Newman shows it takes a steady hand and a clear eye to paint a pot.

During the 19th century, New Geneva, Pa., was a potter's paradise. Located in nearby McClellandtown, the New Geneva Stoneware Company pays homage to the past while meeting the needs of the 21st-century public. Its production facility is in a restored church social hall. The company's own pottery and works from other local and national potters, as well as handcrafted tinware and prints, are for sale on the top floor.

FOOTEDALE

St. Maximilian Kolbe Shrine
528 Footedale Road (PA 3023), Footedale
Outdoors at St. Thomas Church

Dedicated to the memory of a recent Polish saint, this shrine shows the continued connection between the predominantly Polish parish of St. Thomas Church and the homeland of the parishoners' ancestors. The parishoners built the shrine guided by their priest, Father Sebastian Pajdzik, an immigrant who came to St. Thomas in 1977, and had served in the Polish resistance during World War II.

The Shrine evokes the death cell at the Nazi concentration camp in Oswiecim, Poland, where Father Maximilian Maria Kolbe was martyred in 1941 when he chose to die in place of a young Jewish father.

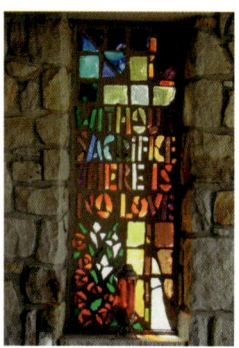

SMOCK

Smock Historical Society
724–677–2528 or 724–677–2415
103 Main Street (2nd floor), Smock
www.orgsites.com/pa/smock
June 1–Oct 31: Sat, 11AM–4PM

Preserving history can be a dirty business. Just ask Pat Myers, president of the Smock Historical Society. When Smock, Pa., was placed on the National Register of Historic Places in 1994, a group of concerned citizens wanted to find a way to tell the stories of the men and women who called this small coal mining town home.

To that end, they set out to transform the long-abandoned H. C. Frick Company's store into a museum. "It was filthy," Pat recalls. "There was no electricity, the windows were boarded up, and I was afraid a ghost would get me any minute."

Despite the ongoing threat of spirits — or maybe because of it — Pat and other members of the historical society kept cleaning and planning for the future. Years later, they finally had something tangible to show for their efforts.

Today, this second-floor space preserves the life and times of Smock through murals, maps, artifacts, antiques, photos, and books. In addition, a typical patch-town living room, kitchen, and bedroom,

and Cicconi's Bar, a former favorite pro-union gathering place, have been recreated in striking detail.

Visitors also will discover Smock's claim to historical fame. Unlike other southwestern Pennsylvania mining towns, Smock's development was fueled by three companies. From the 1880s to the 1950s, the Pittsburgh Coal, Hurst Coal, and H. C. Frick companies kept the area's mines running and beehive coke ovens firing. Another legacy the companies left behind are the coal-patch communities like Hurst Row, Smock Hill, and New Town, which were built to house their workers. Pat Myers says, "In the '50s and '60s, there was a stigma to living in the patch. Now times have changed; we value what our ancestors did here."

In the 1930s, local labor activists held their meetings at Guido Cicconi's Union Beer Garden in Smock. In an attempt to discourage meetings, company police drove past the bar spraying bullets. Although no one was harmed, one bullet struck this framed photo of Franklin Delano Roosevelt — in the heart. This picture became for Smock coke workers a symbol of patriotism and the freedom to organize.

Exhibits emphasize women's role in keeping coal-patch families together during difficult times.

Monongahela Route

FREDERICKTOWN AREA

From Pittsburgh: *Take PA 51 S to PA 43 S to PA 88 S by Fredericktown.*

One-Day Tour: Sites 15–19
Fredericktown Ferry: *PA 88 S into Fredericktown. Quick left at Ferry sign (Frederick St.).* **Coal Miner Memorial:** *Stay on PA 88 S. Go .2 mi. Right on Crawford Rd. at blinking light. Go 2.6 mi. Bear right at "Y." Left on Bulldog Dr. to high school.* **Rices Landing Riverfront:** *Return to Fredericktown. Right on PA 88 S. Go 5.3 mi. Left on PA 188 E. Bear left at "Y" onto Rices Landing Rd. Go 1.1 mi. under viaduct. Right on McClain St. Left on Water St. into parking lot. Explore on foot.* **McCutcheon Monument:** *Return to PA 88 N. Go 11.8 mi. to Centerville exit 30B. Take US 40 W. Go 1.7 mi. Angle left, then bear right up hill on Old National Pk. Go .5 mi. to monument on right in Taylor Cemetery.* **Westerwald Pottery:** *Return to US 40 W. Left 9.9 mi. through Scenery Hill to Westerwald Pottery on right (look for signs).* ***Return to Pittsburgh:*** *US 40 W to I-79 N.*

FREDERICKTOWN

Fredericktown Ferry
Fredericktown (Daylight hours, weather permitting)

Captain Paul Wroule

Once upon a time, the mid- and upper-Monongahela River supported a thriving community of ferryboats. Now, the Fredericktown Ferry (a.k.a. the Frederick) is the lone survivor.

Like most long-term companions, the Mon and the Frederick share a history. Through floods and droughts, economic upswings and spiraling downturns, the two have managed to maintain their business-as-usual love affair.

With the recent opening of a prison on the Mon's eastern shore, business has increased. As a result, three captains now take shifts at the ferry's helm. With 38 years of experience piloting river barges, Paul Wroule is the newest addition.

Working the throttle on a crisp fall day, Captain Paul explains that the Frederick is kept on course by two separate cables — one pulls while the other serves as a guide.

Since bridges on this part of the river are few and far between, the Frederick is a time saver. Licensed in 1948, the diesel-powered ferry makes the 750-foot crossing from Fredericktown to Labelle in just three or four minutes, depending on the current. Crossing via the nearest bridge, one ferry passenger reports, takes nearly 45 minutes one way. Considering the cost of the boat ride — 15 cents for pedestrians, 75 cents per car, and up to $4 for trucks, trailers, or RVs (depending on weight) — it's a bargain.

Except in the most severe weather, about 150 cars and their drivers go along for the ride on the Ferry every weekday.

Southwest from Pittsburgh

16 Coal Miner Memorial
724–267–4948
179 Crawford Road, Fredericktown
www.bc.k12.pa.us/localhistory/index.htm
Outdoors. Open year-round.

Although placing a Coal Miner Memorial at a school might seem unusual, coal was king in this part of southwestern Pennsylvania for generations. Bethlehem Center High School teacher Tim Shimrock, raised in the nearby town of Marianna, sculpted the memorial with the help of his students.

BY THE WAY

Bethlehem Center High School shares the name of the mining company that dominated the area.

Community Museums and Historical Societies

There's a local museum or historical society in almost every town in southwestern Pennsylvania. Each one offers something a little different from the rest — yet each is part of a larger pattern. Some display antique wedding dresses, intricately embroidered clothes from the "old country," or high-school band uniforms, while others have rooms devoted to coal-mining gear, steel mill replicas, or old-fashioned kitchen appliances. One has recreated a turn-of-the-century beauty parlor, another an early doctor's office. Some have a theme, such as fire-fighting or patch-town life. And always there are scrapbooks offering a glimpse of life gone by with family and industry photos and tinted postcards, collected and preserved by dedicated volunteers.

Local museums preserve historic photos such as this one of the Vesta 4 Mine near California, Pa., once the largest bituminous mine in the United States.

Courtesy of California Area Historical Society

These organizations are often a visitor's quickest and friendliest introduction to a community. But, although they welcome guests, their most loyal audiences are their own townspeople. The real purpose of local museums and historical societies is to reinforce a sense of place and pride in those who live there. These institutions are keepers of community identity. And, in America's increasingly transient society, that is an important role to play.

Monongahela Route

RICES LANDING

Rices Landing Riverfront
River Road, Rices Landing

When Rices Landing was incorporated as a borough in 1903, its streets were lined with shops, taverns, and trading posts. Its abundant natural resources — clay, sand, coal, and lumber — helped local businesses prosper. Its proximity to the Monongahela River made it an ideal industrial and transportation hub.

More than 100 years later, the stores, coal mines, and lock and dam that once defined this community are all gone. What remains is a strong connection to the river and the land. Rices Landing serves as one of the entry points to the Greene River Trail. Running parallel to the Monongahela, this rail trail meanders through the countryside for miles.

Many of the town's 500 residents also remain connected to the past. One of those residents is Murray Kline. "When I was a kid," he says, "our house was filled with pictures and stories." Now this former shop teacher takes it upon himself to tell the stories of his hometown and the people who lived and worked there.

A Murray-guided tour begins at the Lock Six Museum, where photographs and memorabilia recount the days when the river was the talk of the town. Next, he suggests a walk through the Hewitt Cemetery. Dating back to 1870, the grounds are the final resting place for the area's most prominent citizens.

Another resting place (of sorts) on Murray's list is W. A. Young & Sons Foundry. William A. Young built the original machine shop in 1900. He added a coke-fired foundry in 1908 and turned on the electricity in 1928.

When the shop closed its doors in 1965, everything — the tools, drills, nails, presses, lathes, wooden molds and patterns, rags, and empty bottles — was left behind. And that's where it's stayed. Although the dust has grown thick and the air stale, the image of what was once a thriving business and a vibrant example of America's industrial heritage remains clear.

Rices Landing riverfront park offers one of the Monongahela River's loveliest views.

Eileen and Ron Nucci are among the many visitors and residents who enjoy hiking and biking along the Greene River Trail from Fredericktown to Rices Landing.

Local historian Murray Kline has led the effort to preserve W. A. Young & Sons Foundry.

Southwest from Pittsburgh

Documented by the National Park Service and listed on the National Register of Historic Places, W. A. Young & Sons Foundry is the site each spring of the Pittsburgh Area Artist–Blacksmiths Association's annual Hammer-In.

Foundries, Machine Shops, and Patternmaking

In the late 1880s and early 1900s, small foundries and machine shops partnered with large steel mills by providing services and parts. The foundries then were only a bit larger than blacksmith shops of the time, although foundries had more machine power and generally more clients.

Around 1900, foundries and machine shops began to grow in size as demand increased the need for more employees and advanced technology. Shops and plants in the Rivers of Steel region included W. A. Young & Sons in **Rices Landing** (Monongahela Route); United Engineer and Foundry in Vandergrift; National Roll Company in Avonmore; Hyde Park Foundry in Hyde Park (Alle-Kiski Route); Latrobe Pattern Company in Latrobe (Youghiogheny Route); Mesta Machine in West Homestead; and Champion Tool & Die in McKeesport (Three Rivers

Wooden patterns for casting machine parts

Route). While there are fewer foundries since the contraction of the steel industry in the 1980s, some, such as Latrobe Pattern Company, Champion Tool & Die, and National Roll Company (now Akers National Roll) are still in business. Many now operate with fewer than 100 employees as "jobbing shops," doing work on demand.

Patternmaking in a foundry is a craft that requires great skill and patience, and takes years to learn. A patternmaker uses both hand tools and power tools to plan and build wooden patterns, or molds. These molds are packed in sand, then pulled out to leave their imprint. Molten iron or steel is then poured into the sand to cast the shape of the pattern. To make the pattern easier to remove from the sand mold, it can be constructed in sections.

Many patternmakers have to complete an apprenticeship by "shadowing" experienced workers. This is often where they learn to read blueprints, an essential skill in itself. Ruth Budosh, whose husband, Charles, worked at the Hyde Park Foundry, explains what a typical day was like for her husband. "Well, he'd start with a blueprint. Then from the blueprint he'd get all the measurements, and then out of wood he would make whatever his blueprint said…[The men] made some patterns that were as big as a house!" Charles's son, Ed, remembers his father crawling on ladders to build certain patterns, and studying the blueprints on the table at home for the next day's work.

Hammers and tongs

Monongahela Route

Pottery

Rich clay deposits have been one of southwestern Pennsylvania's most versatile natural resources. In addition to brickmaking for the steel industry, roads, and home construction, another regional industry's growth depended on clay — pottery. Soon after 1800, German artisans established thriving potteries in riverfront towns in Fayette and Greene Counties, producing salt-glazed stoneware as well as redware for shipping whiskey and other goods to market and for home use. Through the 19th century, pottery production remained an important source of income in the region.

Contemporary local pottery: plate by Craig Roberts, bowls by Laura Schlesinger, and vase by Linda and James Winegar

In southwestern Pennsylvania today, pottery continues to thrive as both an industrial craft and an art form. At the **Westerwald Pottery** and the **New Geneva Stoneware Company** (Monongahela Route), visitors can watch artisans produce handmade salt-glazed stoneware and other pottery, then stop in at the companies' showrooms. Independent local potters display their work for sale at the **Artists' Co-op** gallery (Monongahela Route), and the **Society for Contemporary Craft** (Three Rivers Route), as well as at the region's many craft fairs and festivals. The **Greene County Historical Museum** includes a permanent collection of antique pottery from the region (Monongahela Route). **Touchstone Center for Crafts** (Youghiogheny Route) offers weekend and week-long workshops in ceramics. Classes for young and old are available at the Pittsburgh Center for the Arts and the **Manchester Craftsmen's Guild** (Three Rivers Route).

top: Throwing a pot
bottom: Earthenware mugs ready to be glazed

Pottery Speak

Pottery comes in many different kinds of "wares."

agate ware *pottery made from clays of two differing colors, not completely mixed. The result is a streaked effect resembling agate.*

earthenware *pots that are porous when unglazed. Usually fired at low temperatures, earthenware is softer and more easily damaged than stoneware.*

flatware *plates, saucers, trays, etc.*

greenware *pottery that has not been fired.*

hollow ware *cups, jugs, bowls, etc.*

stoneware *pottery fired at a high temperature to make it non-porous. Unglazed stoneware can hold water, but it is usual to glaze the inside of the vessel, at least. Stoneware is more durable than earthenware, and capable of resolving finer detail.*

redware *terracotta, usually unglazed.*

Southwest from Pittsburgh

CENTERVILLE

18

McCutcheon Monument
Old Route 40, in Taylor Cemetery
1.4 miles east of Centerville

The McCutcheon Monument is a granite memorial located in the Taylor Methodist Episcopal churchyard. James Shannon McCutcheon (1824–1902), a miserly farmer who made his fortune from coal discovered on his land, chose to build a monument to himself rather than leave his money to his family. On July 27, 1936, a tornado ripped through the churchyard, tearing off the granite obelisk that sat atop the monument, leaving only the base. Local people affectionately call what's left the "Spite Monument."

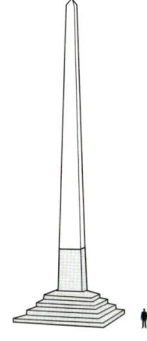

above: The monument stood 85 feet high from its base, about 18 times the height of a man.

below: James Shannon McCutcheon

SCENERY HILL

19

Westerwald Pottery
724-945-6000
40 Pottery Lane, Scenery Hill
Mon–Fri, 8AM–5PM; Sat, 10AM–5PM; Sun, 11AM–5PM,

This shop has it all — books about local pottery history, working studios that welcome visitors, and a wide range of traditional pottery for sale.

Phil Schaltenbrand, historian, craftsman, and owner of Westerwald Pottery, is the author of *Old Pots*, a history of salt-glazed stoneware in the region.

203

Monongahela Route

WASHINGTON AREA

From Pittsburgh: Take I-79 S to Washington.

One-Day Tour: Sites 20–25
PA Trolley Museum: I-79 S to Meadowlands exit 41. Follow blue Trolley Museum signs. **Quail Acres:** From Museum, right 1 mi on N. Main St. Left on SR 4049 (Country Club Rd.). Go 1 mi. to stoplight. Left on Pike St. to first stoplight. Right on Racetrack Rd. Go 1 mi. Left on Quail Acre Ln. Go .5 mi. to shops on left. **Artists' Co-op (in Washington Mall):** Return 1 mi. on Racetrack Rd. Take I-79 S to I-70 E to Murtland exit 19A. Get in right lane for Mall. In parking lot, left at second stop sign around Rex's to Mall entrance. **Washington Tourism Promotion Agency:** From Mall, right on Murtland Ave. (PA 19 S). Go .2 mi. Left on North Ave. Go .5 mi. Right on E. Beau St. Go. 4 mi. Left on S. Main St. Go 3 blocks to railroad crossing. Right into depot parking lot. **Duncan and Miller Glass Museum:** From WTPA parking lot, left on S. Main St. Go 1 block. Left on US 40 W/PA 18 N (Jefferson Ave.). Follow Jefferson Ave. for 1 mi. to Museum on left. ☎ **Side trip to Old Concord Presbyterian Church:** From Museum, right on Jefferson Ave. (PA 18 S). Go 15.5 mi. Church is on left. **Return to Pittsburgh:** PA 18 N to I-79.

WASHINGTON

Pennsylvania Trolley Museum
724–228–9256
1 Museum Road, Washington
www.pa-trolley.org
Memorial Day–Labor Day: Mon–Sun, 10 AM–4 PM (last tour 3 PM);
April–Memorial Day: Weekends only, 11 AM–5 PM (last tour 4 PM)
Adults: $6; Seniors: $5; Children 2–15: $3.50; Children under 2: Free

Visitors can ride on the original "Streetcar Named Desire."

Atrolley by any other name (such as streetcar or cable car) would still take us places — places as routine as the office, as imaginative as Mister Rogers' Neighborhood of Make-Believe or as provocative as our own desires. From the very first clinking clanking trolley of the late 1880s to the high-speed, high-tech systems of the turn of the millenium, this mode of transportation enabled us to travel beyond our own backyards.

With the dawn of the Electric Age, it seemed that the sky was the limit. By 1918, the Pittsburgh Railways Company operated some 2,000 trolley cars, 65 different lines, and more than 600 miles of track. (That same year, 18,000 miles of trolley tracks lined the country.) Back then, a nickel got you where you wanted to go.

The Great Depression hit the lines hard. But during World War II, when the civilian front was facing severe fuel and rubber rationing, streetcars were returned to service. Once victory was declared and the soldiers started marching home, however, the trolley found itself on a collision course with the automobile. As families began moving to the suburbs, more and more highways, shopping malls, and fast-food restaurants were being constructed to accommodate this dramatic shift in lifestyle. The trolley was fast becoming obsolete.

Southwest from Pittsburgh

But thanks to three forward-thinking local streetcar enthusiasts, it was never completely forgotten. In 1949, recognizing the importance of preserving history as well as of restoring actual cars to their former glory, these individuals joined to create the Pennsylvania Trolley Museum. By 1953, the group formally organized the museum into a nonprofit corporation, purchased a 2,000-foot section of abandoned railroad track in Washington County, and counted three discarded trolleys as their entire collection.

Opened to the public in 1963, the museum has never slowed down. Now encompassing 30 acres, the facility features a 3-mile track, gift shop, restoration and repair garage, trolley-car barn, and education center complete with photo displays and diorama.

But at the end of the line, the main attraction remains the trolleys. The museum's collection now numbers 45 (12 in running condition, the rest in various stages of restoration). Standouts include Pittsburgh's own 77/54 (dubbed the "Flying Fraction," it ran from the North Side to Carrick to Bloomfield); 1711 (retired in 1953, it was the last car to make the trek from Washington, Pa., to Pittsburgh); and the "Fred Rogers" trolley (Philadelphia Transit Car 5326 was the star of an episode of *Mister Rogers' Neighborhood*).

Streetcar tokens and vintage advertisements turn back the clock to a time when trolleys took you almost everywhere you wanted to go.

Railroads

Newcomers arriving in southwestern Pennsylvania by car or plane may find it hard to imagine how important railroading was in the region's industrial history. The first tracks were laid here in the 1840s. But it was from the 1870s on that the railroad network spread throughout the region.

During the 100-year Steel Era, rail lines of all sizes crisscrossed the seven-county Pittsburgh Industrial District. In major towns, streetcar lines reached into every neighborhood. Interurban lines connected mine patches and market towns with each other and with Pittsburgh. Long-distance mainlines — the Pennsylvania Railroad, the Baltimore & Ohio, the Norfolk & Western, the Pittsburgh & Lake Erie (often called "P&LE"), and the Bessemer & Lake Erie — carried raw materials, products, produce, and people between southwestern Pennsylvania and the rest of the nation. Huge steel companies built rail spurs to carry coke fuel from their mines to riverfront barge landings and workers from one plant or patch to another. At the mill sites, narrow-gauge "dinky" trains moved tons of material from shop to shop and transported molten iron in insulated "torpedo" cars from blast furnace to rolling mill. Within U. S. Steel's Homestead Works alone there were more than 150 miles of track! Train spotters can still find evidence of this expansive rail network throughout the Rivers of Steel area.

Vast, multi-track railyards can be viewed at Conway (Ohio-Beaver Route) and Pitcairn (Three Rivers Route). Families can ride the rails on tours at the **Kiski Junction Railroad** in Schenley (Alle-Kiski Route), the **Youngwood Historical and Railroad Museum** (Youghiogheny Route), and the **Pennsylvania Trolley Museum** in Washington (Monongahela Route). Many depots have been converted into restaurants, often with exhibits about their railroading past, including **Station Square** (Three Rivers Route), **Tarentum Station Restaurant** (Alle-Kiski Route),

and **DiSalvo's Station Restaurant** (Youghiogheny Route). Almost anywhere, visitors can still hear the penetrating, echoing whistle and deep-throated rumble of a long coal train as it winds its way through the hollows to fuel the region's industries.

Monongahela Route

Quail Acres
724–229–9819
1445 Washington Road, Washington
www.quailacres.com
Tues–Sat, 10AM–5PM; Sun, NOON–5PM
Cattail Coffee & Tea: Tues–Sat, 8AM–5PM

Quail Acres provides an outlet for local traditional artists. Shops include Westerwald Pottery's retail shop, Cattail Coffee & Tea, and Country Confections.

Building on Washington County's long tradition of wool production, this shop in the Quail House Emporium co-op sells quality yarn.

Artists' Co-op
724–229–0365
Washington Mall, Washington
Wed–Sat, NOON–8 PM

Quilting and pottery are among the many crafts from around the region for sale at the Artists' Co-op. Call the Co-op for information on special events.

Southwest from Pittsburgh

Washington County Tourism Promotion Agency
1-800-531-4114
273 South Main Street, Washington
www.washpatourism.org
Mon–Fri, 9AM–4:30PM

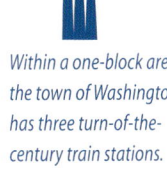

This historic Baltimore & Ohio (B&O) train station in the heart of Washington, Pa., has been restored and now serves as the county's visitor center.

Within a one-block area, the town of Washington has three turn-of-the-century train stations. Look for them as you drive through town.

Washington

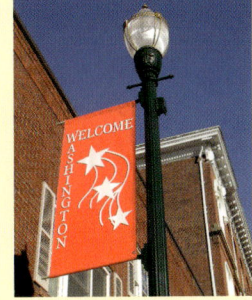

"Little" Washington, as it is known in the region (to distinguish it from Washington, DC), is one of the area's oldest communities. It is located along the Chartiers River, a tributary of the Ohio River. Before European settlement, a Native American village called "Catfish Camp" stood at the site. In 1775, George Washington obtained a land patent for the area. By 1784, 13 families of Scots-Irish "Covenanters" (the most conservative Presbyterian sect) had moved onto the land, claiming squatters' rights. Washington evicted them and held the land until 1796, when he sold off plots to other farmers. Scots-Irish settlers continued to predominate, joined by English Methodists from Virginia, African-Americans, and a small number of Germans. The city played an important role in the Whiskey Rebellion of the late 18th century, and in the early–19th-century movement to abolish slavery.

Industrial activity began early, with a "tin manufactory" founded in 1792 and financed by a local lending co-operative. But the town's main industrialization took place after the Civil War. In the early 1880s, discoveries of oil and natural gas brought wealthy industrialists who built glass factories and firms that made equipment for the oil industry. By the early 20th century, there were 26 glass factories in the city, several of which had relocated from Pittsburgh.

Although glassmaking remained important, after 1890 the industrial spotlight turned to metals, with new tin-plating factories and iron works. By 1900, steel started to replace iron and tin. Mills producing sheet steel and stainless steel sprang up, with new plants being built even into the late 1940s. Connected with Pittsburgh and the rest of the region by a network of freight and passenger railways and interurban tracks, Washington served as the industrial center for its area.

Today, Washington is known as much for commerce and education as for industry. Visitors can still drive through the East Washington Historic District past more than 100 Queen Anne-style industrialists' mansions, or tour the **Duncan and Miller Glass Museum**, with its exhibits on Washington's glass industry. A highlight of the trip will be a visit to the **Pennsylvania Trolley Museum** for a ride into the region's railroad history, followed by a stop at **Quail Acres** or the **Artists' Co-op** gallery to discover the work of regional artists in pottery, metals, and fabric.

Monongahela Route

Duncan and Miller Glass Museum
724–225–9950
525 Jefferson Avenue, Washington
April 1–Oct 31 (except holidays): Th–Sun, 11AM–4PM
By appointment for groups
Admission: $2.50; For groups of 10 or more: $2 each

When Duncan and Miller Glass closed its doors for good in 1955, few suspected this end-of-an-era event would mark the beginning of a new appreciation of the company's products.

Today, authentic Duncan and Miller glassware is a hot commodity. Collectors abound. Conventions are commonplace. Clubs are all the rage. And, thanks to the efforts of the National Duncan Glass Society, Inc., there's even a museum chock-full of sugar bowls and creamers, salt and pepper shakers, ash trays and shot glasses, plates, and vases, in patterns ranging from Caribbean to Tear Drop, Festive to Early American.

The Duncan and Miller Glass Museum opened in 1975 with just two rooms in the Washington County Historical Society building (a.k.a. the LeMoyne House). Over the years, the collection outgrew its space. As a result, the Duncan Glass Society found a new home on Jefferson Avenue, just one block from where the fabled glass plant once stood.

above: A former Duncan and Miller worker's home now houses the glass museum.

right: Glass blower at Duncan and Miller circa 1920. The lamp in the foreground was made at the factory.

The house was the property of a former Duncan and Miller factory worker. According to Shirley O'Brien, president of the society, the owner was thrilled to learn that his address was destined to become the center of an ever-expanding Duncan Glass universe.

Dedicated in 1993, the new Duncan and Miller Glass Museum affirmed its commitment to paying tribute to the company's employees, their skills and craftsmanship, and to the management and its record of productivity—and to the enduring beauty of the glass itself.

That's something Shirley personally appreciates. "When I got married in 1949, one of our gifts was First Love [a tried and true Duncan and Miller pattern]," she says. "Back then, you knew you were getting Duncan Glass." Although Shirley didn't join the Duncan Glass Society until 1977, she's a long-time collector. "I don't even know how much I have," she says. What she does know is that the society's collection is present and accounted for throughout the two-story house.

In addition to countless goblets, animal figurines, oil lamps (some dating back to the 1800s), the museum displays photos, blueprints for the construction of the plant's Washington location, tools, molds, and the original factory clock.

The company's history is traced to 1865, when George Duncan, along with his sons, Harry and James, and his son-in-law, Augustus Heisey, purchased an existing glassmaking business on Pittsburgh's South Side.

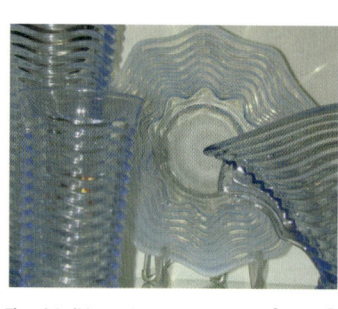

Tinted Caribbean glass

Situated near the Monongahela River, Duncan & Sons had easy access to water transport, as well as to the eastern European glass workers and artisans who tended to settle in this part of town.

Nearly 10 years later, the respected glass designer John Ernest Miller signed on with the company. After a fire destroyed the South Side facility in 1892, the decision was made to move 30 miles south to Washington, Pa., where transportation via the railroads was still readily available.

With 70 of its Pittsburgh-based workers making the move, the new factory was up and running by the winter of 1893. By 1900, Miller was offered a full partnership in the business and the company became known as Duncan and Miller.

Black light brings out the beauty of uranium glass.

During its heyday (1893–1955), it was said that Duncan and Miller Glass employed at least one member of every family in Washington. After the plant shut down, hope remained that another glass company would take over. Those hopes, however, were extinguished when a fire reduced the factory to ashes in 1956. But thanks to the museum and its supporters, the Duncan and Miller legacy lives on not far from where the furnaces once fired.

OLD CONCORD

㉕ ✕ ⋏ Ⓔ
Old Concord Presbyterian Church
724–222–3306
155 Old Concord Road, Old Concord
☎ Phone ahead, or attend service: Sun, 11 AM

Head to Old Concord Church during July and August for homemade peach pies.

Hidden in a New England–style landscape is the delicately painted floral plasterwork of itinerant Italian workmen who passed through southwestern Pennsylvania as they helped to build the region's railroads. Their traditional artistry graces the ceiling of the Old Concord Presbyterian Church, built in 1884.

Monongahela Route

TRAVELING ON I-79

From Pittsburgh: Take I-79 S almost to West Virginia border.

One-Day Tour: Sites 26–30
Welcome Center: I-79 S to Mount Morris exit 1. Left off exit. Left to northbound entrance. Go 5 mi. on I-79 N. Welcome Center is on right.
RAG Cumberland Mine: Continue 1.5 miles on I-79 N. Take Kirby Garards Fort exit 7. Left on SR 2018 W (Kirby Rd.). Go 4 mi. through Kirby to Mine.
Greene County Historical Society: SR 2018 E through Kirby to I-79 N to Waynesburg exit 14. Go 2.5 mi. on PA 21 E. Right on Rolling Meadows Rd. Go 1.5 mi. to Historical Society on left. **Ruff Creek General Store:** Return to PA 21 W to I-79 N to Ruff Creek exit 19. Left .3 mi. on PA 221 N to store.
Spring House: Return to I-79 N to I-70 E to Eighty Four exit 25. Left on PA 519 N. Go 2 mi. to stoplight. Left 1 mi. on PA 136 W. Spring House is on right. **Return to Pittsburgh:** PA 136 W to I-70 W / I-79 N.

26 Welcome Center
724–627–7331
Exit 1, I-79 N, Kirby

Visitors crossing into Pennsylvania will get their first glimpse of the region's coal heritage at the I-79 Welcome Center at Exit 1 near the West Virginia border.

above: Outside, the Coal Miners' Monument honors the region's miners.

right: Inside, artifacts and a mural depict the coal miner's life.

A Miner's Prayer

Down beneath the frozen ground the coal is laying,
  Only waiting till we seek it from its bed,
While above the earth with aching heart we're praying,
  While each wife and mother waits with bowed down head.

— Folk ballad sung by Mrs. Ralph B. Thompson in Pittsburgh, recorded in 1940 by folklorist George Korson

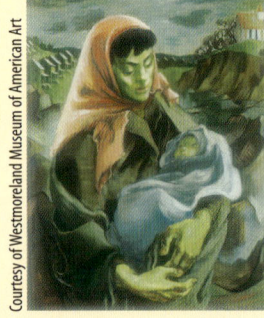

Madonna of the Mines,
gouache on paper,
by Mildred Young Olmes
(b. 1906), 1949

Courtesy of Westmoreland Museum of American Art

Southwestern Pennsylvania Mine Disasters 1884–1962

Date	Mine	Location	Killed
1884	West Leisenring	West Leisenring	19
1884	Youngstown	Uniontown	14
1886	Uniondale	Dunbar	6
1890	Hill Farm	Dunbar	31
1891	Mammouth	Mount Pleasant	109
1899	Grindstone	Grindstone	5
1902	Catsburg	Monongahela	5
1903	Ferguson	Connellsville	17
1904	Harwick	Cheswick	179
1905	Clyde	Fredericktown	6
1905	Hazel Kirk No. 2	Monongahela	5
1905	Braznell	Bentleyville	7
1907	Naomi	Fayette City	34
1908	Rachel and Agnes	Marianna	154
1911	Hazel	Canonsburg	9
1913	Cincinnati	Finleyville	98
1915	Patterson No. 2	Elizabeth	9
1918	Harmar	Harmarville	8
1920	Ontario	Cokesburg	6
1924	Gates No. 1	Brownsville	10
1925	New Slope	Sewickley	5
1927	No. 53	Cokeburg	6
1928	Mather No. 1	Mather	195
1933	Oakmont	Barking	7
1945	Crucible	Crucible	5
1957	Marianna No. 58	Marianna	6
1962	Robena No. 3	Carmichaels	37

www.cdc.gov/niosh/mining/data/discoal.html

Southwest from Pittsburgh

KIRBY

27 RAG Cumberland Mine
Kirby

As you ride through Greene County's rolling farmland near Kirby, you would never know you are in a vast industrial site. But, as you round the bend, spread before you is the sprawling RAG Cumberland Mining Company. Outward evidence of long-wall mining with underground corridors stretching miles beneath the surface, this facility processes 1,600 tons of coal per hour. The coal then is shipped via RAG Cumberland rail lines to company dock facilities on the Monongahela River, where it is loaded onto barges.

Some uses for coal:
Light oil
Gas
Coke
Chemicals
Tar
Medicines
Home heating
Gas engines
Glassmaking
Refrigeration
Household ammonia
Rubber cement
Dyes
Linoleum
Baking powder
Insecticides
Jewelry
Fertilizer
Perfume
Billiard balls
Pencils
Sugar substitutes
Paints and varnishes
Car parts
Plastics
Radio parts
Explosives
Wood preservatives
Food preservatives
Steelmaking
Road paving
Sidewalks
Charcoal
Fuel for power plants
Waterproofing
Roofing

Photos courtesy RAG Cumberland Mine

In Greene County, a beautiful corner of Pennsylvania that is literally built on coal, mining replaced farming as the key industry after the 1880s.

More than 50% of the electricity in the United States is generated by coal.

Monongahela Route

WAYNESBURG

Greene County Historical Society
724–627–3204
918 Rolling Meadows Road, Waynesburg
www.greenepa.net/~museum
May–Aug: Wed–Fri, 10AM–4PM; Sat & Sun, NOON–4PM
Sept–Oct: Th–Sun, NOON–4PM

Explore a maze of 52 rooms to discover the rich agricultural and industrial heritage of Greene County. On site is a W & W narrow-gauge steam locomotive and the one-room, brick Coal Lick schoolhouse built in the 1870s.

above: This steam locomotive was fueled by locally mined coal.

right: Dating from the 19th century, the museum's main building originally housed the county poor farm.

RUFF CREEK

Ruff Creek General Store
724–627–9122
720 Washington Road, Ruff Creek
Mon–Sat, 7AM–8PM; Sun, 10AM–5PM

Before supermarkets, there were general stores. You can still find one at Ruff Creek, where local residents buy everything from penny candy to hunting gear.

Ruff Creek General Store boasts a century of service to its community.

Southwest from Pittsburgh

Two Company Coal Towns: Cokeburg and Marianna

Many rural communities in eastern Washington and Greene Counties, like those across the Monongahela River, began as company towns. Appropriately named, **Cokeburg** can be seen from Route 40 near Scenery Hill, with its company-built frame duplex houses laid out in neat rows. The town was founded in 1902 by the Ellsworth Collieries coal and coke firm, whose brick store building stands at the entrance to the town. Cokeburg is well-known for the annual St. George's Day Festival held by the local Croatian Fraternal Union lodge.

Listed on the National Historic Register, **Marianna** was founded in 1907 by the Pittsburgh-Buffalo Company, a mining and brickmaking firm. Mine ownership later passed to the Bethlehem Mine Corporation, a subsidiary of Bethlehem Steel. The company's huge coal facility and ranks of beehive ovens dominated the center of town, which was home to several Slavic cultural groups including the reclusive "Old Believers," a sect that grew out of a schism in the Russian Orthodox Church several hundred years ago. One of only a few such congregations in North America, the Old Believers in Marianna keep a strict code of plain dress and observe rituals no longer practiced in the mainstream church.

Old Believers Church in Marianna

Croatian and Serbian Heritage

Although their Balkan homeland is small, Croatians and Serbians have contributed greatly to the steel region's heritage. Two organizations, the Croatian Fraternal Union (CFU) and the Serb National Federation, are based in the Pittsburgh area.

These South Slavic groups arrived in the late 19th century to work in the region's milltowns and coke patches. They came united by their shared customs and spoken language, but separated by a long history of religious difference. Croatians are Roman Catholic, while Serbians are Eastern Orthodox. Croatians write their dialect of Serbo-Croatian in the Latin alphabet, while Serbians use the Cyrillic alphabet.

The Croatians (or Croats) settled along the Allegheny River in Pittsburgh's North Side and in Millvale communities, in milltowns such as Rankin and McKeesport along the Monongahela River, and in Aliquippa and Ambridge on the Ohio, as well as in mining towns such as Cokeburg. After work, they would gather at their local "Cro club" to dance to tamburitza bands,

Community kolo dancing on St. George's Day in Cokeburg

watch Croatian-language plays, or attend performances by Croatian choral groups such as Society Javor. The CFU kept club members up to date through its newspaper *Zajednicar*.

Serbians (or Serbs) congregated in milltowns such as McKeesport and in mine patches such as Carmichaels. They, too, started local ethnic clubs, built houses of worship affiliated with the American wing of the Serbian Orthodox Church, and read the latest news in the *American Srbobran*, a weekly newsletter. St. Sava Serbian Orthodox Church in McKeesport (Three Rivers Route) and St. George Serbian Orthodox in Carmichaels (Monongahela Route) continue traditions such as the Slava (Patronal Feast) in November and burning the *badnjak* (Yule log) at Christmas.

Visitors will want to see the striking murals created by immigrant painter Maxo Vanka for **St. Nicholas Croatian Church** of Millvale, and view the exhibits at the **CFU Museum** in Monroeville (Three Rivers Route). Annual summer events such as the St. George's Day festival in Cokeburg (Monongahela Route) feature *kolo* dancing, *tamburitza* music, and spit-roasted lamb. And there are performances of folk music and dance by the world-renowned Duquesne University Tamburitzans, and by junior tamburitza troupes as well.

Monongahela Route

EIGHTY FOUR

Spring House
724–228–3339
Route 136, Eighty Four
Mon–Sat, 9AM–9PM; Sun, NOON–9PM

BY THE WAY

84 ways to name a town! People say that Eighty Four got its name because:

1) *It commemorated President Cleveland's election in 1884*
2) *The town got its post office in 1884*
3) *B&O Engine 84 stopped there*
4) *The Railway Mail Service used to drop bags of mail on platforms, and this town's bag number was 84*
5) *Eighty Four's location is 80 degrees, four minutes west longitude*
6) *Eighty-four men left the settlement to fight the British in the Revolutionary War*

It's the classic story of girl meets boy, girl marries boy, girl and boy live happily ever after, raising their five children and lots of cows.

Bev and Sam Minor met at a livestock fair. She was showing off her Jerseys, he was strutting his Holsteins. It was love at first moo. After tying the knot and starting a family, the Minors wanted to get back to basics. So, about 27 years ago, they set up a produce stand along Route 136 and encouraged their children to pitch in.

The stand and the Minor kids — Marcia, Kristen (Tee), Jody, Jill, and Sam — became a favorite local roadside attraction. But Bev and Sam shared a dream of owning more cows and more processing equipment and building a brand-new, old-fashioned country store.

In 1975, the Spring House — with 80 acres, 35 cows, and the help of friends and family — was born. The first day, the Minors sold 17 gallons of milk. Now they pasteurize and homogenize 2,000 gallons a week. But that's not all that's grown. These days, the Spring House encompasses 420 acres, 200 cows, 60 full- and part-time workers, a 75-seat sunroom, outdoor picnic tables, a hot buffet, homemade baked goods, fresh produce, and cheeses.

Through the years, Bev and Sam's children have expanded their roles in the business as well. Marcia runs the store with her mom, Jill has taken charge of catering, Sam works the farm with his dad, and Sam's wife, Marsha, handles the books. (Tee and Jody live in the Washington, DC area.) "We love sharing our farm with anyone who wants to learn about milking cows, feeding calves, and processing milk," Marcia says. Each year, some 4,000 people take advantage of the Spring House's open-door policy.

In addition to its agricultural roots, the farm is grounded in Washington County's coal-mining past. The property's original farmhouse, built in 1802, stands as a visible reminder. As a consequence of a mine existing under its foundation, one side of the structure is 12 inches shorter than the other.

Although the Minors are looking into restoring the house, for the moment, it's simply part of the scenery. "The farm is just so beautiful," Marcia says, "so Pennsylvania."

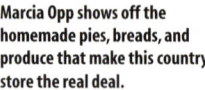

Marcia Opp shows off the homemade pies, breads, and produce that make this country store the real deal.

Southwest from Pittsburgh

AVELLA

From Pittsburgh: *Take I-79 S to Bridgeville exit 54. Left on PA 50 W.*

Half-Day Tour: Sites 31–32
Meadowcroft Museum of Rural Life: *Go 22.5 mi. on PA 50 W through Cecil and Hickory to Avella. Bear right on Cross Creek Rd. Watch for Meadowcroft signs. Go 2 mi. Bear right on Meadowcroft Rd. Go 1 mi. to Museum parking lot.* ☎ ***Tudor Ironworks:*** *From parking lot, return via Cross Creek Rd. to Avella. Right on PA 50 W. Bear left on PA 231 S. Go 1 mi. Right on Sugar Run Rd. Go .2 mi. to Weatherbury Farm sign.* ***Return to Pittsburgh:*** *PA 50 E to I-79 N.*

The Meadowcroft Rock Shelter offers a glimpse inside the oldest and longest continually occupied site in North America, dating back 16,000 years.

Meadowcroft Museum of Rural Life
724–587–3412
401 Meadowcroft Road, Avella
www.meadowcroftmuseum.org
Late May–Early Sept: Wed–Sat, NOON–5PM; Sun, 1–5PM
Adults: $6.50; Seniors: $5.50; Children: $3.50

Meadowcroft Village recreates the 1890s using historic structures. The blacksmith shop, relocated to the museum, offers a look at the once-familiar trade as an interpreter demonstrates iron forging at the anvil.

Tudor Ironworks (Weatherbury Farm)
724–587–3763
Weatherbury Farm, Inc.
1061 Sugar Run Road, Avella
www.tudorironworks.com
☎ Phone ahead.

The blacksmith shed at Meadowcroft

Visit a working forge and learn from a young metalsmith about an age-old trade! Using coke that he bakes in an old coal furnace once used on the railroads, artist–blacksmith Nigel Tudor creates ornamental ironwork for home and garden. Now in his 20s, Tudor got his start at age 13 when he attended a blacksmithing workshop at nearby Meadowcroft Village.

Tudor Ironworks is part of Weatherbury Farm, which offers family-oriented "farm vacations" and regular public programs. The shop includes both a forge for working hot metal and a tool room for cold shaping. The annual "hammer-in" hosted by the Ironworks draws metalsmiths from throughout the region.

Tudor's pieces are available for sale at Weatherbury Farm or through the Ironworks web store. The web site includes a virtual metalwork museum that displays items from Tudor's collection of wrought-iron objects dating back to ancient times.

Blacksmith Nigel Tudor

Monongahela Route

EVENTS CALENDAR

For specific dates and times of events see
www.riversofsteel.com

Recurring Events

Local History Conference
The LeMoyne House
724–225–6740
49 East Maiden Street, Washington
Conference featuring local history
topics such as coal mining or local ethnic history

*African-American and
Italian-American Heritage*
The LeMoyne House
724–225–6740
49 East Maiden Street, Washington
Monthly
African-American Heritage and
Italian-American Heritage round tables

February

Robert Burns Banquets
Donora Borough Building
724–379–6600
49 East Maiden Street, Washington
Events honoring the Scottish poet

April

Syrian Chicken Dinner
Saint Michael's Antiochian Orthodox Church
724–684–7460
1201 Patton Avenue, Monessen

Syrian Bake Sale
Saint Michael's Antiochian Orthodox Church
724–684–7460
1201 Patton Avenue, Monessen

Hammer-In
W. A. Young & Sons Machine Shop and Foundry
724–627–3204 or 724–592–6184
Water Street, Rices Landing

May

Belgian Dayz
Chamber Plaza
724–483–4060
Main Street, Charleroi
Early May
Celebration of Belgian heritage
featuring food, entertainment, and glass blowing

National Road Festival
Route 40
724–437–9877
Towns along Route 40 in Washington County
Early May
Food, arts and crafts, and exhibitions

June

Trax Farms Annual Strawberry Festival
Trax Farms
412–835–3246
528 Trax Road, Finleyville
www.traxfarms.com
2nd weekend

Rices Landing River Festival
Rices Landing
724–592–6184
Rices Landing Lock Wall
Community Festival

St. Anthony Festa
St. Anthony Church
724–258–9710
Behind Sheetz on Main Street, Monongahela
Last full weekend
Ethnic foods, bake sale, games, and entertainment

July

Syrian Chicken Dinner
Saint Michael's Antiochian Orthodox Church
724–684–7460
1201 Patton Avenue, Monessen

Glass Extravaganza
Antiques Downtown
724–222–6800
88 South Main Street, Washington
Features work of local glassware factories,
past and present

Holy Rosary Craft Festival
Holy Rosary Parish
724–745–3531
One Orchard Street, Muse
Mid-July
Juried crafts, ethnic foods, and entertainment

*Duncan Miller Convention Glass
Annual Show and Sale*
724–225–9950
Alpine Club
735 Jefferson Avenue, Washington
Late July
Exhibits and auction

Jacktown Fair
Wind Ridge Fairgrounds
www.vicoa.com/vca/jack.html
Route 21, outside of Jacktown
Late July
The nation's oldest continuing fair

Rain Day
Waynesburg
www.greenemessenger.com/rain
Along East High Street, Waynesburg
July 29
Activities and beauty pageant. In the past
128 years, it has rained on this day in Waynesburg
83% of the time.

Sheep Fest
Weatherbury Farm
724–587–3763
1061 Sugar Run Road, Avella
www.weatherburyfarm.com
Late July – Early August

August

Brownsville Community Days Display
Flatiron Building Heritage Center
724–785–9331
69 Market Street, Brownsville
www.flatironcenter.com
Community Festival

Brownsville Area Community Celebration Festival
Brownsville Wharf
724–785–9331
Riverside Park, Brownsville
Community Festival

Pennsylvania Men and Women Bocce Tournament
Brownsville Sons of Italy
724–785–9982
Race Street, Brownsville
Bocce Tournament open to all

King Coal Festival
Pennsylvania Bituminous Coal Show
Carmichaels
www.vicoa.com/vca/coal.html
PA 21 in Carmichaels
Last Week
Entertainment, coronation of the Coal Queen, a parade, and a mine-rescuing contest

September

Hammer-In
Tudor Ironworks
724–587–3763
Weatherbury Farm, Inc.
1061 Sugar Run Road, Avella
1st weekend

Syrian Bread Sale
Saint Michael's Antiochian Orthodox Church
724–684–7460
1201 Patton Avenue, Monessen
Mid-September

Pennsylvania Bavarian Oktoberfest
Greater Canonsburg Chamber of Commerce
724–745–1812
Main Street, Canonsburg
German bands, foods, and crafts

Washington/Greene County Covered Bridge Festival
Mingo Creek County Park
800–531–4114 or 724–228–5520
10 miles east of Washington, Exit 5 off I-79
3rd weekend
Featuring beautiful old covered bridges, food, and entertainment

Meadowcroft Fall Foliage Festival
Meadowcroft Museum of Rural Life
724–587–3412
401 Meadowcroft Road, Avella
Late September – Late October: Every weekend
Events change each weekend.

Harvest Festival
Greene County Historical Society Museum
724–627–3204
918 Rolling Meadows Road, Waynesburg
2nd weekend in October

October

Apple Festival
Mt. Pleasant Volunteer Fire Company
724–356–3378
106 Main Street, Mt. Pleasant
Early October

Pennsylvania Arts and Crafts Christmas Festival
Washington County Fairgrounds
724–863–4577
2151 North Main Street, Washington
Christmas arts and crafts for sale

Syrian Chicken Dinner
Saint Michael's Antiochian Orthodox Church
724–684–7460
1201 Patton Avenue, Monessen

December

Syrian Baklava Pastry Sale
Saint Michael's Antiochian Orthodox Church
724–684–7460
1201 Patton Avenue, Monessen

Trolleys and Toy Trains
Pennsylvania Trolley Museum
877–728–7655 toll-free or
724–228–9256
1 Museum Road, Washington
www.pa-trolley.org
Late December
Holiday events

Index

A

A & B Bakery, 9, 16
aba'ah (cloak), 156
abolition movement, 207
Abruzzi's, 76
accordion, 112
Acmetonia, 144
Aeolian pipe organ, 164
African-American heritage: Alle-Kiski area, 117; Ambridge, 87; Beaver, 96; Blemahdoo's African Market Place, 17–18; Bloomfield/Lawrenceville neighborhood, 54; festivals and events, 79, 216; Ford City, 143; Hill District, 70–73; Homewood/Point Breeze neighborhood, 58; Pittsburgh area, 41
African-American Heritage Quilters, 73
African Heritage Room, 73
African-inspired clothing, 17
Afro-American Music Institute, 58
Alcoa (Aluminum Company of America), 117, 122, 127
Alcoa Building, 42–45, 51, 53
Alcoa Research Laboratory, 129
Alexander, John White, 67
Aliquippa, 92–95, 113–114, 131
Aliquippa Works (J&L Steel), 81, 93
Allegheny Cemetery, 55, 57
Allegheny County, 5, 32, 49, 160 *See also* Alle-Kiski Route; Three Rivers Route
Allegheny County Rib Cook-Off, 79
Allegheny Ludlum Steel, 10, 116–117, 125–126, 133–134, 136–137
Allegheny River, 5, 41–42, 46, 107, 117, 143
Allegheny Valley, 37–39, 138
Allegheny Valley Association of Churches, 145
Alle-Kiski-Connie Canoe Sojourn, 144
Alle-Kiski Route: Freeport, 138–139; historical background, 117; Kittanning, 141–143; Leechburg/Hyde Park area, 134–137; New Kensington area, 128–131; Slate Lick, 140–141; Springdale, 119–121; Tarentum area, 122–127; Vandergrift, 132–133
Alle-Kiski Valley Historical Society & Museum, 122, 123, 144
Allequippa, Queen, 92
Alpen Schuhpplattler, 85
Aluminum City Terrace, 122
aluminum industry, 117, 122, 123, 127
Amalgamated Association of Iron and Steel Workers, 14–15
Ambridge, 81, 83–88, 113–115, 131
Ambridge area, 83–91
Ambridge Assembly of God, 87
A. M. Byers, 10

American Bridge Company, 81, 86–88
American Friends Service Committee, 194
American Indian Gathering, 114
American Indian heritage *See* Native American heritage
American Indian Pow-wow, 79
American Sheet and Tin Plate Company, 43
American Slovenian Citizens Association, 144
American Steel & Wire Plant, 10, 187
Amish, 85, 150
amusement parks, 26–27, 152, 155
Ancient Order of Hibernians, 49
Andy Warhol Museum, 51, 53
Antiochian Orthodox Chrstian Archdiocese of North America, 156
Antiochian Village, 152, 156, 179–181
Antique Emporium, 102, 106
Apollo, 145
Apollo Iron & Steel Company, 133
Appalachian Mall of America, 172
Applebutter Fest, 114
Apple Festival, 217
Applegate, Brenda, 90
Aranowski, Father, 89
architectural tours, 179
Armstrong County, 5, 137, 141, 143, 160 *See also* Alle-Kiski Route
Armstrong County League of Arts Center, 140–141, 144
Armstrong, Thomas, 46
Arnold, 130
art, American, 104
art auctions, 177, 179–180
art galleries, 104–105, 202
Artists' Co-op, 204, 206, 207
arts and crafts classes *See* Touchstone Center for Crafts
Arts and Crafts Movement, 142
Arts and Heritage Day Festival, 180
Art Space 303, 9, 17
Asian heritage, 31, 32
Ateleta Club, 57
Augoustidis, Mark, 91
Automatic Guided Vehicle, 117
Avella, 215, 217
Avenue Mine, 125
Avonmore, 127, 200

B

Babcock & Wilcox Steel Tube Plant, 97
Bach, Oscar, 94
Back Porch Restaurant, 188
Baden, 89, 113
badnjak (yule log), 213
Bagdad, 137
Baggy Cat craft shop, 188
bagpipe bands, 88, 159, 180
Bakewell & Pears, 160
baklava, 88
Baltimore & Ohio Railroad, 205, 207

Baltzer Meyer Historical Society, 149, 151
Barbershop Chorus, 113
barges, 15, 99, 107, 138, 183, 189
barn dances, 163
Barnes, Oliver, W., 151
Bartholemew & Smith, 94
baseball, 9, 67, 70, 73
basic oxygen furnace, 10, 25
basketry, 177
Battle of Homestead, 15, 19
Beaver, 96, 98–99, 113–115
Beaver area, 96–101
Beaver Area Historical Museum, 98–99
Beaver County, 5, 91–92, 96–97, 100, 160 *See also* Ohio-Beaver Route
Beaver County Flag Plaza, 98, 100
Beaver County Historical Research & Landmarks Foundation, 90
Beaver County Industrial Museum, 100
Beaver County Riverfest, 114
Beaver Division Canal, 96
Beaver Falls, 106–107, 115
Beaver Falls Historical Society & Museum, 102, 106
Beaver River, 5, 81, 96–97 *See also* Ohio-Beaver Route
Beaver Valley Episcopal Outreach, 102
Bedford, Nathaniel, 74
beehive coke ovens, 147, 167–168
beer, 154
Behold the Lamb of God (19th century painting), 129
Belcher, Henry, 71
Belgian Dayz, 216
Belgian heritage, 216
Belleek China, 38
bell, firehouse, 50
Bell, Thomas, 24
Benedictine order, 85
Benedictine Society, 52, 153
Benedum family, 58
Bert's Wooden Angel and Indian, 98, 99
Bessemer, 147
Bessemer & Lake Erie Railroad, 205
Bessemer process, 24, 74
Betchunis, Carrie, 91
Bethlehem Center High School, 199
Bethlehem Mine Corporation, 213
Bethlehem Steel, 213
Beth Shalom Synagogue, 63, 65
Bey, Sharif, 51
B. F. Jones Memorial Library, 92–94
Bhagavatula, Latha, 31
Biblical Botanical Garden, 69
Big Steel, 6
Big Steel Era, 4, 7, 10–12
Billiani, Mr., 194
Birmingham Bridge, 75
biscotti, 54
Blackburn, William Wallace, 43
Black Diamond Works, 10
Blacksmith "Hammer-in," 179
blacksmithing, 177, 179, 201, 215
Blaine, Ephraim, 97
Blarney Stone Restaurant, 37, 38

218

blast furnace, 10, 28
Blattner Brunner, 44
Blawnox, 7
Blemahdoo's African Market Place, 9, 17
Bloom, Dave, 166
Bloomfield, 41, 54–57, 131
Bloomfield Bridge, 55
Bloomfield Bridge Tavern, 54, 56
blown glass, 160, 167
Bluegrass Day, 144
BlueGrass Festival, 144
boat building industry, 167
bobbin lace making, 131
Bob Day, 180
Bobs, The, 158
bocce tournament, 217
bockwurst, 121
Bost Building, 9, 14
botanical gardens, 66, 69
Bowman family, 192
Bowyer, Mary and Charlie, 136–137
Brackenridge, 126
Braddock, 10, 20, 23–25
Braddock Carnegie Library, 22, 23
Brady's Bend, 4
Brady's Run Park, 115
Braovac, Kristina, 101
bratwurst, 121
Braun, Fred, 185
Breton cake, 38
Brewer, John, 59
Brewer, Tina, 73
Bricker, Dick, 103
Bricker's Restaurant, 102, 103
brickmaking industry, 127, 213
Bridge, James Howard, 163
bridges: Birmingham Bridge, 75; cast-iron, 191; covered, 217; Homestead Grays Bridge, 9; Homestead High-Level Bridge, 9; Hot Metal Bridge, 45, 76, 149; Monaca-Rochester Bridge, 97, 101; Monongahela River, 183; P&LE Railroad bridge, 99; Roberto Clemente Bridge, 45; Smithfield Street Bridge, 45
Bridgewater, 96, 99–100
Brodhead Cultural Center, 98, 101, 113
Brown, Byrd, 71
Brownsville, 190–191, 217
Brownsville area, 190–194
Brownsville Area Community Celebration Festival, 217
Brownsville Area Revitalization Corporation, 190, 194
Brownsville Community Days Display, 217
Brown, Thomas, 191
Bruderhof, 85
Bucciero, Joe, 131
Budosh, Ruth, Charles, and Ed, 201
Bulgarian-Macedonian National Educational and Cultural Center, 9, 21, 78
Bulgaro-Macedonian Beneficial Association, 21
Burcin, Chris, 101
Burtner, George A., 123

Burtner House, 145
button box (accordion), 112
by-product coking, 29, 167, 168
Byzantine Catholic Archdiocese of Pittsburgh, 111
Byzantine Catholicism, 173
Byzantine chant, 179–180

C

Calliope Benefit Concert, 78
Camp Dunneback, 177
Candlelight Tours, 115
Canonsburg, 91, 217
capicola, 88
Cappabianco, Mafalda (Muffy), 89
Car and Carriage Museum, 58, 61
Cardwell Dawson Choir, 58
Carlino, August, Sr., 55
Carmichaels, 213, 217
Carnegie, 34, 36, 78
Carnegie, Andrew: biographical information, 69; Carnegie Technical Institute, 66; Carnegie (town), 34; Duquesne Club, 43, 44; heritage, 141; Homewood/Point Breeze neighborhood, 58–60; libraries, 20, 58; marble pulpit commission request, 129; steel industry, 4, 7, 12, 19, 24
Carnegie Library, Homewood Branch, 60
Carnegie Library of Homestead, 9, 20
Carnegie Mellon University, 66, 67, 69
Carnegie Museums of Pittsburgh, 67, 69
Carnegie Music Hall, 69
Carnegie Steel Company, 14–15, 20, 43, 69, 129
Carnegie Technical Institute, 66
Carpatho-Rusyn *See* Rusyn heritage
Carrie Furnaces (U. S. Steel), 7, 11, 12, 14, 22
Carson, Rachel, 120–121
Carson Statesmetal, 138
Carus, Louise, 111
Casino Theatre, 133
Cassatt, Mary, 50, 149
Cattail Coffee & Tea, 206
Cavoulas, Marcella, 95
Cement City, 185, 186–187
Centerville, 203
ceramic crafts, 177, 202
Chadwick, James, 66
Chalk Hill, 179
challah bread, 62
Challinor and Taylor, 123
Chamovitz, Sheila, 63
Champion Tool & Die, 201
charcoal furnaces, 176
Charleroi, 188, 216
Charlton, Brian, 187
Chartiers River, 207
Chatellier's Bakery, 37, 38
Chestnut Ridge, 147, 152, 167, 170
Childs, Adelaide Howard *See* Frick, Adelaide Howard Childs
china industry, 143, 160

Chinese dragon boat, 32
Chinese heritage, 32
Chiodo's Tavern, 9
Christ Episcopal Church, 102
Christmas at the Village, 115
Christmas Dinner Tour, 115
Christmas with Belsnickel (Santa Claus), 114
Christ the King Church, 87
Church Brew Works, 54, 56
churches *See* religion; *specific church*
Cincinnati Mine explosion, 185
cipka (bobbin lace), 112
Ciurlionis, Mikalojus Kastantas, 67
civil rights march, 71
Civil War encampments, 163
Clairton, 7, 29
Clairton Coke Works (U. S. Steel), 4, 7, 11, 22, 29, 168
clay, 127, 202
Clay Hole, 143
Clayton (Frick family home), 60, 61, 85, 106
Clinton Iron & Steel, 10
clothing stores, 139
Coal and Coke Heritage Center, 166, 170–171
Coal and Iron Police, 23
Coal Barges on the Monongahela (Shryock), 183
Coal Center, 189
coal industry, 125–126, 147, 183, 195, 197, 210–213
Coal Miner Memorial, 198, 199
Coal Miners' Monument, 210
coal reserves, 125
coal tipple replica, 170
coal, uses for, 45, 211
Cochran Coal & Coke, 165
Cochran, James, 164–165
Cochran, Philip, 164–165
Cochran, Sarah Moore, 164–165
coffee, 47
Cokeburg, 213
coke plants: beehive coke ovens, 167–168; by-product coking, 167, 168; Clairton Coke Works (U. S. Steel), 7, 22, 29, 168; Cochran Coal & Coke, 165; coke-making process, 147, 167, 168; Connellsville Coke District, 167, 170, 174, 195; H. C. Frick Coke Company, 163, 168; locations, 10–11; Mammoth Park Coke Ovens, 161, 168; maps, 163; Marianna Coke Ovens, 168; Monongahela River, 183; Smock, 197; Youghiogheny Route, 147
Colt Industries, 109
Columbus, Christopher (statue), 55
common sayings, 10
Connellsville, 141, 160, 166–167, 180
Connellsville area, 166–172
Connellsville Coke District, 167, 170, 174, 195
Connell, Zachariah, 167
Conrad's Catering, 9, 16
Construction Junction, 60
Conway Yards, 90, 205

219

Cookman, William, 150
Cook Township, 179
Cooper Mural, 67
Coptic, 87
Corpus Christi Celebration, 122, 144
Corr, Jim, 189
Council of Three Rivers American Indian Center, 37, 39, 79
Country Day, 144
Covenanters, 207
covered bridges, 217
Craft, Isaiah, 194
Crawford Grill, 71, 72
Creighton Works (PPG), 116, 117, 121, 138, 160
Croatian Fraternal Union, 213
Croatian Fraternal Union Museum, 30, 33, 213
Croatian heritage, 22, 33, 213
Crucible Stainless and Alloy Division, Colt Industries, 109
La Cucina Flegrea, 63, 64
Cultural District, Pittsburgh, 45
Curtiss-Wright plant, 98, 99
Czechoslovak Room, 173

D

dams, 107
Dancin' Demons, 71
dancing: barn dances, 163; Brodhead Cultural Center, 113; Dancin' Demons, 71; Eastern European, 101; German, 85; Grecian Odyssey Dancers, 91; Irish, 49, 78; Italian folk, 88; Kalamatiano dance, 91; *kolo* dancing, 213; Ligonier Highland Games, 180; polka music, 112, 144, 159, 179; Poltava Ukrainian Dance Company, 36; square dancing, 140–141
Darlington, William, 155
Daughters of Erin, 49
Davidson Mine, 170
Dawson, 164–165, 180
Dawson, Mary Cardwell, 58
Deer, Fred, 39
Delany, Martin, 73
Delaware Indian *See* Lenape (Delaware Indian)
Del's Bar and Restaurant, 57
Derry, 180
Derry Station Railroad Days, 180
Desmond, Mike, 71
Dickens, Charles, 46
DiIanni, Antonella, 131
DiSalvo's Station Restaurant, 152, 154, 205
Ditka, Mike, 101
Divine Redeemer Church, 87
Donatelli's Italian Food Center, 54, 57
Donner, William, 186–187
Donora, 186–187
Donora Historical Society, 187
Donora Smog, 187
Dorsett, Tony, 101
Dorseyville, 39, 79
Doughboy Square, 55
dragon boat, Chinese, 32

Dragon Boats Race, 79
Dravo, John F., 99
drawing, 177
dreidels, 63
driving routes: general information, 5; Alle-Kiski Route, 118; Monongahela Route, 184; Ohio-Beaver Route, 82; Three Rivers Route, 8; Youghiogheny Route, 148
Duke Energy, 195
Dunbar, 172
Dunbar's Knob, 175
Duncan and Miller Glass, 160
Duncan and Miller Glass Museum, 160, 204, 207, 208–209
Duncan family, 208
Duncan Miller Convention Glass Annual Show and Sale, 216
Duquesne, 26–27
Duquesne Club, 43, 44
Duquesne Incline, 74, 76, 77
Duquesne University Tamburitzans, 101, 213
Duquesne Works (U. S. Steel), 7, 11, 27

E

Earle, George, 93
Early American Farm Implements Museum, 172, 178
East Connellsville United Methodist Church, 165
Easter eggs, 173 *See also pysanky*
Eastern Europe, 101
East Pittsburgh, 91
East Vandergrift, 144
East Vandergrift Ethnic Days, 144
East Washington Historic District, 207
Ebenezer Baptist Church, 72
Edgar Thomson Works (U. S. Steel), 4, 7, 11, 20, 22, 24, 54
Edison, Thomas, 186
Edith Furnaces, 10
Eighty Four, 214
Eliza Furnaces (J&L Steel), 7, 10, 149
Eljer Company, 143
Ellington, Duke, 71
Ellsworth Collieries, 213
Ellwood City, 114
Elmo's, 190, 193
Emil's Lounge, 22
English heritage, 18, 96, 117, 160
Enon Valley, 112, 113
Enterprise (steamboat), 191
Environmental Education Center, 153
environmental events, 78
Epic Metals Corporation, 22
Erntefest Harvest Festival, 114
Eruv, The, 62
Ethnic Days, 114
ethnic groups *See* immigrants; *specific ethnic group*
Etna, 7, 38
Evanstown SNPJ Picnic Grounds, 179, 180

Expo Center at Greengate Mall, 179–180

F

Faiella, Egidio, 131
Falcione, Sandy, 54
Fall Festival, 114
Fall Hike, 145
Fallingwater, 178, 179
Farmers Home Administration (FHA), 161
Farmers' Markets, 113–115
Farmington, 85, 177–178, 179
Fayad, Mike, 95
Fayette Bank Building, 174
Fayette County *See also* Monongahela Route; Youghiogheny Route: coke plants, 168; historical background, 174; immigrants, 49; pottery, 202; Rivers of Steel National Heritage Area, 5; steel industry, 10, 73
Fayette County Courthouse, 174
Fayette County Fair, 180
Fayette County Fairgrounds, 179–180
Fayette Springs Hotel, 178
Fazio's Italian Foods, 128, 130
Fenstermacher, Steve, 166–167
ferries, 183, 198
Ferri, Kathleen, 26
Festa Italiana, 79
Festival of St. Vincent Basilica Parish, 180
Festival of Trees, 115
festivals and events: Alle-Kiski Route, 144–145; Ambridge, 88; Monongahela Route, 216–217; Ohio-Beaver Route, 113–115; Three Rivers Route, 78–79; Youghiogheny Route, 179–181
fiddle music, 141, 179
Finleyville, 216
fire company water battles, 193
firefighting, 150
firehouse bell, 50
First Fridays at the Frick, 78–79
First Night Pittsburgh, 79
First Presbyterian Church, 43, 44
Fitzgerald, London, 59
flatboat building, 167
Flatiron Heritage Center, 190–191, 217
Fleatique/Antiques Market, 144–145
flint china, 160
Folk Festival (Allegheny Valley Association of Churches), 145
football, 53, 101
footbridge, 134
Footedale, 49, 196
Forbes Field, 67
Ford City, 122, 143–145, 160
Ford City Heritage Days, 143, 144
Ford City Plate Glass Company *See* PPG (Pittsburgh Plate Glass)
Ford, John B., 122, 143
Ford Motor Company, 159
Fort Allen Antique Farm Equipment Association, 180
Fort Armstrong Folk Festival, 144

Fort Mason Historical Society, 195
Fort McIntosh, 96
Fort Palmer mines, 155
Foster, Stephen C., 50, 56, 73
Foster, William B., 54, 56
Foster, William Z., 25
Founder's Day, 179
foundries, 117, 134, 135, 200–201
Foxfire, vol. 5, 176
fraktur, 85
Fredericktown, 198–199
Fredericktown area, 198–203
Fredericktown Ferry, 198
Freedom, 90, 114–115
Freedom Corner, 71, 72
Freedom Vicary Days, 114
Freeport, 138–139
Freeport Brick Company, 127
French and Indian War, 175
French patisseries, 38
French, Patricia Penka Jordanoff, 21
Frick, Adelaide Howard Childs, 61, 163
Frick Art and Historical Center, 61, 78
Frick Art Museum, 59
Frick Building, 42, 45
Frick, Elizabeth Overholt, 162
Frick family, 58
Frick, Helen Clay, 163
Frick, Henry Clay *See also* H. C. Frick Coke Company; biographical information, 162–163; coke plants, 147, 163, 168, 195; Duquesne Club, 43; heritage, 85; Homewood/Point Breeze neighborhood, 58–61; steel industry, 4, 19–20
Frick, John W., 162
Frick Park (Homestead), 9, 19, 20
Frick Park (Pittsburgh), 59, 60–61
Friendship Farms Bakery, 153
From the Drums Came All That Jazz (Brewer), 73
Fry Glass Company, 106
Fueling a Revolution, 183
furnaces: basic oxygen furnace, 10, 25; blast furnace, 10, 28; Carrie Furnaces, 7, 12, 22; charcoal furnaces, 176; iron industry, 176; locations, 10–11; naming process, 11; operation process, 176; Wharton Furnace, 172, 176
Fusco, Monsignor Nicola, 129

G

Gaelic Arts Society, 49
Gateway Center, 42
Gatrell, Frank, 140
Gatto Cycle Diner, 123, 124
GCU (Greek Catholic Union) St. Nicholas Chapel, 108, 110–111
Geiger, Robert "Bob," 158
gelato, 141
George Cupples Stadium, 74
George Westinghouse Museum, 30

German heritage: Alle-Kiski area, 117; Ambridge, 87–88; artisans, 202; Beaver, 96; Bloomfield/Lawrenceville neighborhood, 54; churches, 18; festivals and events, 217; German Mennonites, 162; glass and china craftsmen, 160; Greensburg, 150–151; Harmony Society, 83–85, 90; Kleiner Deutschmann, 121; North Side/Troy Hill neighborhood, 50, 52; Pittsburgh area, 41; Strip District, 46; Tarentum, 122; Wimmer, Boniface, 152
Gettamy, Mr., 158
Gilpin Township, 137
Glass Extravaganza, 216
glass houses, 160
glassmaking: Antique Emporium, 106; general discussion, 42, 74, 122–123, 159–160, 207–208; Rochester, 97; Touchstone Center for Crafts, 177; West Overton Museums, 162–163; Youghiogheny Glass Company, 166–167
Glassport, 7
Glazer, Joe, 115
Glenn, John, 43
Glen's Frozen Custard, 119
glory hole, 166
Golden Triangle, 40–45
Good Samaritan Church, 49
Good Samaritan Parish Ethnic Days, 87
Gorson, Aaron Harry, 149
Gospel Mass, 78
gospel music, 54, 72, 73, 78, 88
Gossler, Anna Maria *See* Vicary, Anna Maria Gossler
Grace Presbyterian Church, 141, 142–143
Graham, Martha, 50
Grape Festival, 181
grape leaves, stuffed, 95
Great Cross of Christ, 175
Greater Pittsburgh Arts and Crafts Festival, 181
Greater Pittsburgh Coliseum Complex, 59
Great "Hunky" Steel Strike (1919), 23, 25, 130
Great Rail Strike (1877), 25
Grecian Odyssey Dancers, 91
Greek Food Festival, 78, 79, 113–114
Greek heritage, 35, 78–79, 91
Greek Mini-Festival, 114
Greene County, 5, 168, 202, 211, 213 *See also* Monongahela Route
Greene County Historical Museum, 202, 210, 212, 217
Greene, Nathaniel, 151
Greene River Trail, 200
Greenfield Bend, 189
Greensburg, 149–151, 175, 179–181
Greensburg Fire Department Museum, 149, 150
gristmill process, 152

Groceria Italiana, 57
guidebook symbols, 5, 83, 119, 149, 185
Guido Cicconi's Union Beer Garden, 197
Gulf Building, 42
Gypsy, 28
gyros (lamb-filled pitas), 88, 91

H

Haas Mural, 43, 44
Hall, Charles Martin, 46
haluski, 173
Hammer-In, 201, 215, 216, 217
Harbison-Walker, 11
Harmony Society, 81, 83–87, 90, 96–97
Harris, Charles "Teenie," 59, 71
Harvest Festival, 145, 217
Harwick Mine Memorial, 119
Hawes, Hunney, 174
Hazelwood Coke Works (J&L Steel), 10
HBC Barge, 190
H. C. Frick Coke Company, 163, 168, 197
Heart of Glass, 78
Heinz Chapel, 66, 68
Heinz family, 58
Heinz Field, 52, 53
Heinz, Henry J., 43, 58
Heinz History Center *See* Senator John Heinz Pittsburgh Regional History Center
Heisey, Augustus, 208
Helveti, Francis, 97
Henninger, F. W., 26
Heppenstall, 54
Heppenstall Forge, 10
Heritage Musical, 181
Heritage Wine Cellars, 188
Herminie, 179–181
Herron, John, 70
Hetzel, George, 149
Hewitt Cemetery, 200
Hill District, 41, 70–73
Hindu beliefs and customs, 31
historical societies, local, 199
history, 4
H. J. Heinz Company, 50, 52
Hmong folk arts, 52
holupki (stuffed cabbage roll), 16
Holy Family Parish Festival, 113
Holy Ghost Byzantine Catholic Church, 173, 185, 188
Holy Ghost Russian Orthodox Church, 86, 156
Holy Martyrs Catholic Church, 122, 144–145
Holy Rosary Craft Festival, 216
Holy Spirit Byzantine Catholic Church, 66, 69
Holy Trinity Greek Orthodox Church, 79, 86, 87, 114
Holy Trinity Roman Catholic Church, 87
Homegrown Crafts Fair, 79
Homer, Winslow, 149
Homestead, 9–20, 78
Homestead Grays, 73
Homestead Grays Bridge, 9

221

Homestead High-Level Bridge, 9
Homestead Steel Strike (1892), 15, 25
Homestead Steel Works (U. S. Steel), 6, 7, 11, 12–15, 19, 205
Homestead Strike, The (song), 15
Homewood, 58–61, 114
Homewood Cemetery, 32, 58, 60, 61
Homewood Heritage Days, 114
Hookstown, 114
Hoover, Herbert, 43
Hopwood, 175
Horne, Elisabeth, 94
Horne, Lena, 71
Hot Metal Bridge, 45, 76, 149
Hovanec, Evelyn, 170
Hudson River School, 104
hump yard, 157
Hungarian heritage, 28, 78, 117
Hungarian Nights, 78
Hungarian Reformed Church, 19
Hunky Alley, 122
Hunky Steel Strike, 23
Hurst Coal, 197
Hyde Land Company, 134
Hyde Park *See* Leechburg/Hyde Park area
Hyde Park Foundry & Machine Company, 134, 135, 201
Hyde Park Museum, 135
Hyde, W. H., 134

I

I-79 corridor, 210–214
I-79 Welcome Center, 210
Ice Cream Festival, 180
iconography, 36, 110, 156, 188
Idlewild Park and Soak Zone, 152, 155, 180
Immaculate Conception Catholic Church, 54
Immaculate Heart of Mary Church, 46, 48
Immigrant Mother Raises Her Sons for Industry, The (Vanka), 37
immigrants: Aliquippa, 92–95; Allegheny Valley, 37–39; Alle-Kiski area, 117; Ambridge, 86–87; Beaver County, 110; Bloomfield/Lawrenceville neighborhood, 54; Brownsville, 191; coke plants, 168; dialects, 16; Donora, 187; Ford City, 143; Greensburg, 151; Hill District, 70–73; historical background, 7, 19; Homewood/Point Breeze neighborhood, 58–61; immigrant wards, 7, 16, 19; Kittanning, 143; labor unions, 25; Leechburg/Hyde Park area, 134; Monongahela River area, 183; Monroeville area, 30–33; Mt. Pleasant, 159; New Kensington, 122; Oakland neighborhood, 66–67; Ohio-Beaver Route, 81, 96; Ohio Valley, 34–36; planned ethnic communities, 81, 92, 95; Polish Hill, 41; religion, 18–19, 21, 31–32; Rusyn, 173; Slovak, 173; South Side, 41, 74–75; Squirrel Hill, 41, 62–65; steel strike, 23; Strip District, 46–49; Tarentum, 122; Washington, 207
Indian, American *See* Native American heritage
Indian, Asian, 31
Indian Head, 147, 169
industrial pollution, 187
ingots, 7, 10
Inside History of the Carnegie Steel Company, 163
International Village, 79
Irish Centre of Pittsburgh, 49
Irish heritage *See also* Scots-Irish heritage: background information, 49; Blarney Stone Restaurant, 38; Cochran, Philip, 164; festivals and events, 78–79; Greensburg, 151; Kittanning, 141; Strip District, 46; workers on Pennsylvania Canal, 138
Irish Room, 49
Irish Rowing Club, 49
Iron City Brewery, 51
iron industry, 10–11, 42, 105, 176
Irvin Works (U. S. Steel), 7, 11
Isabella Furnaces, 10
Italian Day, 145
Italian Day Festa, 180
Italian folk dancing, 88
Italian heritage: artisans in church building, 100, 128–129, 209; Ateleta Club, 57; background information, 130–131; Bloomfield/Lawrenceville neighborhood, 54–55; DiSalvo's Restaurant, 154; festivals and events, 79, 145, 216; firefighters, 150; glass workers, 160; Greensburg, 151; Mancini's Bakery, 34; Nationality Days, 88; Pittsburgh area, 41; planned ethnic communities, 92; stonecutters, 164; stonemasons, 194; Tony's Specialty Meats & Market, 88
Italian wind band, 131

J

J&L Steel *See* Jones & Laughlin Steel Company
J&L Steel Works, 10, 54 *See also* South Side Works
J&L Structural Steel, 92
Jacktown, 216
Jacktown Fair, 216
Jacobs Creek, 110
jallabiyah (caftan), 156
Jameson Coal & Coke Company, 150
Jamestown Crystal Outlet, 157, 160
Javor, 213
jazz, 73
Jeannette, 131, 151, 160
Jerry's Curb Service, 96, 98, 100
jewelry making, 177
Jewish Community Center, 63
Jewish heritage, 19, 41, 62–65, 70, 78, 88
Jewish Museum (Jewish Community Center), 63, 64
J. H. Shoop & Sons, 116, 138, 139
jinky tin, 168
Joe Grkman Band, 112
"Johnny Bull," 19
Johnston, Hartley, 123
John White Alexander Murals, 69
Jones & Laughlin Steel Company: Aliquippa, 92–95; Aliquippa Works, 81, 93; Eliza Furnaces, 7, 10, 149; Hazelwood Coke Works, 10; J&L Steel Works, 10, 54; J&L Structural Steel, 92; South Side Works, 7, 41, 76, 92
Jones, B. F., 4, 43, 94
Jones, Mary Harris "Mother," 25
Joseph, Tony, 88
Jozsa Corner Hungarian Restaurant, 28, 65, 78
Jumonville, 175
Jumonville Methodist Training Center, 172, 175
Juneteenth, 122, 144

K

Kalamatiano dance, 91
Kapeluck, Michael, 36
Kaplan, Leslie, 55
Kaulen, Tim, 27
Kazansky's, 65
Kazincy, Father Adalbert, 23
Kelley, Jim, 101
Kennametal, 151
Kennywood Park, 22, 26–27, 78
Kennywood Park Corporation, 155
Kentuck Knob, 178, 179
Keshok, Sister Rita, 173
kibee, 95
kielbasa, 49
Kier Brick Company, 127
Kier Rock Creek Oil, 118
Kimisis Tis Theotokou Greek Orthodox Church, 113–114
King Beaver *See* Tamaqui
King Coal Festival, 217
King, Martin Luther, Jr., 58
Kipling, Rudyard, 96
Kirby, 211
Kiski Junction Railroad, 116–117, 135–137, 205
Kiskiminetas River, 5, 117, 133, 134, 136–137 *See also* Alle-Kiski Route
Kittanning, 141–144
Kittanning Brick Company, 127
Klein, Barbara, 95
Kleiner Deutschmann, 85, 119, 121
Klein, Morris, 95
klezmer music, 88
Kline, Murray, 200
Klondike Coal Field, 195
knitting, 194
knockwurst, 121
kolachi (filled pastry), 172
Kolenda (Polish Christmas Caroling), 145
kolo dancing, 213
Kontoulis family, 35

222

Koppel Steel Corporation, 89
Korson, George, 15, 181, 210
krofi (doughnuts), 112
Krushchev, Nikita, 9
Kubachka, Josephina Rudinska, 171
Kuhler, Otto, 149
Kundar, Cynthia, 104
Kurtik, Larry, 125

L

labor terms, 94
labor unions: Amalgamated Association of Iron and Steel Workers, 14–15; Guido Cicconi's Union Beer Garden, 197; historical background, 25; Sellins, Fannie, 130; steel industry, 81, 92-93; United Mine Workers of America, 191; United Steelworkers of America, 43, 44
lace, 112
Lackovic-Croata, Ivan, 33
Lacock, Abner, 99
Lamb of God Christian Ministries, 18
Langenbaker, Romelius, 84
La Prima Espresso Company, 47
larry cars, 161, 168, 171
lasagna, 88
Latrobe, 151, 152–154, 180
Latrobe Brewing Company, 152, 154
Latrobe Coal Company, 153
Latrobe Electric Steel, 151
Latrobe Pattern Company, 201
Lauderbaugh, Judy, 188
Laughlin, Alexander, Jr., 94
Laughlin, James, 4, 43, 94, 141
Laughlin Library, 94
Lawrence, James, 54, 57
Lawrenceville, 41, 54–57
Lawson, Ernest, 149
Lebanese Club, 93, 95
Lebanese heritage, 32, 92, 93, 95 *See also* Middle Eastern heritage
Leechburg Area Museum and Historical Society, 135
Leechburg/Hyde Park area, 134–137
Leechburg-Hyde Park footbridge, 134
Leech, David, 134
Leisenring, 147
lekvar, 35
LeMoyne House, 216
Lenape (Delaware Indian), 39, 96, 99
Lenox China, 159, 160
Lenox Crystal, 167
Lenox Outlet, 157, 160
Lenox, Walter Scott, 160
Lenten kitchens, 173
L. E. Smith Glass Company, 157, 159, 160
Lewis, John L., 25
Ligonier, 155–156, 180–181
Ligonier Highland Games, 180
Ligonier Valley Railroad, 155
limestone works, 4, 117
Linden Hall, 162, 164–165, 180

Linford, Charles, 149
Linn, Robert P., 99
Lithuanian Room, 67
Little Athens of Sewickley, 34, 35, 91
Little Frick Park, 9, 20
Local History Conference, 216
local museums and historical societies, 199
locks and dams, 107
Lock 6 Landing Restaurant, 107, 108
Lock Six Museum, 200
Lopreiato, Giuseppe, 126
LTV Corporation, 75, 92
Lucy Furnaces, 10
Lynch Field, 180

M

machine shops, 54, 200–201
Madonna of the Mines (Olmes), 210
Magarac, Joe, 14, 27
Magyar, 28
Mallorca Restaurant, 77
Mammoth, 161
Mammoth Park Coke Ovens, 157, 161, 168
Manchester Craftsmen's Guild, 51, 53, 202
Mancini's Bakery, 34
mandolin music, 88
Maple Creek Mine explosion, 191
maps: Alle-Kiski Route, 118; Bloomfield/Lawrenceville, 56–57; coke plants, 163; Golden Triangle, 40, 44; Hill District, 72; Homewood/Point Breeze, 60; Klondike Coal Field, 195; Monongahela Route, 184; North Side/Troy Hill, 52; Oakland, 68; Ohio-Beaver Route, 82; Pittsburgh, 40; South Side, 76–77; Squirrel Hill, 64; Strip District/Polish Hill, 48; Three Rivers Route, 8; Youghiogheny Route, 148
Marcello, Beth, 75
March of the Rolling-Mill Men (song), 145
Marianna, 213
Marianna Coke Ovens, 168
Marietta, Bill, 157
Marino, Dan, 101
Maronite Catholic, 32
masons *See* stonemasons
Masontown, 195
Masontown area, 195–197
Matasich, William, 34
Mavuno African-American Visual and Performing Arts Festival, 79
Max's Allegheny Tavern, 53, 85
Mayer China, 106, 160
Mazda lights, 30
Mazziotti Bakery, 128, 130, 131
McClellandtown, 196
McCready, Andrew, 159
McCutcheon, James Shannon, 203
McCutcheon Monument, 198, 203
McIntosh, Lachlan, 99
McKeesport, 7, 28, 78–79

McKeesport Heritage Center, 22, 28
McKees Rocks, 7, 34–35
McKenna Metals, 151
McMurtry, George, 132, 133
McSwigan, A. S., 26
Meadowcroft Fall Foliage Festival, 217
Meadowcroft Museum of Rural Life, 215, 217
Meadowcroft Rock Shelter, 215
medveniki (travelers' cookies), 180
Melega, Frank, 183, 191
Mellon, Andrew, 26, 187
Mellon family, 4, 58, 169
Mellon, Richard B., 128, 129
Mellon, Thomas, 70, 155, 186
Mennonites, 85, 159, 162–163
Mercurio, Anthony, 141
Merrick, Charles, 104–105
Merrick, Edward Dempster, 104
Merrick, Family 104–105
Merrick Free Art Gallery, 102, 104–105
Merrick, Robert Silas, Sr., 104–105
Mesta Machine, 11, 21, 54, 201
metalsmithing, 177, 215
Metamorphosis Sculpture Park, 22, 27
Metropolitan Philip, 156
Mexicans, 143
Mexican War Streets Society, 50
Mickey's Mill, 138
Middle Eastern heritage, 32, 92, 95, 156, 216–217
Midland, 109, 114
Midland area, 108–111
Miller, John Ernest, 209
miller's knot, 152
Millvale, 7, 37–38
Mina, Mila, 188
mine disasters, 210
Mine Explosion (Melega), 191
mine explosions, 119, 185, 191
Mineo's Pizza House, 64
Miner's Prayer, A, 210
Minor Family, 214
Mollinger, Father Suibertus Goddfried, 50
Monaca, 97, 101, 106, 113–114
Monaca-Rochester Bridge, 97, 101
Monastery Bread, 153
Monastery Run Improvement Project, 153
Monessen, 131, 216–217
Monongahela, 131
Monongahela Incline, 76, 77
Monongahela River: coal and coke industries, 168; general discussion, 5, 183; glass and china industries, 160; Golden Triangle, 41–42; locks and dams, 107; steel industry, 7, 12
Monongahela Route: Avella, 215; Brownsville area, 190–194; Fredericktown area, 198–203; historical background, 183; I-79, 210–214; maps, 184; Masontown area, 195–197; Venetia-Donora-Charleroi area, 185–189; Washington area, 204–209

223

Monongahela Street Railway Company, 26
Monongahela Valley, 9–21
Monroeville, 33
Monroeville area, 30–33
Montana, Joe, 101
Mon-Yough Riverfront Entertainment and Cultural Council, 79
Moore Metal Works, 175
Moore, Sarah *See* Cochran, Sarah Moore
Morewood Mine Massacre (1891), 25, 159
Morgan, J. P., 4, 7, 69, 141
Mosaic of Industry, 117
Mountains of Fire, 146
Mountain Top Campgrounds, 144
Mt. Gallitzin Academy, 83, 89
Mt. Pleasant, 158–160, 180, 217
Mt. Pleasant area, 157–161
Mt. Pleasant By-Product Coal Company, 153
Mt. Pleasant Coke Company, 153
Mt. Pleasant Glass and Ethnic Festival, 159, 181
Mt. Pleasant Presbyterian Church, 159
Mt. St. Macrina, 180
Mt. St. Macrina Retreat Center, 172, 173–174
Mt. St. Peter Roman Catholic Church, 127, 128–129, 131, 145
Mt. Washington, 74–77
Mulberry Street Creamery, 141
Mullaney's Harp and Fiddle, 48, 49, 78
Müller, Bernard, 90
murals, 67, 69, 123
Murat, Gioacchino, 57
Murray Avenue Kosher, 62, 64
Murray, Philip, 25
Muse, 216
museums, local, 199
mushball, 122
music festivals, 144, 159, 179
Muto, Antonio, 129
Myers, Pat, 197

N

Namath, Joe, 101
Napoleon, Ellen, 89
National Duncan Glass Society, 208
National Historic Places: Ambridge, 84; B. F. Jones Memorial Library, 92–94; Bost Building, 14; Carnegie Library of Homestead, 20; Cement City, 186–187; Kennywood Park, 27; Linden Hall, 164–165; Marianna, 213; Mt. St. Peter Roman Catholic Church, 128–129; Nemacolin Castle, 192; Old Economy Village, 83–84; Penn-Craft Historical District, 194; Redstone Knitting Mill, 194; St. Nicholas Croatian Church, 37; St. Peter's Roman Catholic Church, 190, 192; Smock, 197; Vandergrift, 133; W. A. Young & Sons Foundry, 200–201; West Overton Village, 163; Youghiogheny Station Glass, 167
Nationality Days, 27, 78–79, 88, 113
Nationality Days, Kennywood Park (Ferri), 26
Nationality Rooms, 173
National Negro Opera Company, 58, 73
National Road, 172, 174, 179, 190–191
National Road Festival, 179, 216
National Roll Company, 201
National Steel Company, 10
National Trust for Historic Preservation, 75
National Tube Works (U. S. Steel), 7, 11, 28
Native American heritage: background information, 39; festivals and events, 114; former settlements, 96, 122, 143, 151, 207; murals, 99; Nationality Days, 88; treaties, 117
Natrona Heights, 145
nature tours, 179–181
Negro League baseball, 9, 70, 73
neighborhood plans, 92
Nemacolin Castle, 190, 192
Nemacolin's Trail, 190–191
Neville Island, 7
New Brighton, 102–105, 113
New Brighton area, 102–107
New Geneva Pottery, 195, 196, 202
New Haven Hose Company Bagpipe Band, 159
New Kensington, 15, 122, 128, 131, 144–145
New Kensington area, 128–131
Newman, Lynn, 196
Nimick Nature Center, 179
Nine Mile Run Watershed Association, 78
Nordhoff, Charles, 83
Norfolk & Western Railroad, 205
Norfolk Southern Railway, 136
North Apollo, 124
North Side, 41, 50–53
Norvelt, 161
Norvelt Community, 157, 161
nut roll, 112, 173 *See also potica*

O

Oak Hill, 173–174
Oakland, 32, 41, 66–69, 91
O'Brien, Shirley, 208
Ohio-Beaver Route: Aliquippa, 92–95; Ambridge area, 83–91; Beaver area, 96–101; Enon Valley, 112; historical background, 81, 96; maps, 82; Midland area, 108–111; New Brighton area, 102–107
Ohio River, 5, 41–42, 81, 107, 207
Ohio Valley, 34–36
Ohioville, 110–111
Oktoberfest, 79, 85, 114, 217
Old and New Westmoreland, 151
Old Believers, 213
Old Concord, 209
Old Concord Presbyterian Church, 204, 209
Old Economy Village, 83–84, 113–115
Old Economy Village Family Festival, 113
Old Europe Restaurant, 75, 77
Old Freeport, 138
Old Time Fiddlers' Jamboree, 141, 179–181
Oliver Bath House, 74, 76
Oliver Iron and Steel Company, 10, 76
Olmes, Mildred Young, 210
Olmsted, Frederick Law, 132, 133
O'Mahoney Stainless Steel Company, 124
Omni William Penn Hotel, 44, 45
Open Hearth #5 (U. S. Steel), 7
Oram's Donuts, 102, 107
Ormsby, John, 74
Orslene, Lou, 190–191, 194
Osterling, Frederick J., 61, 106
O'Toole, James, 75
Out of This Furnace (Bell), 24
Overholt, Abraham, 162
Overholt, Christian, 163
Overholt, Elizabeth *See* Frick, Elizabeth Overholt
Overholt, Henry, 162
Overholt Homestead, 162
Overholt Museum, 85

P

P&LE Railroad bridge, 99
P&LE Railroad shops, 10
paczki (doughnuts), 49
painting, 177
Pajdzik, Father Sebastian, 196
Palmer, Arnold, 43, 152
Panther Hollow, 131
papermaking, 177
Parade Circle display, 150
parades, 78
Pargny, Eugene W., 43
Parish Festival, St. Rita Church, 180
Park Place AME Church, 18
patch towns, 65, 147, 168–171, 197
Patch/Work Voices Project, 170–171
Pat Lyon pump wagon, 150
pattern making, 201
Patti, Sam, 47
Pechin Shopping Village, 166, 172
Penn Avenue Wholesalers, 48
Penn-Craft Historical District, 161, 190, 194
Penn Hills, 31–32
Penn Station, 45
Pennsylvania Arts and Crafts Christmas Festival, 217
Pennsylvania Bavarian Oktoberfest, 217
Pennsylvania Bituminous Coal Show, 217
Pennsylvania Brewing Company, 52, 79, 85
Pennsylvania Canal, 122, 123, 134, 137–138
Pennsylvania Department of Environmental Protection, 153

224

Pennsylvania Historical and Museum Commission, 84
Pennsylvania Landmark Register, 192
Pennsylvania Macaroni Company, 47
Pennsylvania Men and Women Bocce Tournament, 217
Pennsylvania Mountain Service Corps, 153
Pennsylvania Railroad, 47, 69, 137, 150–151, 157, 205
Pennsylvania State University, Fayette Campus, 170
Pennsylvania Trolley Museum, 204–205, 207, 217
Peters Creek Historical Society, 185
Peterson, Carlos F., 71
Petro, Frederick, 111
pewter ware, 138
Philadelphia Toboggan Company Carousel, 155
Philip Cochran United Methodist Church, 165
Phillipsburg, 97
Phillips, Stephen, 97
Phipps Conservatory & Botanical Gardens, 66, 69
Phipps family, 66
Phoenix Glass, 106
photography, 177
Piedmont Oil Company, 174
pierogi, 7, 34–35, 49, 54, 89, 113–115
Pierogies Plus, 34, 35
Pilgrimage Honoring Our Lady of Perpetual Help, 180
Pinkerton guards, 15
Pinskers Judaica, 62, 64
Pioneer Crafts Council, 177
pipe organ, 164
pita (Slovak apricot pastry), 16
Pitcairn Yards, 205
Pittsburgh neighborhoods: Bloomfield/Lawrenceville, 54–57; cultural center, 66–67; festivals and events, 78–79; Golden Triangle, 40–45; Hill District, 70–73; historical background, 41–43; Homewood/Point Breeze, 58–61; neighborhood history, 41; North Side/Troy Hill, 50–53; Oakland, 66–69; South Side, 74–77; Squirrel Hill, 62–65; Strip District/Polish Hill, 46–49
Pittsburgh & Lake Erie (P&LE) Railroad, 93, 97–99, 167, 205
Pittsburgh area: Allegheny Valley, 37–39; Monongahela Valley, 9–21; Monroeville area, 30–33; Ohio Valley, 34–36; Rankin-Clairton route, 22–29
Pittsburgh Area Slovaks (PAS), 173
Pittsburgh Athletic Association, 67
Pittsburgh Brewing Company, 154
Pittsburgh-Buffalo Company, 213
Pittsburgh Center for the Arts, 202
Pittsburgh Coal, 197
Pittsburgh Crawfords, 70
Pittsburgh Folk Festival, 49, 79
Pittsburgh Folk Music Society, 78
Pittsburgh Glass Center, 55, 57, 78, 160
Pittsburgh Industrial District, 4
Pittsburgh Irish Festival, 79
Pittsburgh Islamic Center, 32
Pittsburgh (Kuhler), 149
Pittsburgh Monongahela River (Lawson), 149
Pittsburgh Pirates, 45, 67
Pittsburgh Point, 4
Pittsburgh Railways Company, 204
Pittsburgh School of Ukrainian Studies, 36
Pittsburgh Steelers, 53
plate glass industry, 117, 121, 122, 143, 160
Plotnikova, Tatyana, 35
PNC Park, 45
Poale Zedeck Synagogue, 65
Point Breeze, 58–61
Point State Park, 44
Point, The, 41
Polish Arts League, 49
Polish Christmas Caroling, 145
Polish Day, 49
Polish Falcons Club, 49
Polish heritage: background information, 49; Bloomfield Bridge Tavern, 56; festivals and events, 145; firefighters, 150; Pierogies Plus, 35; St. Anthony Catholic Church, 19; St. Maximilian Kolbe Shrine, 196; Strip District, 46; Tarentum, 122; workers, 54
Polish Hill, 41, 46–49
Polish National Alliance, 49
polka music, 88, 112, 113, 144, 159, 179
Poltava Ukrainian Dance Company, 36
Posey, Cumberland "Cum," 73
potica (nut roll), 112
pottery, 163, 183, 195–196, 198, 202–203
Powdermill Nature Reserve, 179–180
Pow-wow, 39
PPG (Pittsburgh Plate Glass), 44, 117, 121–123, 125, 143, 160
PPG Place, 42, 44
pressed glass, 160
Pressed Steel Car Works, 10, 34
Primanti Brothers, 47
printmaking, 177
Priory–A City Inn, The, 50, 53
professional sports: baseball, 9, 67, 70, 73; football, 53, 101
pull-tabs, 51
Pump House and Water Tower (U. S. Steel), 9, 14
pump wagon, 150
punty rod, 166
pyrohi, 173 *See also* pierogi
pysanky, 36, 78, 88, 113, 179 *See also* Easter eggs
Pysanky Easter Egg Sale, 78

Q

Quail Acres, 204, 206, 207
quilting: African-American heritage, 73; Redstone Knitting Mill, 194; Scots-Irish heritage, 141; Scottdale Fall Festival, 180; Touchstone Center for Crafts, 177; West Overton Museums, 179; West Overton Village, 163
Quilt Patch, The, 163
Quilt Show, 179
Quinn, Andy, 27

R

R & R Station Restaurant, 157, 158
Rachel Carson Day, 144
Rachel Carson Homestead, 119, 120–121, 144
radio stations, 173
RAG Cumberland Mine, 168, 210, 211
railroads: Baltimore & Ohio, 205, 207; Bessemer & Lake Erie Railroad, 205; Connellsville, 167; Kiski Junction, 116, 117, 135, 136–137, 205; Ligonier Valley, 155; Norfolk & Western, 205; Norfolk Southern, 136; Pennsylvania Railroad, 47, 69, 137, 150–151, 157, 205; Pittsburgh & Lake Erie (P&LE), 93, 97–99, 167, 205; station restaurants, 124, 150, 154, 158; Westmoreland Scenic Railroad, 205; Youngwood Historical & Railroad Museum, 157–158, 180
Rain Day, 216
Rankin, 22
Rapp, Father George, 83–84, 86, 90, 97
Raymond Walls' Intercultural Choir, 58
Rea, Marilyn and Red, 140
recipes: La Prima's Espresso Recipe, 47; Spaghetti all'aglio e olio, 130
Rededication of St. Nicholas Church (Vanka), 37
Red Star Brewery & Grille, 150
Redstone Knitting Mill, 194
Reintgen, Robert "Bob," 158
religion, 18–19, 31–32, 64–65, 87 *See also specific church;* synagogues; temples
Renaissance (Pittsburgh), 42
Republic Steel Company, 10
Resh's General Store, 166, 169
Reynolds, Jane Ross, 142
Rices Landing, 198, 200, 216
Rices Landing River Festival, 216
Rices Landing Riverfront, 198, 200
Richard Beatty Mellon Mansion, 128–129
Richards & Hartley, 123
Rich, Ellen, 88
Rich, Tony, 88
Ridna Shkola of Pittsburgh, 36
Riverfront Park & Boat Landing, 75, 77, 98
Riverfront Park (Kittanning), 145
Riverfront Park (Rochester), 114
Riverside Village Shops, 188

225

Rivers of Steel National Heritage Area, 4–5
Roaring Run Trail Pavilion, 145
Robert Burns Banquets, 179, 216
Roberto Clemente Bridge, 45
Roberts, Craig, 202
Robinson, Rev. Jimmy Joe, 71
Rocca's Homestyle Pasta, 108, 109, 131
Rochester, 96, 97, 100–101, 114
Rodef Shalom Biblical Botanical Garden, 69
Rodef Shalom Temple (Homestead), 19
Rodef Shalom Temple (Pittsburgh), 64, 66, 67, 69
Rogers, Fred, 152
Rolladin Bakery, 62, 64
Rolling Rock beer, 154
Roman Catholic Diocese of Greensburg, 151
Romani language, 28
Rooney, Art, 53
Roosevelt, Eleanor, 161, 194
Rosalind Candy Castle, 102, 103
Route 28, 4, 138
Rowley's Market, 116, 132
Ruff Creek, 212
Ruff Creek General Store, 210, 212
Ruggiero, Renee, 85
Russian Orthodox Church of the Holy Ghost, 87
Rusyn Food Festival, 114
Rusyn heritage, 19, 52, 156, 173, 187

S

Sacred Art Series, 179
Sacred Music Institute, 180
saganaki, 35
St. Anthony Catholic Church, 19, 85
St. Anthony Festa, 216
St. Anthony's Chapel, 50, 52
St. Benedict, 152
St. Benedict the Moor Catholic Church, 70, 72, 78
St. Blaise Catholic Church, 114
St. Francis of Paola Church, 145
St. George Antiochian Orthodox Church, 144–145
St. George's Day Festival, 213
St. George Serbian Orthodox Church, 213
St. Gregory Russian Orthodox Church, 19
St. John-Mark Lutheran Church, 18
St. John's Evangelical Lutheran Church, 54
St. John's Greek Catholic Church, 87
St. John's Lutheran Church, 83, 87
St. John's Russian Orthodox Church, 113–114
St. John the Baptist Byzantine Catholic Cathedral, 19
St. John the Baptist Church, 83, 86, 89
St. John the Baptist Roman Catholic Church, 113
St. John Ukrainian Catholic Church, 74, 76
St. Joseph's Academy, 151
St. Joseph's Roman Catholic Church, 54, 57
St. Joseph the Worker, 18
St. Mary Magdalene Catholic Church, 18, 19
St. Mary's Carpatho-Russian Orthodox Church, 156
St. Mary's Coptic Orthodox Church, 87
St. Mary's Forty-Sixth Street Church, 54
St. Maximilian Kolbe Parish, 18
St. Maximilian Kolbe Shrine, 195, 196
St. Michael, 173
St. Michael Church Auditorium, 78
St. Michael/Good Shepherd Church, 22, 23
St. Michael's Antiochian Orthodox Church, 216–217
St. Michael Slovak Catholic Church, 18
St. Nicholas, 111
St. Nicholas Chapel, 108, 110–111
St. Nicholas Croatian Church, 37, 213
St. Nicholas Greek Orthodox Cathedral, 67, 68, 78
St. Nicholas Greek Orthodox Church, 19
St. Patrick's Catholic Church, 46, 48
St. Patrick's Day Parade, 49, 78
St. Paul Roman Catholic Cathedral, 67, 68
SS. Peter and Paul Chapel, 156
St. Peter and Paul Ukrainian Catholic Church, 86
SS. Peter and Paul Ukrainian Orthodox Church, 34, 36
St. Peter and Paul Ukrainian Orthodox Greek Catholic Church, 78
St. Peter's Roman Catholic Church, 190, 192
St. Pudentiana Roman Catholic Church, 98, 101
St. Rita Church, 180
St. Sava Serbian Orthodox Church, 213
St. Stanislaus Church, 87
St. Stanislaus Kostka Church, 46, 48
SS. Thekla and Raphael Pilgrimage, 181
St. Thomas Church, 196
St. Vincent Archabbey and Grist Mill, 85, 150, 151–153
St. Vincent Basilica Parish, 153, 180
St. Vincent College, 153
St. Vincent Grove, 180
St. Vladimir Ukrainian Orthodox Church, 87
salami, 88
salt extraction, 117
Salute to the Classics, 180
San Rocco Cultural Committee, 114
San Rocco Festa, 114, 131
Sarah Bell, The, 50
Sargent, John Singer, 149
Sarkis, June, 95
sarma (stuffed cabbage roll), 16
Saturday schools, 7
sauerbraten, 121
sauerkraut, 85, 89
sausage, 88, 121
sawdust carpets, 122
Scenery Hill, 203, 213
Schaltenbrand, Phil, 203
Schenley, 136–137
Schenley, Mary Croghan, 66, 137
Schenley Park, 55, 66, 69, 137
Schenley Whiskey Distillery, 137
Schlesinger, Laura, 202
Schoen Wheel & Axle, 10
Scots-Irish heritage: Alle-Kiski area, 117; Beaver, 96; churches, 18; Greensburg, 151; immigrant settlement, 207; Kittanning, 141; Tarentum, 122
Scottdale, 162, 168, 180
Scottdale area, 162–165
Scottdale Fall Festival, 180
Scottish heritage, 141, 179, 180
See also Scots-Irish heritage
scrip, 171
sculpture classes, 177
Sebastian, Bert and Julia, 99
Sellins, Fannie, 25, 130
Senator John Heinz Pittsburgh Regional History Center, 48, 73, 132
Seneca, 151
Seneca Oil, 118
Serbian heritage, 213
Serb National Federation, 213
Seton Hill University, 151
Seven Principles of the Harmony Society, 84
Sewickley, 35, 79
Shadyside Arts Festival, 79
Shahn, Ben, 161
Sharpsburg, 7
Shaw, Joseph and Elizabeth, 194
sheepdog trials, 180
Sheep Fest, 217
sheet glass, 167
Sheltering Tree, The, 138
Shimrock, Tim, 199
Shipman, Alecia, 51
Shippingport Nuclear Power Station, 109
shish kebab, 35, 95
Shlyakovskaya, Tatyana, 35
Shoop Family, 139
Shoop, John E., 139
Shryock, John, 183
Shute, Henry Damon, 43
Silent Spring (Carson), 120
Sisters of St. Joseph, 89
Sisters of St. Basil, 173–174, 180
Skrbin, Aaron, 101
Slate Lick, 138, 140–141, 144
Slava (Patronal Feast), 213
Slavjane, 173
Slovak Association, 173
Slovak Festival, 173

Slovak heritage: A & B Bakery, 16; Ambridge, 87; Andy Warhol, 51; background information, 173; Dunbar, 172; festivals and events, 145, 180; immigrant workers, 187; St. Michael/Good Shepherd Parish, 23; Slovakian design in church, 111; Strip District, 46; Tarentum, 122; Uniontown, 171
Slovak Heritage Association, 122
Slovak Sokol, 187
Slovak Stedry Vecer, 145
Slovene Day at Kennywood, 112
Slovenefest, 113
Slovenian heritage, 112, 179–180
Slovenian National Benefit Society, 112, 179, 180
Slovenian Polka Dance, 179, 180
Smithfield Bridge, 45
Smith, Nate, 71
Smock, 197
Smock Historical Society, 195, 197
snake oil, 118
SNPJ (Slovenian National Benefit Society) Borough Recreation Center, 112, 113
soaking pits, 10
Society for Contemporary Craft, 47, 48, 59
Society Javor, 213
Solidarity Forever (song), 115
Somayajula, Lakshmi, 31
Sony Technology Center, 162
Soul Food Luncheon & African Market, 78
soup kitchens, 102
Soup Sega, 21, 78
South Asians, 31
Southern fried chicken, 88
South Side, 41, 74–77
Southside Historical Village Days, 114
South Side Local Development Company, 75
South Side Market House, 75, 76
South Side Slopes, 75
South Side Works (J&L Steel), 7, 41, 75–76, 92
Southwestern Pennsylvania Landscapes collection, 149
souvlaki, 35
spaetzle, 121
spanakopita, 91
Spang-Chalfant, 10
Sparks Supply Store, 169
Speers Street Shops, 185, 188
Spiritual Form (Peterson), 71
Spite Monument *See* McCutcheon Monument
Springdale, 85, 119–121, 144
Spring House, 210, 214
square dancing calls, 140
Squirrel Hill, 41, 62–65
Sri Venkateswara Temple, 30, 31–32
stained glass windows, 33, 142, 165, 167, 192
Standard Horse Nail Company, 104, 105
Stanish, John, 128

State Theatre Center for the Arts, 174
Station Square, 74, 77, 79, 205
Station Street Reunion, 95
steamboat travel, 191
steel industry *See also* coal industry; coke plants: Bessemer process, 24, 74; coke plants, 29; historical background, 4, 10–12, 81; labor unions, 93; railroads, 205; steelmaking process, 10–11; steelmaking terms, 13; strikes, 15, 23, 25, 93; Washington, 207
Steelmark logo, 53
Steel Mill Blues (song), 115
Steel Valley, 7, 9–29
Steel Valley Heritage Trail, 14
Steelworkers' Monument, 75, 77
Steel Workers Organizing Committee (SWOC), 93
Stein, Gertrude, 50
Stephen Foster Memorial, 68
Steuben Crystal, 167
Stickley, Gustav, 142
Stone House Restaurant & Country Inn, 172, 178
stonemasons, 55, 100, 129, 164, 168, 170
stoneware, 183, 196, 202
storytelling festivals, 88, 163
"Streetcar Named Desire" (trolley), 204
streetcars, 204–205
strikes, 15, 23, 25, 93
Strip District, 41, 46–49
Strongland Chamber of Commerce, 144
stuffed cabbage, 88
subsistence homesteads, 161, 194
sweet potato pie, 88
Sweetwater Center for the Arts, 79
Swissvale, 7
synagogues, 64, 65, 67 *See also* churches; temples
Syrian Bake Sale, 216
Syrian Bread Sale, 217
Syrian Chicken Dinner, 216–217
Syrian Food Festival, 144
Syrian heritage, 32, 156 *See also* Middle Eastern heritage
Syrian Picnic, 145

T
tailoring, 139
Tamaqui, 98, 99
tamburitza bands, 22, 33, 88, 213
Tamburitzans, 101, 213
Tanner, Henry O., 50
Tarbell, Ida, 132
Tarentum, 122, 144–145
Tarentum area, 122–127
Tarentum Glass, 123
Tarentum Station Restaurant, 123, 124, 205
Taylor Methodist Episcopal Church, 203
temples, 31–32 *See also* churches; synagogues

terminology: barges, 189; coal industry, 125–126; cokemaking process, 168; furnaces, 176; glassmaking, 166; labor unions, 94; pottery, 202; steel industry, 13
Teutonia Männerchor, 50, 52, 85
Thompson House Restaurant and Tavern, 190, 193
Thompson, J. V., 168, 173–174
Thompson, Mary, 173
Thompson, Mrs. Ralph B., 210
Three Rivers Art Festival, 79
Three Rivers Route: Allegheny Valley, 37–39; historical background, 6–7; maps, 8; Monongahela Valley, 9–21; Monroeville area, 30–33; Ohio Valley, 34–36; Pittsburgh, 40–79; Rankin-Clairton route, 22–29
Three Rivers Rowing Association, 79
Thunder Mountain Lenape Nation, 39
Thunder of Protest, 81
Tiffany, Louis Comfort, 142
tin-plating, 207
tinware, 196
Tony's Specialty Meats & Market, 83, 88, 101, 131
Touchstone Art Auctions, 177, 180
Touchstone Center for Crafts, 160, 172, 177, 179, 202
Tour-Ed Mine & Museum, 117, 122, 123, 125–126, 168
towboats, 108, 189
Traditional Musicians Jam, 144
trails: Council of Three Rivers American Indian Center, 39; Ford City, 143; Frick Park, 58; Greene River Trail, 200; Indian Head Trail, 169; Riverfront Trail, 75; Steel Valley Heritage Trail, 14; Youghiogheny Trail, 167
Train Station at Greensburg, 149, 150
Trax Farms Annual Strawberry Festival, 216
Treble Clef Club, 58
Trinity Cathedral, 43, 44
Trinity United Presbyterian Church, 174
trolleys, 204–205
Trolleys and Toy Trains, 217
Trolley Station Oral History Center, 59, 60
Trout, Mary Beth, 120
Troy Hill, 50–53
Troy Hill Fire Station, 50
"Tube City," 28
Tudor Ironworks, 215, 217
Tudor, Nigel, 215
Tunnel and Shrine, the, 81, 92, 93
Tunney, Glenn, 193
Turkovich, Kara, 101
Tuscarawas Trail, 96
Twain, Mark, 7
Twin Lakes Park, 180
Two-Cent Coal (song), 181
Two Kings Mural (Ciurlionis), 67

U

Ukrainian heritage, 36, 87
Union Beer Garden, 197
unions *See* labor unions
Union Steel Company, 186
Uniontown, 170–171, 173–174, 180
Uniontown-Farmington area, 172–178
Union Trust Building, 43, 45
Unitas, Johnny, 101
United Engineer and Foundry, 201
United Jewish Federation, 78
United Mine Workers of America, 130, 191
United Steelworkers of America, 43, 44, 165
University of Pittsburgh, 66–68, 151
Upper & Lower Union Mills, 10
Urban, Marta, 85
U. S. Highway 40, 172, 179, 190–191, 216
U. S. Steel Corporation: Alcoa (Aluminum Company of America), 127; background information, 10; Carnegie Library of Homestead, 20; Carrie Furnaces, 7, 11, 12, 14, 22; Clairton Coke Works, 4, 7, 11, 22, 29, 168; Coal and Coke Heritage Center, 170–171; Coal and Iron Police, 23; Duquesne Works, 7, 11, 27; Edgar Thomson Works, 4, 7, 11, 20, 22, 24–25, 54; Homestead Steel Works, 6, 7, 11, 12–15, 19, 205; Irvin Works, 4, 7, 11; Leechburg, 134; National Tube Works, 7, 11, 28; Open Hearth #5, 7; Pump House and Water Tower, 9, 14; Vandergrift mill, 133
U. S. Steel Donora Zinc Works, 187
U. S. Steel News, 13
U. S. Steel Tower, 42, 44, 45

V

vacuum tumbling, 88
Valley of Work: Scenes of Industry collection, 149
Vandergrift, 132–133, 144
Vanka, Maxo, 37, 213
Van Meter, 110
vecherinka (Bulgarian evening events), 21
Venetia, 185
Venetia-Donora-Charleroi area, 185–189
Veronica's Veil Passion Play, 76, 78
Vesta 4 Mine, 199
Vibo's Italian Bakery, 123, 126, 131
Vicary, Anna Maria Gossler, 90
Vicary House, 83, 90, 114–115
Vicary, William, 90
Victorian Vandergrift Museum and Historical Society, 132
Virgin Hodegetria, 156
vocabulary *See* terminology
Voegtly Cemetery, 50, 53

W

Wagner Act (1935), 25, 92
Wagner, Honus (statue), 55
Wahlen, Pete, 125
Wall Street Journal, 172
Warhol, Andy, 51
Warhola, Paul, 51
Warmack, Gregory, 59
Washington, 160, 204–207, 216–217
Washington area, 204–209
Washington County *See also* Monongahela Route: coal industry, 214; coke plants, 168, 213; glassmaking, 160; immigrants, 28, 91; Rivers of Steel National Heritage Area, 5; trolleys, 205
Washington County Tourism Promotion Agency, 204, 207
Washington, George, 54, 175, 207
Washington/Greene County Covered Bridge Festival, 217
water battles, 193
Waterfront redevelopment, 4
Waynesburg, 212, 216–217
W. A. Young & Sons Foundry, 200–201, 216
Weatherbury Farm, 215, 217
weaving, 91, 177
WEDO 810-AM radio, 173
weisswurst, 121
West End–Elliott Overlook, 76, 77
Westerwald Pottery, 198, 202, 203, 206
West Homestead, 7, 21, 78
West Homestead Electrical Machine Company, 21
Westinghouse Air Brake, 11, 30
Westinghouse Building, 44
Westinghouse Electric, 11
Westinghouse Electric and Manufacturing Company, 43
Westinghouse, George, Jr., 30, 43, 46, 58
Westinghouse Memorial, 69
Westinghouse Standard Control Division, 98
West Mifflin, 78
Westmoreland and Fayette Coal Company, 153
Westmoreland Arts and Heritage Festival, 180
Westmoreland Columbus 500, 180
Westmoreland County, 5, 49, 151, 160, 162, 168 *See also* Alle-Kiski Route; Youghiogheny Route
Westmoreland-Fayette Historical Society, 163
Westmoreland Homesteads, 161
Westmoreland Museum of American Art, 149, 151, 179
Westmoreland Scenic Railroad, 158, 205
West Overton Museums, 85, 162, 179–181
West Overton Village, 163
Wharton Furnace, 172, 176
Wheeling-Pittsburgh Steel Company, 10
Which Side Are You On? (song), 181
whiskey making, 162–163
Whiskey Rebellion, 207
William Penn Hotel *See* Omni William Penn Hotel
Williams, David, 151
Wilmerding, 30
Wilson, Ruth, 99
Wilson's Bar-B-Q, 53
Wimmer, Boniface, 152–153
Winegar, Linda and James, 202
Wood Coal Company, 125
Wood, Ira, 125
Woodruff, Frank, 105
Woods, James, 157
Woodwell, Joseph, 149
woodworking, 177
Works Progress Administration (WPA), 161
Wright, Enoch, 185
Wright Family, 185
Wright, Frank Lloyd, 142, 178
Wright House, 185
Wroule, Paul, 198

Y

Yakkity Yak Diner, 124
Yankovich, Frankie, 112
yarn shop, 206
Yiddish, 65
Youghiogheny Glass Company, 160, 166
Youghiogheny River, 5, 167 *See also* Youghiogheny Route
Youghiogheny Route: Connellsville area, 166–172; Greensburg, 149–151; historical background, 147; Latrobe, 152–154; Ligonier, 155–156; maps, 148; Mt. Pleasant area, 157–161; Scottdale area, 162–165; Uniontown-Farmington area, 172–178
Youghiogheny Station Glass, 167
Youghiogheny Trail, 167
Young, John, 157
Young's Oriental Grocery Store, 65
Young, William A., 200
Youngwood, 157–158, 180
Youngwood Historical & Railroad Museum, 157–158, 180, 205
Ypapanti Greek Food Festival, 79
yule log, 213
YWCA of McKeesport, 78

Z

Zachos, Gust, 103
Zagar, Father Albert, 37
Zimmerman, Philip, 156
zither, 156